THE CANADIAN HORROR FILM

Terror of the Soul

From the cheaply made "tax-shelter" films of the 1970s to the latest wave of contemporary "eco-horror," Canadian horror cinema has rarely received much critical attention. Gina Freitag and André Loiselle rectify that situation in *The Canadian Horror Film* with a series of thought-provoking reflections on Canada's "terror of the soul," a wasteland of docile damnation and prosaic pestilence where savage beasts and mad scientists rub elbows with pasty suburbanites, grumpy seamen, and baby-faced porn stars.

Featuring chapters on *Pontypool*, *Ginger Snaps*, 1970s slasher films, Quebec horror, and the work of David Cronenberg, among many others, *The Canadian Horror Film* unearths the terrors hidden in the recesses of the Canadian psyche. It examines the highlights of more than a century of horror filmmaking and includes an extensive filmography to guide both scholars and enthusiasts alike through this treacherous terrain.

GINA FREITAG is an independent scholar and the founder of the Cellar Door Film Festival in Ottawa.

ANDRÉ LOISELLE is a professor in the Film Studies program and Assistant Vice-President (Academic) at Carleton University.

THE CANADIAN HORROR FILM

Terror of the Soul

Edited by
Gina Freitag and André Loiselle

UNIVERSITY OF TORONTO PRESS
Toronto Buffalo London

ISBN 978-1-4426-5054-1 (cloth)
ISBN 978-1-4426-2850-2 (paper)

Printed on acid-free, 100% post-consumer recycled paper.

Library and Archives Canada Cataloguing in Publication

The Canadian horror film : terror of the soul / edited by Gina Freitag
and André Loiselle.

Includes bibliographical references.
ISBN 978-1-4426-5054-1 (bound)   ISBN 978-1-4426-2850-2 (paperback)

1. Horror films – Canada – History and criticism.   I. Freitag, Gina, 1985–,
editor   II. Loiselle, André, 1963–, editor

PN1995.9.H6C36 2015   791.43'61640971   C2015-905674-8

This book has been published with the help of a grant from the Federation
for the Humanities and Social Sciences, through the Awards to Scholarly
Publications Program, using funds provided by the Social Sciences and
Humanities Research Council of Canada.

University of Toronto Press acknowledges the financial assistance to its
publishing program of the Canada Council for the Arts and the Ontario
Arts Council, an agency of the Government of Ontario.

 Canada Council
for the Arts
Conseil des Arts
du Canada

 ONTARIO ARTS COUNCIL
CONSEIL DES ARTS DE L'ONTARIO
an Ontario government agency
un organisme du gouvernement de l'Ontario

Funded by the   Financé par le
Government   gouvernement
of Canada   du Canada

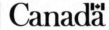 Canada

Contents

THE CANADIAN HORROR FILM

Terror of the Soul

Terror of the Soul: An Introduction

GINA FREITAG AND ANDRÉ LOISELLE

I have long been impressed in Canadian poetry by a tone of deep terror in regard to nature ... it is not a terror of the dangers or discomforts or even the mysteries of nature, but a terror of the soul at something that these things manifest. The human mind has nothing but human and moral values to cling to if it is to preserve its integrity or even its sanity, yet the vast unconsciousness of nature in front of it seems an unanswerable denial of those values ... Confronted with a huge, unthinking, menacing, and formidable physical setting – such communities are bound to develop what we may provisionally call a garrison mentality ... The real terror comes when the individual feels himself becoming an individual, pulling away from the group, losing the sense of driving power that the group gives him, aware of a conflict within himself far subtler than the struggle of morality against evil.

(Frye 1971, 225–6)

An Introduction to Deep Terror

Northrop Frye's famous commentary on the peculiar anxieties that have apparently shaped the Canadian imagination suggests that people living in this country find themselves in a horrifying conundrum. On the one hand, the world "out there" is so threateningly indifferent to our existence that we are compelled to huddle in tiny dark holes, hiding from the enormity of our devastating irrelevance. On the other hand, our paralyzing fear of the uninterested exterior turns us into obsessive-compulsive shut-ins who impose unbearably constrictive rules of good behaviour on one another. This seemingly makes it impossible for us to *either* live as free individuals moving liberally in wide open spaces (as Americans are able to do) *or* thrive as a cohesive group gathered in a protective, self-contained space (like the British). Being Canadian, therefore, is a veritable nightmare! But it is a polite, law-abiding, and pleasant nightmare. For as perpetually terrified as Canadians might be, they do seem to live rather happy, quiet, and comfortable existences. And this is one of the many paradoxes of the Canadian imagination: our minds might be filled with horrible visions of physical torture, moral filth, and mental agony, but we also cherish our pristine natural landscapes and quaint little neighbourhoods.

It is very possible that Frye's reading of the Canadian mentality is a woefully inaccurate interpretation of the way the people of Canada *actually are*. But it does not really matter. The fact of the matter is that the – real or imaginary – tension between the "terrifying outside" and the "unbearable inside" has had such a deep influence on how intellectuals and artists have envisioned Canadian culture that it has come to express something of the Canadian ethos: a terror of the soul at what we *fantasize* ourselves to be. As Margery Fee argues in her contribution to the anthology *Northrop Frye's Canadian Literary Criticism and Its Influence*, "the widespread belief of critics, writers, artists, and readers that Canada's harsh northern climate in some sense explains our culture may be total nonsense … but it has supported some good art (the painting of the Group of Seven), and almost all English-Canadian literary criticism, both good and mediocre" (2009, 187). A manic apprehension of the outside world, coupled with an agonizing case of cabin fever, might have no grounding in Canadian reality. But it certainly makes for a hot and juicy counter-narrative to the otherwise rather lacklustre experience of living in God's frozen country.

Taking its cue from Frye's evocative insight, this anthology offers a theory of the Canadian horror film that locates the "terror of the soul" in the interval between external threat and internal dread. This is an interval where sensible prudence intersects with rabid exasperation, and rugged resilience clashes with childish cowardice; a liminal space where paralysing contradictions animate the nationalist fervour of meek bureaucrats and shatter the mettle of adventurous *coureurs de bois*. From this position of overlapping pleasures and pains, the Canadian horror film projects a disturbing image of malicious civility, brutal modesty, and cruel tolerance. In this ordinary wasteland of docile damnation and prosaic pestilence, savage beasts and mad scientists rub elbows with pasty suburbanites, crusty seamen, and baby-faced porn stars. The Canadian horror film, we argue over the following thirteen chapters, produces a discourse of paradoxes where familiar places lose their proper names, monsters behave like self-righteous victims, and heroes prove to be perverts. This is the stuff of an "uncanny nation" as Justin D. Edwards (2005, xix) characterizes (gothic) Canada. Canadian horror is a genre where the urge to erect borders, assert rules, and preserve decency is equalled only by a defiant impulse to challenge limits and throw caution to the frigid northern winds. Decidedly centrifugal in its hostile distortion of sublime natural vistas, the Canadian horror film thrives on the centripetal iconography of a monstrously protective homestead.

One hundred years after the 1913 release of the first Canadian horror film, Henry MacRae's short *The Werewolf*, Canada has produced and co-produced a significant body of scary movies that have both reflected the dark fantasies of Canadians and impacted the filmic practices of other nations. Some films, such as *Ginger Snaps Back: The Beginning* (2004, Grant Harvey) and *Le poil de la bête* (2010, Philippe Gagnon), explicitly evoke Frye's idea of the "garrison mentality" by depicting the frightful experience of early European settlers in Canada, huddling in small isolated communities, threatened by the metaphorical lycanthropes that roamed the dark, uncharted forests of the far-flung colonies. Other films modernize the image of the garrison by transforming the old colonial barracks into urban apartment buildings or office towers that shelter, imprison and dement fearful Canadians. Films ranging from Maude Michaud's unsettling *Dys-* (2014) to David Cronenberg's classic *Shivers* (1975) are striking examples of this practice.

Cronenberg's surprisingly consistent reliance on the conventional tropes of Canadian horror has often been examined by critics. Piers Handling (1983), Bill Beard (1994), Gaile McGregor (1992) and Bart Beaty (2008), have all shown that "from a thematic perspective, Cronenberg's work can be argued to be very close to the archetypal profiles of Canadian culture as advanced by Northrop Frye [and] Margaret Atwood" (Beard 2002, 147). Beyond self-imposed isolation in the garrison to hide from a threatening environment (see *Shivers*, *Dead Ringers* [1988], and *Spider* [2002]), all the other neurotic obsessions of Canadians also appear in Cronenberg's oeuvre: a deep anxiety about rampant technological progress, prototypically expressed in the writings of Marshall McLuhan, Harold Innis, and especially George Grant[1] (see *Videodrome* [1983], *Crash* [1996], and *eXistenz* [1999]); a pathological fixation on emasculation as showcased in canonical Canadian films like Don Shebib's *Goin' Down the Road* (1970)[2] (see *Rabid* [1977], *Scanners* [1981], and *Eastern Promises* [2007]); a paralyzing insecurity before creativity and innovation[3] (see *The Fly* [1986] and *Naked Lunch* [1991]); and a ridiculous need to hide violence and perversion behind the veil of good conduct and respectability (see *The Brood* [1979], *M. Butterfly* [1993], *A History of Violence* [2005], and *A Dangerous Method* [2011]). Over the past forty years, Cronenberg has tapped into our prosaic anxieties to create the grammar and syntax of national dread that film scholars endlessly venture to dissect and decipher.

Aside from Cronenberg's films, a few other entries in the canon of Canadian horror cinema have attracted scholarly attention. *Cube* (1997, Vincenzo Natali) and *Ginger Snaps* (2000, John Fawcett), as genuine international hits, have been discussed at some length by serious critics.[4] And as an early prototype of the "teen slasher," *Black Christmas* (1974, Bob Clark) has secured a place in the pages of horror film history books.[5] But by and large, Canadian horror cinema has not received sustained critical scrutiny. This is especially true of those cheaply made "tax-shelter " films that hide all references to Canada whatsoever, as in *Deadly Eyes* (1982, Robert Clouse) in which Toronto masquerades as Any-town, USA, and dachshunds masquerade as giant rats . However, from the perspective of this anthology, such films are worthy of attention; for concealed in the shadows of ostentatious Americana lurk evil beasts that incarnate fears and apprehensions deeply repressed in the recesses of the Canadian psyche. One of the goals of *The Canadian Horror Film: Terror of the Soul* is precisely to unearth the secrets of the petrified Canadian body that years of intellectual doubt and academic suspicion have buried under the dirt of critical paranoia and neurotic acculturation.

If, as Robin Wood (1979, 14) has famously suggested, the horror film can be essentially summarized as when "normality is threatened by the monster," then normality in the Canadian horror film is "peace, order and good government"[6] and the monster is everything that unsettles this boring civil society. The most obvious threat to dreary Canadian normality is, of course, bipolar American radicalism. This menace is literalized in the French-Canadian tale of terror *Le collectionneur* (2002, Jean Beaudin) in which a psycho killer from the US panics the sleepy bureaucracy of Quebec City. But more often than not, the American peril takes the insidious form of frightening omnipresence, with conspicuous American flags on the front lawns of anonymous Winnipeg bungalows and blue mailboxes on the generic streets of Ottawa, which exacerbate the Canadian fear of disappearance under the crushing weight of the colonizing monster to the south. Made-in-Canada films such as Don

McBrearty's *American Nightmare* (1983), Mary Haron's *American Psycho* (2000), and the Soska sisters' *American Mary* (2012) make explicit in their very titles this omnipresent dread of being swallowed up by Uncle Sam (Loiselle 2014).

Dull Canadian peacefulness is also threatened by the legendary malevolence of our indifferent natural environment, which, at the drop of a hat, can turn from bucolic melancholia into either a flaming blizzard that burns the skin of an innocuous scientist, as in the remake of *The Thing* (2011, Matthijs van Heijningen Jr.) or an undead beast that tears out the flesh of a self-righteous environmentalist, as in Carl Bessai's logging camp zombie nightmare, *Severed: Forest of the Dead* (2005). Similarly, mundane but safe Canadian secularism can be threatened by excessive religiosity and perverse devoutness, usually expressed in the form of devil worship, as in Jean Beaudin's *Le diable est parmi nous* (1972), Harvey Hart's *The Pyx* (1973), Éric Tessier's *Sur le seuil* (2003), and Maurice Devereaux's *Blood Symbol* (1992) and *End of the Line* (2007). Perhaps most disturbingly, the normality that is threatened by the monster in the Canadian horror film is represented by the superficial rationalism, prudence, and level-headedness that conservative British North Americans are so proud of, but which collapse like a house of cards under the pressures of repressed lust, anger, and madness. This is brilliantly evoked in *The Dark Hours* (2005, Paul Fox), in which a relentlessly rational and coldly clinical psychiatrist snaps when she catches her cheating husband and sister in each other's arms and axes them to pieces (and, incidentally, also shoots the family dog in the head). These and other forms of "typical" Canadian terrors are explored in the following chapters.

The Canadian Horror Film: Terror of the Soul is divided into six sections. It begins with a general consideration of some of the most basic questions and concerns which are at the heart of Canadian horror cinema, from the diversity of "Canadian Monsters," to the reactions against the threatening presence of the American film industry. The second section delves deeper into Canadian culture, drawing essential connections between the collective imagination as it is interpreted through literature, and the way in which it bleeds into cinematic representations from the industries of both of our official languages. Following this analysis is a brief historical look at the gory slashers produced during the notorious "tax shelter" era, which then gives way to a reflection on Canada's preoccupation with its image of environmentalism, which translates into a distinct form of eco-horror. We then take an uncertain turn away from the mainstream of Canadian horror films – such as it is – towards animation and the avant-garde as unexpected vehicles for the macabre and the grotesque. Unsurprisingly, we conclude our journey through pain, anguish, and agony with an homage, of sorts, to the single most important figure of Canadian horror cinema: David Cronenberg. Each chapter of this book scrutinizes a small body of films whose common style, thematic concerns, or auteurist signature are dissected to identify the various limbs of a corpus that is hauntingly recognizable as Canadian.

Dissecting the Canadian Horror Cinema Body

The first section of *Terror of the Soul* opens with Caelum Vatnsdal's "Monsters up North: A Taxonomy of Terror." This chapter takes the form of a (crypto-)zoological inspection of the myriad creatures roaming the snowy landscapes of Canadian cinema – and, as the films and their makers seem to attest, our collective Canuck consciousness. From Cronenberg's protean-rage creatures in *The Brood* to the pubescent were-women of *Ginger Snaps*, Canadian monsters have a way of bursting forth unexpectedly from within our mild-mannered psyches, as though their primary mission were to rend asunder our fawning, self-congratulatory, and increasingly inaccurate profile as a global force for moderation, reason, balance, and restraint. The chapter also discusses more realistic creatures. The giant rat upsetting a Toronto family's upper-middle-class harmony in *Of Unknown Origin* (1983, George P. Cosmatos); his partners-in-chaos in *Deadly Eyes*; the mangy accessories to a young boy's vengeful anger found lurking in *The Pit* (1981, Lew Lehman); the necrotarian shag monster of *The Dark* (1993, Craig Pryce): all of these vicious mutants have something to tell us about the fears and ferocities to be found in the Canadian soul. Still other beasts leap forth from the mists of history and Aboriginal myth, as we see in movies like 1913's *The Werewolf*, or more recent efforts like *Ghostkeeper* (1986, Jim Makichuk). Sometimes the monsters are the products of weird science, as in *The Brain* (1988, Ed Hunt) or Cronenberg's remake of *The Fly*. This chapter is dedicated to discussing two central questions: where do the monsters in Canadian cinema come from, and what do they mean?

Vatnsdal's essay identifies proper fantastical monsters, but of course there are other threats at work in Canadian horror cinema. The notion of cultural empowerment, or lack thereof, informs Andrea Subissati's "Viral Culture: Canadian Cultural Protectionism and *Pontypool*." For Subissati, cultural identity is a slippery thing that becomes even more difficult to articulate in the context of globalization and virtualization processes. For the most part, being Canadian is understood in negative terms as a counterpoint to being American. In addition to their constant reactions against cultural assimilation with the United States, Canadians also have to contend with cultural tensions from within, especially in terms of relations between Quebec and the rest of the country. Thus, the Canadian experience is one of shaky cultural identity where cultural assimilation or cultural implosion is an increasingly real fear. Bruce McDonald's 2009 horror film *Pontypool* examines this fear of cultural assimilation in inventive and thought-provoking ways. In the film, a deadly virus sweeps through the small Ontario town, turning its residents into mindless homicidal carriers of the disease. But this is no T-virus, trioxin, or even tetrodotoxin responsible for making people this way. The virus is transmitted through speech, or more specifically, through the complex processes of verbal comprehension. As the characters in the film struggle to survive the bizarre disease, they encounter confusing intervention from Europe as well as the French-Canadian authorities. This chapter explores the allegorical links between the virus and the infectious nature of culture with reference to the ways in which the film speaks to our heritage of seeking to preserve our loosely defined concept of what it means to live on the margins of the Anglo-American linguistic empire.

The danger of cultural assimilation, but of a different form, is a theme which reappears in section two, at the core of Aalya Ahmad's chapter "Blood in the Bush Garden: Indigenization, Gender, and Unsettling Horror." Ahmad notes that both the absences and appearances of indigenous people in canonical English Canadian literature have been traced by Frye and Margaret Atwood. Frye explains the absences by saying that "Canada has not had, strictly speaking, an Indian war: there has been much less of the 'another redskin bit the dust' feeling in our historical imagination" (Frye 1971, 224), and contends that our imagination has instead concentrated on the conquest of nature rather than the conquest of Native peoples. Margaret Atwood discusses the anxiety of "going Indian – in a more literary sense," arguing that the impersonation of Native people stems from "the feeling of being alien, of being shut out" (Atwood 1995, 60). It is at "that imaginative frontier, where the imported European imagination meets and crosses with the Native indigenous one" (1995, 64) that Atwood sees monsters beginning to appear as a topographic feature of the Canadian wilderness. Ahmad's chapter takes as its starting point the inescapable fact that what we speak of as "Canadian" identity is defined by settler cultures that have figured Native people as simultaneously monstrous and desirable. Following Atwood, Ahmad argues that this "indigenism" can be discerned in the Othered identities that pervade Canadian horror fictions, film being no exception. Using the work of horror theorists such as Judith Halberstam and Robin Wood, she discusses various ways in which indigenism figures in horror films, such as *Ginger Snaps Back* and Ryszard Bugajski's *Clearcut* (1991). If horror produces national identity in particular ways, according to "imagined communities" which are "conceived in language not in blood" (Halberstam 1995, 14), the language of Canadian horror produces a troubled Canadian identity that disrupts the boundaries between monstrous "savagery" and "civilization" governing Frye's "garrison mentality."

André Loiselle's contribution, "Pure Laine Evil: The Horrifying Normality of Québec's Ordinary Hell in the Film Adaptations of Patrick Senécal's 'Romans d'Épouvante,'" continues to explore the relationship between horror literature and film. But here the focus is narrowed down to three screen adaptations of novels by "le Stephen King Québécois," Patrick Senécal: *5051, rue des ormes* (1994), *Sur le seuil* (1998), and *Les 7 jours du talion* (2002). What Loiselle's analysis reveals is that, unlike the terrifying Wendigo and the other fantastical northern monsters discussed by Vatnsdal and Ahmad, the fiends that people Senécal's "romans d'épouvante" and their film versions are ordinary men. Horror in these novels and films is not caused by some formidable creatures emerging from dark, mythical forests. Rather, both heroes and villains are "Canadien français pure laine," old-stock French Canadians, who share cultural values and historical heritage. In these texts, fear emerges from the inconceivable personal and cultural affinity between monster and victim.

In section three, we narrow down the focus even further to zero in on the anxiety and struggles of a specific type of villain who thrived in the 1970s and early 1980s: the psychotic killer of the tax-shelter slasher. One of the strangest films of the 1970s, *Death Weekend* (1976, William Fruet), is the first case study presented in this section. As Paul Corupe argues in "(Who's in the) Driver's Seat: The Canadian Brute Unleashed in *Death Weekend*," perhaps the film's most peculiar characteristic is its director, William Fruet, who, with this tale of terror, shifted away from the respected realist dramas (*Goin' Down the Road* [1970, Don Shebib] and *Wedding in White* [1972, Fruet]) he had been involved with to concentrate on more lucrative genre movies. The result is an uncompromising horror film: a harrowing narrative about a woman who takes revenge after she is brutally attacked and raped by a gang of hoodlums. *Death Weekend* was vilified by Canadian film critics, who felt Fruet had sacrificed his interest in home-grown themes to focus on the international market. But careful examination shows this film closely follows the ideas established in the director's earlier work. This chapter looks at how *Death Weekend*'s gang and their vicious leader, Lep (played by Don Stroud), follow in a long line of ineffectual, frustrated male characters that dominate not only Fruet's scripts, but many other industry-defining Canadian films of the early 1970s, including *The Rowdyman* (1972, Peter Carter) and *Paperback Hero* (1973, Peter Pearson). Specifically, the chapter demonstrates how Fruet takes the insecurity and misguided idealism that marked *Goin' Down the Road*'s anti-heroes Pete and Joey to horrific extremes by having an emasculated Lep track down and attack a female model in a show of macho bravado. This theme is further illustrated by contrasting the portrayal of Lep's gang in *Death Weekend* to the four rapists in the infamous 1978 American horror equivalent, *I Spit on Your Grave* (Meir Zarchi).

Central to the terror effect of *Death Weekend* is the unsettling tension between the urban sensitivities of the protagonists and the threatening rural environment in which they find themselves victims of socially and physically impotent hillbillies. A similar tension is at the core of an entire subgenre known as the "forest slasher." As Mark Hasan explains in *"Rituals*: Creating the Forest Slasher within the Canadian Tax Shelter Era," these films expose the endemic Canadian tension between a fascination with, and petrifying fear of, our natural environment. Generally, the forest slasher begins on the positive note of a recreational retreat suggesting that, indeed, Canadians love their luxuriant forests, pristine lakes, and soaring mountains. But things soon go grievously wrong when an assailant starts viciously attacking our heroes. Significantly, this aggressor is based in reality. Unlike Michael Myers in *Halloween* (1978, John Carpenter), who dons a bleached William Shatner mask, or Jason Voorhees, who outfits himself with a skull-gripping hockey mask in *Friday the 13th Part 3* (1982, Steve Miner), the villains in the forest slasher sport neither a mask nor uniform for their violent endeavours; they just wear their everyday hillbilly clothes. Furthermore, the aggressor in a forest slasher is often a member of an extended family, living off the land, and fuelled by hatred of city folks. These rustic families see no difference between the acquisition, processing, and consumption of the meat of bear, deer, or a wandering hiker attempting to find some spiritual connection with nature.

With this fixation on our natural landscape in mind, section four contemplates the horror inherent in our physical and cultural environments. In "The [Hostile] Nature of Things: A Cultural Dialogue on Environmental Survival," Gina Freitag addresses the discourse on survival, initiated by the ideas of Atwood, by creating a comparison between the works of iconic environmentalist David Suzuki and instances of Canadian eco-horror, such as *Severed: Forest of the Dead, Kaw* (2007, Sheldon Wilson), and *The Thaw* (2009, Mark A. Lewis). These cultural artefacts form a discussion around the concern that "solutions are in our nature," that it is in our power to take action against environmental destruction. More significantly, this essay allows for a criticism of the underlying attitude that nature is "the solution." Evidently, our collective imagination suggests that not only do we believe that it is too late to instil change, but we tend to envision violent environmental retribution as necessary punishment for our failure to prevent the extent of our current environmental crises.

Peter Thompson's essay offers another element to our ecological image by placing the notion of environmental retribution along the margins of the east coast in his chapter "Eco-Horror and Boundary Transgressions in *Orca: The Killer Whale.*" Thompson notes that Newfoundland has long held a sense of awe for people from outside the province. Writers and artists such as Farley Mowat and Rockwell Kent often move to the province to be inspired by its remote and rugged landscape, and film crews from the United States and other parts of Canada often use Newfoundland's dramatic scenery as backdrops. In spite of this, depictions of the province by "outsiders" often cause controversy. For example, many critics, novelists, scholars, and residents of Newfoundland responded with bitterness to the romanticized version of outport life in *The Shipping News* (2001, Lasse Hallström). Reaction to the cult film *Orca* (1977, Michael Anderson), however, has been much different. While *Orca* seems incongruent with much of the cultural production that has come out of Newfoundland in the past fifty years, this chapter examines how it actually fits into conventional depictions of Newfoundland and images of the province produced by the tourism industry in unexpected ways. The film's hunt for killer whales parallels the province's popular whale-watching industry, the rugged northern landscape evoked in the film is similar to depictions of the province in tourism videos, the municipalities of Terranova and St John's commemorate the production of the film with signs, and tour guides to the region take visitors to locations where filming took place. Perhaps more than this, the film fits in with received narratives about both Canada and Newfoundland: the "eco-horror" genre – in this case, a whale that looks to exact revenge on the crew of a ship who kill the unborn fetus carried by his mate – certainly matches Northrop Frye's description of the immense fear of nature characteristic of Canadian cultural production, and whaling adventures in the north fit in with romantic depictions of Newfoundland provided by writers such as Mowat.

From eco-terrorism and geographical margins we move, in section five, to generic margins and the terror of commercialization, with Kier-La Janisse's "A Song from the Heart Beats the Devil Every Time: The Fear of Selling Out in Nelvana's *The Devil and Daniel Mouse* and *Rock and Rule.*" The title of this chapter is taken from a line in one of the films produced by the animation company Nelvana, *The Devil and Daniel Mouse* (1974), a rock-infused supernatural television special whose preoccupations would later be elaborated upon in Nelvana's feature film *Rock and Rule* (1983). The chapter is devoted to these two films as a means of examining how the three artists who founded Nelvana in 1971 – Michael Hirsch, Clive A. Smith, and Patrick Loubert – emerged from the radicalism of the 1960s with the goal of making intelligent children's animated films informed by their mutual interest in underground filmmaking and early Canadian comic book art. The three shared a unique aesthetic and artistic sensibility that made Nelvana internationally renowned as a dynamic complement to the animation being produced by the National Film Board of Canada, but they were constantly dogged by their fear of selling out to the mainstream. It was this fear of being hegemonized and artistically neutered by the lure of mainstream money that made its way into the narratives of *The Devil and Daniel Mouse* and *Rock and Rule* – both of which feature singers who sell their souls – or more specifically, their *voices* – to the devil. These cautionary rock-operatic horror tales for kids reflected a larger Canadian fear of being silenced by US-dominated corporate interests.

Resistance to the mainstream and commercial interests is also central to the Canadian avant-garde. But the fear expressed in the experimental films studied by Scott Birdwise in "Where is Fear? Space, Place, and the Sense of Horror in the Canadian Avant-Garde Film" is not that of "selling out," but rather the dread of the ontological violence of the real. The experimental approach to film is often said to foreground the medium and its aesthetic possibilities; avant-garde films are deemed to serve a kind of art-for-art's-sake project that is disconnected from the real world. But, as Birdwise argues, Canadian avant-garde films are often deeply immersed in the real's inescapable brutalities. Deploying horrific imagery to create an intensification of the cinematic experience through a located manifestation of repressed violence, films like Bruce Elder's *Crack, Brutal Grief* (2000) and Jack Chambers's *The Hart of London* (1968–70) are directly engaged with the unending struggle between the self, nature, and community. Like Cronenberg's *Shivers*, *Crack, Brutal Grief* and *The Hart of London* explore the latent violence of communities trapped in a world evermore driven by destructive technological mastery, a world where humanity has effectively abdicated its responsibility to others.

It is no coincidence, then, that the most renowned Canadian horror film director would have emerged from the experimental cinema tradition of the 1960s. It is only after having explored issues of perverse communal ontology and toxic technological epistemology in his avant-garde features *Stereo* (1969) and *Crimes of the Future* (1970) that David Cronenberg could move on to direct his landmark cinematic tales of terror: *Shivers*, *The Brood*, *The Fly*, and *Dead Ringers*. It is only fitting that this anthology should close on a broad assessment of the work of Canada's horror meister.

From the start, Cronenberg has sought to destabilize the generic conventions of horror. But over the past several years, his relation to the genre has become even more complicated and idiosyncratic. In the first chapter of section six, "Traces of Horror: The Later Films of David Cronenberg," Bill Beard examines Cronenberg's more recent productions to argue that, in spite of their superficial difference from his earlier output, they still remain horrific in a way that is clearly recognizable as Cronenbergian, and in a vein that is traceable back all the way to his earliest genre movies. Starting with *Dead Ringers*, and even more so with *Naked Lunch* on, we recognize a profoundly uncomfortable feeling attached to events that are not in themselves exclusive to the cinematic tale of terror but are completely in keeping with the uneasiness that always characterizes Cronenberg's horror. Indeed, if *A History of Violence* and *Eastern Promises* seem at first sight not particularly Cronenbergian, a closer view reveals them as bearing their director's mark exactly in this realm of queasy spectator discomfort. This essay describes the genre position of the later Cronenberg films, places them relative to his earlier body of work, and traces those disturbing elements which cause us as Canadians to find a kinship with that oeuvre.

In "The Physician as Mad Scientist: A Fear of Deviant Medical Practices in the Films of David Cronenberg," James Burrell discusses how the auteur taps into the fear and resentment that Canadians secretly harbour against their health care system. Placing implicit trust in their doctors' abilities and intentions, Canadians have rarely questioned the health care provided to them by public medical practitioners. However, misguided ethics and abuse of power by various medical and governmental bodies have resulted in several instances since the 1920s whereby Canadians have been subjected to – oftentimes without their consent – various forms of harmful, systematic, and unauthorized medical experimentation. As such, the fear of deviant, irresponsible medical behaviour (with the modern physician/surgeon supplanting the traditional mad scientist of American and European cinema) is a theme that resonates within Canadian horror, especially in Cronenberg's *Shivers*, *Rabid*, and *Scanners*. All three films comment on and denounce new and untested bioscientific procedures that aid in the creation and proliferation of a catastrophic medical and societal threat.

Younger filmmakers have been deeply influenced by Cornenberg's vision of a dreadfully unreliable medical establishment. Vincenzo Natali's *Splice* (2009) is but one example of this persistent Cronenbergian theme. But his influence has not been merely thematic. He has also taught new generations of cineastes to challenge and criticize this country's government-funded film industry through extra-filmic choices. This is the topic of the book's final chapter, Sean Moreland's "Contagious Characters: Cronenberg's *Rabid*, Demarbre's *Smash Cut* and the Reframing of Porn-fame." *Rabid* was the first non-pornographic film role for actress Marilyn Chambers. Similarly, Lee Demarbre's slasher-film parody and homage to Herschell Gordon Lewis, *Smash Cut* (2009), features not only a number of well-known B-horror celebrities, but also "porn star" Sasha Grey. While both Cronenberg and Demarbre emphasize that they selected their lead actresses for their ability to capture the characters they portray, it is nonetheless undeniable that their association with the porn industry is one of the ways the films attempt to critically engage the generic competence, and critical awareness, of their audiences. The narratives of both films frame issues of governmental authority, *Rabid* by emphasizing the mingled indifference and inadequacy of the government's response to its virulent, sexually transmitted contagion, and *Smash Cut* by satirizing the bureaucracy involved in funding film projects in Canada (as its fictional film-within-a-film's producer comments, "Now we can stop making tax cuts and start making money!"). Building on these themes, the promotion and reception of both films suggestively link their adult film–associated actors with anti-authoritarian sensibilities. Furthermore, the analysis highlights the way the filmmakers mobilized the association of their "leading ladies" with the porn industry as part of their critical play with cinematic genre. This chapter considers the economic and cultural context in which both these films were produced, and the way the clashes, both real and imagined, that they created with Canadian funding and production agencies contributed to their reception.

In the Conclusion, we reflect one last time on our intention to flesh out the nuances of Canadian horror cinema from a critical perspective, so as to uncover the more obscure sources and intricate manifestations of the deep terror of the soul that petrifies our collective imagination. Another crucial, if indirect, objective of this book is also to *decolonize* Canadian cinema, and particularly Canadian genre cinema. By addressing Canadian horror cinema as *horror cinema*, rather than as the *horror cinema of a minor cinema*, we wish to assert that after fifty years of commercial filmmaking, Canadian cinema should no longer have to apologize for itself. It should no longer have to be merely an "artisanal" auteur cinema. It has earned the right to develop a genre industry that can thrive and be analysed as such. Hollywood does not have to constantly justify its own existence; scholars of Italian cinema do not always have to contextualize their work within a broader context in order to be taken seriously; critics of Korean horror films do not have to refer to canonical works in the genre to demonstrate that films like *The Host* (2006, Joon-ho Bong) and The Pang Brothers' *The Eye* (2002) deserve to be analysed. The editors of this anthology chose to take a stand and declare that Canadian cinema *does* exist and that it has developed its own generic traditions. We unapologetically claim that if *Halloween* matters then so does *Shivers*. This is a performative act, which we hope our readers will appreciate.

NOTES

1 See, for instance, Arthur Kroker's celebrated book *Technology and the Canadian Mind: Innis/McLuhan/Grant* (New York: St Martin's Press, 1985).

2 See Christine Ramsay, "Canadian Narrative Cinema from the Margins: The Nation and Masculinity in Don Shebib's *Goin' Down the Road*," *Canadian Journal of Film Studies* 2, no. 2–3 (1993): 27–49.

3 As Frye argues, when we succumb to our self-centred insecurities, "something anti-cultural comes into Canadian life, a dominating herd-mind in which nothing original can grow" (Frye 1971, 226).

4 See Suzie Young, "Snapping Up Schoolgirls: Legitimation Crisis in Recent Canadian Horror," in Steven J. Schneider and Tony Williams, eds, *Horror International* (Detroit: Wayne University Press, 2005), 235–56.

5 See, for instance, Richard Nowell's "Chapter Two – Slay-Ride to Small-Town, USA. The Advent of the Teen Slasher Film, *Black Christmas* (1974) and *Halloween* (1978)," in his *Blood Money: A History of the First Teen Slasher Film Cycle* (New York: Continuum, 2011), 57–106.

6 This is the often-quoted phrase which introduces section 91 of the Constitution Act of 1867 authorizing Parliament to "make laws for the peace, order, and good government of Canada."

PART ONE

Shaping the Canadian Horror Landscape

1 Monsters up North: A Taxonomy of Terror

CAELUM VATNSDAL

Whenever another Canadian serial killer or mass murderer hits the news it is as though it were the first aberration ever to our otherwise mind-numbingly boring ethos, and everyone is breathless with surprise: Canada has monsters too!?! Indeed we do. A society that had no real monsters of its own, if such a place existed, would scarcely need to act them out on film, much less as compulsively and self-analytically as is done north of the 49th. Any portrayal of a monster is at its foundation an attempt to understand the origins of our deep-rooted fears; and Canadian filmmakers have frequently employed monsters in their fictions to explore their own obsessive anxieties, from the broadest and most symbolic sort, to the half-glimpsed figures lurking in the background when we look in the mirror, to the literal fanged and furred variety which are the ostensible topic of this essay.

It is a common fantasy among film scholars that a country's cinema is also its shared dream: flickering reflections of a cohesive national psyche. As a hard and fast claim, it does not stand up (a country's borders these days contain little more than a politically fabricated nation-state, irrespective of any collective imaginary). But as an abstraction, it can serve as a convenient instrument to consider a nation's body of films. Where Canada is concerned, this abstraction arises from a shared experience of wilderness as constant presence: in a nutshell, it is easier to get out of the city and away from population here than it is in most places. As a result of this proximity to untamed nature, most of us have felt the terror of the woods, of the hungry bear waiting in the forest just beyond the campfire's glare, or the still worse unknown thing whose slavering maw will be the last thing we ever see. Large, powerful, aggressive, and totally unpredictable things tend to frighten us, for we all collectively live next door to one, which is all the more dangerous now for being wounded, howling, and in decline. And sudden surprises, such as monsters provide, are a natural threat to our typically safe and orderly lives. The Olsens, the Bernardos, the pig farmers, the killer Colonels, the maniacs like Magnotta, and all their loathsome confrères, are a shock in placid old Canada each time a new one is revealed because it is in the character of the country to assume such creatures to be strictly the product of more brutal cultures.

It's worth noting that for every dingy serial killer the United States produces, several equally dingy low-budget films result; but, aside from Denis Villeneuve's serious and understated *Polytechnique* (2009), our filmmakers have left it up to Americans to trade in seedy dramatizations like *Killer Pickton* (2005) and *Karla* (2006), both of which attracted no small amount of scorn from Canadians appalled at the lack of taste required to exploit these horrific figures and the tragedies they caused. But that doesn't mean our filmmakers do not feel compelled to put monsters on the screen, and here, in the journey between reality and cinema – and in the form these monsters ultimately take – is where national peccadilloes reveal themselves further. (The absence of rougher beasts on screen, the two-legged ones which exist in real life, may be a byproduct of these national quirks.) Perhaps the best way to examine our Canadian bestiary is monster by monster, as a sort of a Horrorland Who's Who, complete with menacing flute theme. Accordingly, this survey of Canada's cinematic monsters will take the form of a zoological guide, broken down by species, which we may use in comparing our country's monster offerings with the Frankensteins, the Draculas, the giant apes, gelatinous blobs, and bandaged mummies of other, stranger lands, and also in self-examining our own society, what it has become, and what it fears.

Werewolves

Werewolves, or lycanthropes, are human beings who will turn into wolves either at the full moon or, by some accounts, at their pleasure. They roam the earth entire, and in particular eastern Europe and anywhere within the range of Gypsy peoples. Unlikely as it may seem, they have been known to stalk Canada as well, though their documented territory has so far largely been limited to the most populous region of the country, southern Ontario. Werewolves are Canada's earliest cinematic monsters, and still among its most resonant. It is a historic monster in motion picture terms: the very first Canadian lycanthrope to appear on screen, in a lost picture called *The Werewolf* (1913), is also the very first of its kind to appear on screen anywhere; and the creature itself, named Watuma, is larded with symbolic significance that is still relevant today. Watuma is a young Aboriginal girl whose mother had taken up with, and then was deserted by, a white man. The mother's consequent hatred of all white men is transferred to the daughter, who, in vague and inaccurate accordance with Native shape-shifting myths, expresses her displeasure by transforming into a wolf and ravaging all the Europeans she can find. She is apparently vanquished by a priest's hokum but returns a century later, now both a werewolf and a kind of ghost, to continue her mission. As the film has been lost, we can never know Watuma's reaction to the sudden, shockingly irreversible increase in white men across what was previously her people's land. In this context, turning into a werewolf seems a reasonable action, though this was probably not the picture's intention.

The Toronto area again felt the hirsute grip of the werewolf upon the release of *Ginger Snaps* in the year 2000. Here too, the werewolf is a young woman, and here too, given her insufferable (suburban) circumstances, lycanthropy seems the only sane choice. Moreover, the transformation coincides with the belated onset of her first period: transformation on top of transformation. Ginger the werewolf and her mousy sister Brigitte, by now a fellow shapeshifter, moved westward to Alberta for the film's sequels, *Ginger Snaps II: Unleashed* (2003) and *Ginger Snaps Back: The Beginning*. This final instalment, which took place in a nineteenth-century fur trading fort, was the true "period piece" horror film that wags had been calling the series from the start. Aalya Ahmad discusses this piece of colonial horror in her contribution to this anthology.

That werewolves figure so prominently in our horror film mosaic is not surprising, given that lycanthropy is nothing less than the sloughing off of a civilized veneer which, in the process, is revealed to be not nearly so deep or impenetrable as we would assume, a return to the state of nature from which our still startlingly young country is not very far removed. The sole Quebec entry into the werewolf subgenre, *Le poil de la bête*, is a striking, if somewhat crude, indictment of the hypocritical civility that hides bestial perversion and savage cruelty under the guise of culture and courtesy. These are understandable concerns in a country as close to the wild as Canada is, both geographically and temporally, and the theme weaves its way merrily through much of our genre cinema, particularly when monsters are involved.

Rats

For an ostensibly (though relatively recently) developed country, Canada has a dilly of a rat problem. Not only are the rats plentiful, they range in size from extraordinarily large up to the approximate bulk of a Cadillac. They have been found as far west as Bowen Island, BC, and as early as 1976, appearing in American filmmaker Bert I. Gordon's would-be H.G. Welles adaptation *The Food of the Gods*. In this picture, the rats have become enlarged by eating chicken feed laced with a curious subterranean paste; fowl, wasps, and even maggots have been affected too, but it is the rats which represent the chief threat, and mainland Canada is to be thankful that all this occurs on an isolated island.

In eastern Canada, however, the problem is worse yet. Toronto, its streets gaily festooned with American flags, is subjected to an invasion of steroid-inflated rodents in 1982's *Deadly Eyes*. These rats are the size of dogs, and with good reason: they were played by dachshunds in shaggy rat coats for the film. Another large urban pest appeared in Montreal, in the townhouse of a character played by Peter Weller, and while this lone rodent may not have been of monstrous proportions, it was able to cause a good deal of havoc by using its teeth and claws and by forcing the Weller character to, like a werewolf, abandon his civilized facade and regress to the state of a primitive man defending his cave with a club. Though the Montreal-shot *Of Unknown Origin* is set in New York, features an American actor in the lead, and is directed by Italian-born, Greek-blooded, Egyptian-raised, British-educated George P. Cosmatos, the Weller character's unwilling discovery of the savage self beneath his skin seems a very Canadian theme.

Back in Ontario, the giant rats of *Food of the Gods* reappeared in that film's sequel, *Gnaw: Food of the Gods II* (1989, Damian Lee), in which York University, or a miniature recreation of same, is overrun by cattle-sized rodents. And in a lonely small-town cemetery somewhere near Toronto, in a 1994 picture called *The Dark*, a corpse-eating rat creature lurks in tunnels beneath the graves and is sought both by a Canadian scientist who wants to study it and by an American government agent who wants to kill it. The nationalities of the characters aren't mentioned in the film, but the peace-loving rock-'n'-roll scientist is played by Canadian Stephen McHattie and the homicidal agent by American Brion James; this casting works well enough for anyone who may attempt a cultural reading of the movie.

Sasquatch and Monsters of Myth

If Canada has a national monster, it is surely Bigfoot, or Sasquatch, the legendary wild man of the woods who peeks out at our so-called civilized communities from the deep and dark woods that surround them. Sasquatch is like an emissary from our recent past, the wild and untamed past from which we've spent the last two hundred years trying to escape; and it may also be considered an avatar of Aboriginal resentment and/or white guilt. Somewhat strangely, the creature has not been used as a subject in very many Canadian films, though it has reportedly been sighted over and over again in every province and territory the Dominion can boast. What few cinematic appearances it has made correspond roughly with the locations of reported real-life encounters however: Jonas Quastel's mediocre 2002 British Columbia production *Sasquatch*, known also as *The Untold*, still stands, rather dismally, as the country's major contribution to the subgenre. Other efforts include a 2008 Abominable Snowman picture by Paul Ziller called *Yeti: Curse of the Snow Demon* and William Burke's 2011 production entitled *Sweet Prudence and the Erotic Adventures of Bigfoot*. Neither of these have much to do with the Aboriginal myths (and white anxiety?) from which the creature originally sprang.

Other monsters of indigenous myth have appeared on Canadian movie screens, but as with the Sasquatch, only with a peculiar infrequency and half-heartedness of execution. There is perhaps a reluctance on the part of white filmmakers to extend the plunder of Aboriginal nations from merely their lands and livelihoods to their myths. *Ghostkeeper*, an Alberta-made picture from 1981, is a minor exception, presenting a distinctly appropriated version of the Wendigo story but giving the audience little of the legend's rich back story and capitalizing on none of its horrific potential. Moving even further from any basis in established legend, we find more hairy humanoid monsters in pictures such as *The Pit* (1981) and *Humongous* (1982, Paul Lynch). These creatures share Bigfoot's hirsute savagery and do the job that they, as monsters, are expected to perform, but no more. They seem rather shy in fact, hiding in quick cuts and shadowy lighting (just as the Sasquatch obscures himself in shaky cameras and blurred footage), unwilling to show themselves plainly to the camera, and preferring to eat in peace.

Purely supernatural monsters, such as demons, are not and have never been popular in Canada. We are in general a secular people; our churchgoing, such as it is, is our own affair, at least for the nonce.

Demonic creatures in our films tend not to be Catholic in character, and our few possessees, in films such as Jean Beaubin's *Le diable est parmi nous* and Harvey Hart's *The Pyx*, come from Quebec and from a time (1972 and 1973 respectively) when the influence of the Church on that province could still be felt by audiences there. Perhaps this influence still remains in La Belle Province. Case in point: *Sur le seuil*, the only relatively recent film that uses Catholicism as a source of horror. André Loiselle explains it all in his chapter on the film adaptations of horror novels by Patrick Senécal – the "Québécois Stephen King."

But the country has its share of denominationally unaffiliated demons, such as John Hough's *Incubus* (1982), a priapic rapist which hides itself in a possessed human, only exposing itself to its chosen victims. A giant snake demon, originally of South Pacific aboriginal origin but fulfilling the same clash-of-'savage'-and-'civilized'-cultures function as would one of North American provenance, menaced Torontonians such as Oliver Reed and Peter Fonda in William Fruet's *Spasms* (1983). Tibor Takács's *The Gate* and *The Gate II*, made in the late 1980s and set in roughly the same neighbourhood as the first *Ginger Snaps* picture, gave us legions of cartoonish, non-sectarian and joyfully pre-CGI demons, upending suburbia and its quiet conventions with playful low-budget glee.

More recently, *Jack Brooks: Monster Slayer* (2007, Jon Knautz) features an anger-challenged prole who finds his true calling when he's revealed to be a natural-born slayer of demons from a nameless beyond. This skill set comes in handy when Ottawa suddenly becomes overrun by just such creatures, a scenario which unwittingly prefigured the 2011 federal election that saw the sulphuric Conservatives win a majority in Parliament. In the film, as in real life, it is up to ordinary people such as plumber Jack Brooks to recognize the threat they face, discover their own previously unsuspected courage and abilities, and stand up to the danger before it becomes irrevocably entrenched.

Finally, *Monster Brawl* (2011, Jesse Thomas Cook) brings us not only a shaved Sasquatch played by Art Hindle, but all the classic monsters of literature and film – Dracula, Frankenstein's monster, a werewolf, a mummy, a zombie, and so on – together in one movie, and puts them in a wrestling ring for a battle royal from which only one may emerge victorious. The film, with its traditional creatures engaging in activities harmful to one another but not the general public, serves as a counterpoint – or better yet, a remonstrance – to the general trend of insidiousness and originality in Canadian monster movies.

Aliens and Monsters of Science

Canada, being capacious and ever in need of skilled newcomers, does not have a great history of alien encounters, or at least of a fear of alien encounters. Aliens are perhaps scarier in crowded countries, or countries in which uninvited immigrants are regularly made objects of fear and political posturing. Still, we have had visits from interested extraterrestrial parties, from *The Christmas Martian*'s (1971, Bernard Gosselin) peculiar holiday sojourn in rural Quebec to the southern Ontario mind control and voracious appetite of *The Brain* in 1988. This latter creature is of interest for its refreshing duality: it is a literally cerebral creature with mind-control abilities, an interstellar intellect, and an ability to use technology to achieve its ends; but it is also a simple rampaging monster with sharp teeth and an abiding interest in swallowing people whole. It forces this duality on its follower-victims as well, who fall prey to tentacle-filled hallucinations and are made savage killers as a result.

A fellow traveller operating in the same territory at the same time as *The Brain* was William Fruet's *Blue Monkey* (1987). This creature is not a monkey but a giant doodlebug, and it has no telepathic capabilities and no broader goals than survival and sustenance. It acts like an alien – in fact, it acts precisely like the one from the popular Ridley Scott movie of the same name – but it is merely a mutation of some sort that has become inflated by steroids poured onto it by a pre-teen Sarah Polley. And Polley again helped create a monster using weird science in Vincenzo Natali's 2009 film *Splice*. Dren, as the creature is named, initially operates as a substitute child for the scientist-couple played by Polley and Adrien Brody, but, as might happen with any child, puberty brings on monstrous and destructive behaviour and ultimately brings an end to this genetically engineered family unit. Once again, an underlying violent nature asserts itself in rural southern Ontario, and the fantasy of control is blown to flinders.

An obscure British-Canadian co-production from 1967 is worth a mention in this context. Lawrence Huntington's *The Vulture* presents a monster, in this case a man-bird hybrid, whose origins involve both ancient legend and a newfangled scientific process, "nuclear transmutation." Again we see that the appearance of civility is as removable as the cloak worn by the grandfatherly historian whose true raptorial nature is revealed at the picture's climax.

Monsters from Within

Here perhaps are the monsters which most precisely reflect our country and the fears of our collective consciousness: the monsters which erupt from within ourselves. (Of course, as we have seen, this description applies in one way or another to most of our monsters.) In the films of David Cronenberg, which are analysed at more length in the last section of this book, the eruption is often literal, and the monsters themselves are merely catalysts to (as in *Shivers*) or offshoots of (as in *The Brood*) the bestial natures we cannot always successfully hide, no matter how hard we might try.

Shivers presents us with shit-coloured worm creatures created by a rogue scientist (who else, in a Cronenberg picture?) which, after intruding their way anti-excrementally into human bodies, give their hosts the perfect excuse to act out their (naturally) savage and sexual inner selves. Like another groundbreaking Canadian genre picture, the deeply and wonderfully ironic *The Mask* (Julian Roffman, 1961), it takes only a single alien element for the house-of-cards society we've constructed to fall down around us and, in the case of Cronenberg's accomplished debut feature, to render Nun's Island, of all places, ground zero for a new and savagely hedonistic stage in human development – a high-tech Garden of Eden where the forbidden fruit eats you.

The Brood is a much more sophisticated refinement of Cronenberg's themes. Elegantly yoking together the dangers presented by science (in this case an invented pseudoscience called "psychoplasmics") and procreation, *The Brood* presents us with the don't-think-about-it-too-hard conceit that concentrated anger may be expressed in the form of, you guessed it, monsters. These "children of rage" act out against anyone whom their progenitor is annoyed by, and provide Cronenberg's characters with perhaps the prototypically reserved Canadian's greatest and most secret wish: the ability to cause revengeful mayhem and wreak general havoc with not only the plausible moral deniability offered by an outside scientific or supernatural agency, but now without even having to get up from the chesterfield.

Cronenberg's final monster (setting aside the weird creatures of *Naked Lunch* and *eXistenZ*, which operate under separate cover) was *The Fly*, in which the scientist and monster are finally fused into one. The film is a ninety-six-minute exercise in determining that precise point where humanity is lost, and the great revelation it presents is that this point comes a lot later in the process than one might have thought from viewing previous Cronenberg pictures. This is the filmmaker's slime-dripping offer of comfort to his audience: civilized behaviour may indeed be a paper-thin veneer easily stripped away by one daft scientific gambit, but there is, deep within, a core of decency that will resist our bestial instincts to the last.

Conclusion

Clearly, Canada is not lacking for cinematic creatures, and they are as nasty and bloodthirsty as any found elsewhere. Many are startling and original creations, not beholden to dusty Victorian novels or established foreign mythologies; almost all of them serve as expressions of fear that our calm civility and rational control are tentative propositions at best, and contend that as natural as it may be, their loss is to be mourned. Is the homicidal maniac horrified at his own loss of control? We who present ourselves as civilized and non-violent can only hope they are, for that is something we can at least relate to; and the rich pageant of monsters on display in Canadian cinema operates as a fantastical backup to this hope. The loss of control represented by these creatures is horrific, it is undesirable, it comes when least expected; but it is also regretted by all, and, at least occasionally, manageable and even ostensibly conquerable.

But such succour is limited, for it is in the nature of horror movies to end with the suggestion that the horror must continue, and it is even more in the nature of Canadian monster movies to end this way. *Shivers* ends just as the horror is really beginning; *The Brood*'s final shot demonstrates how quickly destructive instincts are weaned of their scientific genesis to become hereditary; and *The Fly* comes to a similar conclusion. Werewolves are never truly destroyed; incubi simply find another host; space-brains are waiting for you in the basement; and there are always more rats, demons, and Sasquatches out there somewhere, waiting to make their move. Worst of all is the monster within, which dies only when we do, and reminds Canadians constantly, more than any other bestial creation we can come up with, that however much we may preach peace and tranquillity, however assiduously we may practise it, our country has its monsters like any other, and they are not going anywhere.

2 Viral Culture: Canadian Cultural Protectionism and *Pontypool*

ANDREA SUBISSATI

Among the monsters that Caelum Vatnsdal describes in the previous chapter, one is conspicuously absent: the zombie. Perhaps this is understandable, for the zombie does not seem, at least on the surface, to evoke a particularly "Canadian" fear. The mindless consumerism that the walking dead symbolize is a plague that afflicts all modern capitalist societies and has nothing to do with Canada in particular. But come to think of it, is there even a particularly Canadian object of dread that any monster could incarnate? What scares Canadians, besides cracks in the ice of our outdoor skating rinks? Desocialized medicine? Ineffectual gun-control regulations? Light beer? Quebec separation? No. American cultural imperialism seems to be the only real "monster" that Canadians actually fear. If the conventional wisdom on Canadian cinema, as expounded by authors such as Michael Dorland (*So Close to the State/s: The Emergence of Canadian Feature Film Policy*, 1998) and Manjunath Pendakur (*Canadian Dreams and American Control: The Political Economy of the Canadian Film Industry*, 1990) is to be believed, then the only "terror of the soul" ever expressed by Canadian film producers and Telefilm bureaucrats is indeed related to the behemoth to the south.

This chapter will investigate 1) the fundamental anxiety that afflicts Canadians, one that has lurked in our collective unconscious since our independence as a nation – cultural extinction – and 2) how this fear has ironically led to a type of protectionism that has deeply hindered our cinematic culture. Kier-La Janisse also elaborates on this topic in her contribution to this book. The fear of cultural extinction is broader and deeper than the mere trepidation at the thought of an "invasion" from the US. It is the fear that a huge, unthinking force will swallow us up, and there will be nothing left of what we understand ourselves to be.

There will only be emptiness, an emptiness that we always feel to be just around the corner. And it is that sense of our culture having been emptied of its meaning that a particularly Canadian kind of zombie might connote.

The fear of extinction generally takes the form of anti-Americanism, resulting in desperate attempts to articulate our distinction from the United States. The Canadian film industry, as a set of policies, practices, and productions, has long attempted to fill the emptiness of our national screens and show our place in the world. The difficulties faced by the Canadian motion picture industry have had real and tangible ramifications on Canada's ability to manifest itself in culturally meaningful ways. Canada's persistent failure to assert its permanence on screen and elsewhere has translated into an inferiority complex that leaves us wandering around like empty shells, unable to express ourselves verbally or otherwise. The aim of this chapter is to show how the Canadian fear of assimilation and extinction is reflected in Bruce McDonald's Canadian horror film *Pontypool*, in which our cultural emptiness is incarnated by zombified language. But *Pontypool* also provides a bold antidote to our protectionist tendencies in the form of a daringly alternative (linguistic) culture.

I – Oh. Canada.

Living next to you is in some ways like sleeping with an elephant. No matter how friendly or temperate the beast, one is affected by every twitch and grunt.

Pierre Trudeau, on Canada's relationship with the US[1]

Trudeau could have easily substituted the elephant in the above euphemism for a lion or a tiger, any beast whose ire you don't want to rouse. On the surface, Canada and the United States share a successful international partnership, with migration and large-scale tourism that benefit both sides. Any bad blood caused by the American invasion to then British North America and the resulting counter-invasion of British-Canadian forces have long been smoothed over since the United States Free Trade Agreement in 1988 and NAFTA in 1994. For the world's largest trading partners, quibbles about minor things like the environment, the eminent oil crisis, and Canada's risk of losing its cultural identity are easily swept under the rug in favour of maintaining economic prosperity ... that, and NAFTA of course. This section will introduce Canada's literary and motion picture industry with reference to the complex relationship between Canadian and American popular culture, and the tensions therein that caused Canada to lose its footing.

As a Canadian child growing up in the 1980s and 90s, I thought popular culture was another American export. Canadian-made movies and TV shows lacked the gloss of American production, and like so many of my Canadian comrades, I came to dismiss homegrown media as second-rate, symptomatic of what is referred to as *cultural cringe*: a term originally coined by literary critic and social commentator A.A. Phillips, who described it with reference to Australian culture in his 1950 essay entitled "The Cultural Cringe."[2] In the case of Australia, the pervasive sense of cultural inferiority came about because of the British domination of Australian theatre, music, and art. As is the case in Canada, many Australian artists and performers left their native soil for a time in order to develop their careers in countries with increased opportunity and a stronger entertainment infrastructure. Before Phillips coined the term, Canadian playwright Merril Denison had already described a similar situation with reference to the Canadian crisis of cultural self-esteem in his 1949 address to the Empire Club of Canada. He noted that Canadians gave little attention to their own domestic media due to an overarching belief that their culture or national identity is not worth expressing (Denison 1949).

The Canadian cultural cringe is nothing new, nor are its manifestations restricted to motion pictures. The man whose dark vision of our national imagination inspired the title of this anthology, Northrop Frye (1971, 226) noticed early on the devastating effects of the Canadian cultural cringe on the creative development of Canadian literature. Frye's collection of Canadian-scribed essays written between 1940 and 1969 entitled *The Bush Garden: Essays on the Canadian Imagination* meant to provide a composite view of the Canadian imagination and also contains an edited version of Frye's conclusion to Carl F. Klinck's *Literary History of Canada*. It is here that he first articulates his now-famous garrison mentality, where the archetypal Canadian sentiment was one of living in fear of being overpowered by the hostile and foreboding outside environment (Frye 1965, 224 and 342). According to Frye, it is because of this garrison mentality that "classic" Canadian literature often contains outward-looking characters who fail to overcome metaphorical walls which simultaneously shelter and segregate. He feared that the deeply ingrained Canadian tendency towards "protectionism" threatened to stunt Canadian literary development as a literature that was decidedly hegemonic: displaying deep discomfort with the "uncivilized" aspects of life and reinforcing social norms towards things like self-centred communities and narrow-minded politics. He wrote of his hope that Canadian literature would move beyond the constraints of the garrison mentality with the help of the forces of urbanization, whereby greater control of the environment and decreased reliance on the civic sphere would produce a society capable of more confident writing, "detached" from the boorish trappings of the classic Canadian imagination (1965, 236). For Frye, the menace that causes the Canadian cringe is our over-whelmingly indifferent environment, which in the dead of winter can obliterate us in a Saskatchewan minute. Given his fixation on the terri-fying Canadian climate, Frye did not write much on the threat of assim-ilation by American cultural imperialism. But both perils amount to the same thing: extinction.

In 1972, Margaret Atwood picked up where Frye left off with *Survival: A Thematic Guide to Canadian Literature,* her own effort to describe the Canadian imagination. Atwood agreed with Frye's assessment that Canadian literature was still looking for solid grounding, a concrete and distinct national literary identity freed from cowardly protection-ism that would bring "CanLit" on par with, say, British or American literature (Atwood 1972, 25). She isolated the theme of *survival* as cen-tral to Canadian literature, just as the image of the "island" is to British literary tradition and the "frontier" is to American (1972, 41). She found Canadian authors to be preoccupied with building a sense of "here" to fill cultural, physical, and emotional emptiness through a central protagonist who grappled with four positions of victimhood, echoing Frye's descriptions of the struggling survivor trapped within the gar-rison (Frye 1971, 45).

Atwood's positions begin with a state of denial, wherein the victim will deny that they are, in fact, a victim and may try to accuse oth-ers in their group of their own victimhood (1972, 46). The final posi-tion is the "non-victim," a recovered and self-actualized victim, for whom creativity is finally possible now that the walls have been torn down and nothing is inhibiting them (1972, 49). For Atwood, "the vic-tim" is the Canadian version of the American anti-hero or the German Romantic doppelgänger. Her observations echo Frye's garrison mental-ity: the Canadian inferiority complex and the Canadian cultural cringe that plague the country's creativity and threaten the development of a distinctly Canadian culture. What is important about their contribu-tion is that they imply a positive way out of this cultural void, through the conjuring up of tangible, robust, and evocative metaphors that can break with the twin traditions of self-imposed isolation and victim-hood. It will be argued below that Bruce McDonald's film *Pontypool* finds such a tangible expression for Canadian culture in the peculiar figure of the zombie, whose condition emerges from the viral material-ity of words emptied of their functional meaning – especially, English words. But there is more to be said on the Canadian cultural cringe and how some attempts to quash the threat of assimilation wound up dwarfing Canada's motion picture industry.

II – "Hollywood North"

While Frye and Atwood contribute much to an understanding of how Canadian literature grappled with the cultural cringe, they have little to say about Canadian cinema. The story of Canadian filmmaking is wrought with more material complications of production, birthright, and government intervention than its literary counterpart. Geographi-cally, Canada rests atop the most aggressive disseminator of movies in history, one that has a reputation of being able to dodge or bully its way through attempts to ban or even limit the influence of Hollywood ideology on foreign populations (Segrave 1997, 204). Hollywood got a head start cementing its foothold in the industry in the 1910s and 1920s while Canada was still a sparsely populated wilderness, which is why most Canadian films from that time were actually nation-building propaganda films rather than a source of entertainment and glamour (Vatnsdal 2004, 21). Starting up the country and surviving the harsh climate took priority over mythmaking and fantasy, and this pragmatic, constructive approach to filmmaking continued for years.

The spectre of cultural assimilation and the compulsion to insulate our young nation against outside cultural influence was already mate-rializing in the late 1920s when a British quota legislation declared that a certain percentage of films exhibited in the UK and the British Commonwealth (including young Canada) had to be of British origin. This quota caused ties to be temporarily severed between the thriving American motion picture industry and Canada's fledgling counterpart, which had up till then been working amicably together. But Hollywood quickly adjusted to the situation by producing a string of "quota quick-ies" (Morris 1978, 181) in BC that could circumvent the new regula-tions. While not strictly speaking a "Canadian" policy, this was the first instance of failed cultural protectionism in this country, and would set the stage for the future of the industry, exacerbating the cultural cringe for generations.

By the 1950s, lethargy in Canadian filmmaking had become so dismal that many promising Canadian artists simply relocated to the United States to pursue their careers. To counteract this, the Canadian government attempted several strategies throughout the 1950s and 60s to simultaneously promote Canadian cultural production and limit the effect of American culture on the domestic audience while maintaining precious trade agreements with the US. In the 1960s, Parliament Hill resounded with impassioned pleas for a newfangled feature film industry in Canada, citing the potential economic value as well as the cultural necessity of telling Canadian stories to Canadian audiences. Their solution was to form the Canadian Film Development Corporation (the CFDC, now known as Telefilm Canada) in 1967, which was given 10 million taxpayers' dollars to promote the development of a Canadian-owned and -controlled film industry (Vatnsdal 2004, 52). The problem with films being funded by the government is that it introduces the necessity of making defensible films, movies that are artistic, refined, and "safe" enough to appease most tastes. Evidently, this is not a recipe for great creative leaps. Critiques of the films that came out of this governmental creature became critiques of the CFDC itself and of Canada in general: a noteworthy example is Robert Fulford's (writing as Marshall Delaney) damning review in *Saturday Night* magazine of David Cronenberg's *Shivers* (1975). He titles his article "You Should Know How Bad This Film Is. After All, You Paid for It." Suddenly Canadian culture became a matter of taste and Cronenberg's lynching made it abundantly clear that racy horror films were not what Canada had in mind for promoting and *protecting* Canadian culture.

Government-mandated attempts at cultural protectionism were well intentioned but only served to exacerbate the problem in the end. Creativity and cultural identity cannot be forced, bought, or assigned. As Seth Feldman puts it, "The problem with film as an art is that it is a business and the problem with film as a business is that it is an art."[3] Frye and Atwood have scratched at the surface of what they claim to be a consistent thread in Canadian literature: the theme of victimhood stemming from a garrison mentality. How does this assessment hold up in the twenty-first century? Certainly, Canada is no longer the vast, uncultivated wilderness it once was, and the majority of the country's residents who dwell in the highly populous Quebec City–Windsor corridor might not enjoy the harsh winters but they certainly don't worry about surviving them. But many Canadians are still concerned about survival: the survival of Canada as a unique and distinct country from the US, and the survival of Canadian cinema as a separate and different industry from Hollywood.

Of course, many Hollywood movies are filmed on Canadian soil or written/directed by Canadian filmmakers and are still considered American movies. This occurs for a variety of reasons, one of which is simply to please the more affluent country. As an example, Caelum Vatnesdal points out that one of the reasons the American horror film *The Fly* (1958, Kurt Neumann) and its two sequels were set in Canada was to serve dramatic purposes, in an effort to make the setting remote enough to be considered foreign, but culturally similar enough to be relatable (Vatnsdal 2004, 28). Most Canadian films, at least since the creation of the CFDC (now Telefilm), have been funded with a complex array of government subsidies and incentives, governmentally mandated resources from broadcasters, broadcasters themselves, and film distributors. International co-productions are increasingly common, and Canadian films driven by American producers and distributors have dubbed this part of the industry "Hollywood North." Ironically, when Cronenberg remade *The Fly* in 1986, he shot it in Canada but with American funding, and opted to show American money and city skylines so as not to confuse and disturb American audiences (Vatnsdal 2004, 14–15). Would *The Fly* have been such a huge hit if the CN Tower was glimpsed in the distance? It seems unlikely that such a detail could have a profound effect on a good film, but somebody sure thought so.

The current Canadian criteria for film and television as set by the Canadian Audio-Visual Certification Office (CAVCO) specifies that all producers, and any person fulfilling a producer-related function, must be a Canadian citizen.[4] There have been disputes as to the Canadian-ness of certain films, the most recent example being 2007's *Juno*, a highly successful comedy-drama that was filmed in Vancouver by a Canadian director and yet was omitted from the Canadian Genie awards due to American financing.[5]

Pontypool does not have such identity problems. The writer, Tony Burgess (who adapted his own novel), and director are Canadians, as are lead actors Stephen McHattie and Lisa Houle. The film was shot on location in Ontario, in Pontypool as well as Toronto. Most importantly, the money behind the film was Canadian. But beyond the birthplaces of the wallet holders, Bruce McDonald's film is Canadian for other reasons too. The fact that the filmmaker is a well-known Canadian auteur brings to *Pontypool* a local perspective rooted in his deep connection to Canadian space. McDonald's other films, such as *Roadkill* (1989), *Highway 61* (1991), *Hardcore Logo* (1996), and *The Tracey Fragments* (2006), are marked by a profound sense of Canada as a geography that is constitutive of character (even when the place in question is explicitly *not* Canada, as in *Highway 61*). *Pontypool* is similarly anchored in a region that could only be Canada, in particular, southeastern Ontario. Furthermore, the film is thoroughly Canadian because it is all about survival – both literal and cultural, as expressed through the collapse of language as a meaningful mode of expression. The film is set in the small town of the same name, where a population of less than 36,000 resides. In the film, Pontypool is besieged by a strange virus that turns its residents into bloodthirsty zombies, but this is no zombie plague like any we've seen before. The remainder of this chapter will discuss the film with reference to Canadian cultural cringe and the trappings of cultural protectionism.

III – *Pontypool*

The movie begins with radio announcer Grant Mazzy driving to work in a nasty blizzard. He drives to the radio station, where he greets his young technical assistant, Laurel-Ann Drummond, and the station manager, Sidney Briar. Once on the air, they consult their weather correspondent Ken Loney, who describes a small riot occurring outside the office of a Dr Mendez in Pontypool before being abruptly cut off. He calls back with descriptions that are increasingly frightening, and he is eventually interrupted by an audio warning transmission in French. Laurel-Ann translates the message, which advises the radio station occupants and the population to avoid using terms of affection, phrases that conflict, or the English language in general. As confusion quickly escalates to fear, Grant tries to leave the radio station but is attacked by a horde of people as he reaches the front doors. Sidney and Grant barricade themselves, while Laurel-Ann starts stuttering and repeating herself. When Dr Mendez breaks into the station for refuge from the mob, he immediately recognizes Laurel-Ann's symptoms and blocks himself off in the recording booth with Sidney and Grant.

Dr Mendez explains that a virus has found its way into the English language, infecting certain words and spreading to others through their comprehension of the words. As he explains, they watch in increasing horror as Laurel-Ann slams herself against the booth window, mangling her own face and spitting blood. When the zombie mob breaks into the station, Grant and Sidney record a diversion in the studio and broadcast it to lure the infected away from the recording booth while Dr Mendez starts repeating words and appearing confused. Grant and Sidney hide in the kitchen upstairs, clumsily killing an infected little girl who attacks them en route. Stricken with horror and guilt, Sidney gets stuck on the word "kill," repeating it miserably. Grant is able to confuse her by repeating the word "kill is kiss!" until her symptoms dissipate. Confident that they now understand how to cure the epidemic, they go on the air and broadcast nonsensical phrases, ignoring warnings that the French will attack the station if these transmissions continue. Sydney and Grant embrace as the transmission counts down from 10 and the screen goes dark, leading us to believe that the French have attacked. However, a brief epilogue after the credits depict a hypothetical conversation between Sidney and Grant had they survived.

Pontypool has a distinctly Canadian feel to it – proud, or at least unapologetic, of its humble northern heritage. It is common knowledge that Canada suffers longer and more punishing winters than most of the United States, a fact that is reflected so beautifully in the scene where Grant Mazzy is driving to work, the cranked-up heat competing with the anti-fog while the windshield wipers fight a losing battle against the pounding snow. Laurel-Ann is the only one in the radio station who is fluent enough in French to be able to translate the emergency transmission, but Grant and Sidney are able to communicate (albeit haltingly) with the language when they're afraid to speak English later in the film. The lived experience of dealing with the snow and proximity to French-speaking Canadians contribute to what feels so Canadian about the film, but they only form the start of this analysis. Apart from the Canadian humour and the quaint little moments of familiarity, the disease afflicting Pontypool is all too familiar, reverberating with a dark cloud that has loomed over this country for over 150 years: the shared language and British ancestry with the US has made it challenging for English Canada to distinguish its cultural productions from those south of the border. Just as linguistic comprehension can be interpreted as a metaphor for culture, Sidney and Grant's impossible fight to protect their minds from the verbal disease speaks to Canada's noble efforts to retain a distinct culture, free from American influence and domination. Our two heroes' story taps into the Canadian cultural cringe while satirizing Canadian cultural protectionism.

Winters in southern Ontario are particularly punishing, and Ponty-pool is no exception, as exhibited by Grant's treacherous drive to the radio station and calling on the weatherman to report on the "cold, dull, dark, white, empty, never-ending, blow-my-brains-out, seasonal affective disorder, freaking kill-me-now weather front." In an especially candid and honest moment, Grant tells Sidney how long Canadian winters make him feel isolated and confined: "These late winters I feel like I'm in the basement of the world. It's so cold and so *dark*." Grant complains of feeling trapped before he is actually hemmed in by a bodily threat, speaking to a sentiment that exists intrinsically in the harsh environment. Later, when panic sets in and Grant becomes unglued, it is his isolation that plagues him most: "I need to know that there's more happening to everyone than what's happening to just me!" Most zombie movies make reference to feelings of claustrophobia as zombie hordes tend to barricade people in, cutting them off from outside resources, but Grant's remark echoes Frye's assessment of the isolation due to the garrison mentality of the gruelling winter environment. His unease is present before the actual bodily threat appears, representing the soulless emptiness of a country that is never at ease, never quite comfortable with its cultural identity both from within and with the rest of the world.

At the start of *Pontypool*, we have little knowledge about our central protagonists. Grant Mazzy was apparently fired from his last job for his dramatic flair on the airwaves, a flair that is also earning him the ire of his current station manager, Sidney. Their main tension is one of communication: his desire to gather an audience through controversial topics versus Sidney's reading of what their small town needs to hear on the radio in the morning. Grant craves expression and wants to make a name for himself but Sidney censors him for rational and utilitarian needs. Essentially, Grant is thinking Hollywood, and Sidney must bring him back to Pontypool. Their tension reflects those experienced by the CRTC: the desire to promote Canadian art while simultaneously regulating it in order to keep it within reason and artistically defensible in the eyes of its citizens. The irony here is the same as it is in Pontypool: playing it safe and appeasing everyone will keep the masses content, but it is not fertile ground for creative expression. This situation sets the stage for the main tension underpinning the film: the barricades that protect are also the walls that isolate and entrap.

Incidentally, the weather man Ken Loney is believed by his listeners to report on the weather from his aerial view on the "sunshine chopper."

Later, Sidney reveals to Grant that Ken is actually sitting atop a hill in his Dodge Dart, the small-town Canadian equivalent of a major city station's weather chopper. Grant is flabbergasted and visibly embarrassed for having believed the sham. The station's first breaking news story that morning is also a hoax: news comes in on the wire about a hostage situation that turns out to be a group of drunken old boys getting silly at the end of ice-fishing season. When Grant reports the story as such, roaring laughter and calling the culprits by name, Sidney admonishes him for humiliating members of their local police force who are known in the community to be barely functioning alcoholics. Grant quickly learns that his gig doing local radio out of an old church basement is a far cry from a big-city job, with imitated choppers and a community that tolerates a drunken police chief out of small-town rules of privacy and respect. He seems set apart from Pontypool, an outsider looking in on the town as though through a snowglobe. Admonished for his honesty and his Hollywood approach, he learns that Pontypool is not the place for showmanship.

Just as Grant must censor what he transmits on the air, incoming information is painfully limited and scattered. At the onset of the confusing crisis, the station is visited by a troupe of performers who are slated to be interviewed and perform on the radio show. Grant is furious at having to patronize his audience in a time of possible crisis, but Sidney and Laurel-Ann are unable to find reliable reports on the wire about what's happening outside until BBC World calls in. In clipped British tones, BBC news correspondent Nigel Healing asks Grants if it's true that French Canadians have set up roadblocks preventing entry and exit to rural Canada, and if these occurrences have anything to do with "Canada's history of separatist terror groups." Grant, Sidney, and Laurel-Ann exchange baffled glances, and Grant replies that there is absolutely no evidence of any political motivation to the swarming. They don't understand what's going on but they are now aware that the crisis has escalated to the point of global interest, or at least the attention of mother Britain. Healing's theory represents the limited viewpoint from even further outside the snowglobe, a view that assumes this rural Canadian disturbance *must* have to do with a French-English dispute because this is the only serious intracontinental conflict Canadians have ever had to face.

It is almost as if to corroborate Healing's theory that a French-language transmission cuts into their signal, warning them not to use terms of endearment, rhetorical discourse, and the English language in general. Grant's morning news broadcast has been entirely in English, of course, and also contained an anecdote about a missing local cat named Honey. When Dr Mendez, Grant, and Sidney are in the sound booth, they are able to discuss the epidemic while their live specimen, Laurel-Ann, demonstrates the culmination of the illness by mutilating herself, vomiting blood all over the sound booth window, and eventually dropping dead. They learn that the virus can only live by spreading, and that staying trapped in one host for too long will kill it. In this, we see an important connection between the virus and culture, as both must be sufficiently practised and reproduced in order to survive. Later in the film, Grant and Sidney learn that transmission of the disease lies in the function of *comprehension* and not merely of sound waves or of hearing. Language only has meaning when interpreted within a cultural context, a shared network that is practised and learned and constantly renewed by its inhabitants. Pontypool's virus is not one that can coexist peacefully in the Canadian cultural mosaic; nor will it mix well in the American cultural melting pot. The virus is a culture that takes over its host completely and represents a deadly threat to individual identity and survival.

When Grant and Sidney determine what they believe to be the key to surviving the disease, they resolve to bring it to the airwaves in spite of the French authorities who would silence them. They mean to save Pontypool, while the military opts for a slash-and-burn method to control the situation. Their voices are not heard because the military believes it knows best how to handle the crisis, just as the Canadian government sought to implement national policy to insulate Canadian culture. In this final climax of the film, Grant and Sidney represent a brave and desperate defiance against censorship and regulation. Fighting fire with fire, they take the zombified words, now emptied of their communicative function and existing as pure infectious materiality, and push language even closer to meaninglessness by further emptying terms of their conventional meanings through a chain of mixed-up significations: "Kill is kiss, kill is kiss," Grant repeats. Rather than seeking to *protect* the singular meaning of words – now that this has proved deadly – the only option left is to exacerbate the threat of meaninglessness until meaning takes on a different shape altogether.

In an epilogue after the end credits, we see Grant and Sidney in a highly stylized black and white scene. The scene is strange and mostly nonsensical, which contributes to the overall disorienting terror that the film seeks to convey. Snow falls behind them but the decor and atmosphere suggest they are somewhere far from Pontypool. There appearances have changed: they are now polished and suave; Grant wears sunglasses while he plays with a large pistol. They speak in eccentric terms of embarking on a sort of adventure: "We're breaking the limits, stealing cars, leaving the world behind to figure out what's black and white." This is a strange-looking Hollywood film noir, which both borrows and rejects the conventions of American cinema. Just like "kill is kiss," this American film noir looks like an Asian piece of New Wave Eurotrash that seeks to emulate Hollywood through Canadian irony. Grant and Sidney's proposed crime spree and devil-may-care attitude hearken back to their rebellious disobedience of the French military warnings, but also suggest that they were successful in their efforts and that casting off the shackles of reason, order, and protective Canadianness was their salvation and the key to their survival.

As such, the film ends on a decidedly radical and optimistic note, where Frye's garrison is conquered and Atwood's victims become victors, now free to be creative and explore the boundaries of their potential. At the radio station in Pontypool, Grant and Sydney discovered that the cure to the verbal epidemic was to break with reason – to shatter the shared, understood foundation upon which language is possible. Blurting nonsense onto the airwaves was strangely difficult to do because it required them to abandon their naturalized sense of linguistic association and reason. They were forced to act with the utmost creativity, unshackled by syntax or the laws of language, and the tragedy of the film is that their creative solution was quashed by the military before they could use it to save Pontypool. The tension here is in the opposing forces of censorship and creativity, and the message (if we choose to hear it as such) is that if Canadian culture is to survive, it must do so organically and on its own terms, free of governmental intervention.

This chapter has sought to describe how one Canadian horror film explores some of the cultural tensions that have materialized due to the American domination of the motion picture industry and the resulting looming threat of cultural assimilation. Canada is particularly at risk of being assimilated into American culture due to its inability to compete with American cultural sprawl. But interventionist efforts towards cultural protectionism have actually made the problem worse. As Canada faces the very real threat of losing its sense of creative autonomy, these tensions manifest themselves in art and literature. As early as the 1950s, Frye took note of a certain sentiment in Canadian literature that he termed the garrison mentality. In the 1970s, Atwood renewed his project and elaborated with an analysis of the recurring positions of victimhood that have appeared in Canadian stories. Their analyses speak to an innate sense of persecution and a resulting protective defensiveness ... but why? Canada has had a relatively harmonious past with little by way of epic warfare, natural disaster, or civil conflict. The battle Canadians face is one of identity and self-expression, and our best efforts to combat this through cultural protectionism have only stunted our culture industry and made the problem worse.

Just as this fear manifested itself in the Canadian literature studied by Frye and Atwood, Canadian horror movies have also tapped into this sense of dread as evidenced in the film *Pontypool*. As Canadian small-town residents struggle to survive a virus that attacks the socio-cultural instead of the physical, the movie presents an uneasy allegory of Canada's troublesome cultural identity. Just as Frye wrote of his hope that urbanization would set Canadian writing free, one can be reasonably optimistic that the increasing number of film festivals will provide a venue for the otherwise-unseen independent movies, and internet piracy will aid in distribution woes (sorry filmmakers, but wouldn't you rather be appreciated than paid?). The task at hand is not to bemoan the demise of Canadian culture, nor invent an identity that has no real foundation in Canadian history. If Canadian culture is built on assimilation anxiety and collective self-deprecation, so be it. There are uniquely Canadian stories to tell, and if *Pontypool* is any example, they are stories worth telling.

NOTES

1 Pierre Trudeau, speech to Press Club in Washington, DC, 25 March 1969.
2 See Arthur Angel Phillips', "A.A. Phillips on the Cultural Cringe," in *The Australian Tradition: Essays in Colonial Culture* (Melbourne: Cheshire, 1958): 89–96.
3 Seth Feldman, "Canadian Movies, Eh?" The Fifteenth Annual Robarts Lecture (Toronto: York University, 2001).
4 Broadcasting Regulatory Policy CRTC 2010-905, http://www.crtc.gc.ca/eng/archive/2010/2010-905.htm (accessed 18 February 2015).
5 CanWest MediaWorks Publications, "No Genie Nominations for Vancouver's Juno," accessed 10 December 2011, http://www.canada.com/vancouversun/news/business/story.html?id=fd0f69cc-a564-413f-9535-d25f0546d1c2.

PART TWO

The Territories of Horror: Terror Stories on Page and Screen

3 Blood in the Bush Garden: Indigenization, Gender, and Unsettling Horror

AALYA AHMAD

Using the word ghost is good because that's what the old people say when they talk about white people in this country: "Ghosts trying to find their clothes"
(Griffiths and Campbell 1997, 60)

In his seminal history of Canadian horror cinema, *They Came from Within*, Caelum Vatnsdal finds a significant absence of indigenous folklore's "blood-chilling traditions and legends." (Vatnsdal 2004, 22) In a telling metaphor, Vatnsdal frames this absence as a regrettable neglect of valuable natural resources, explaining that "a richly veined lode of indigenous myth remains largely unexplored by Canadian filmmakers, Native or otherwise" (2004, 22). If we look to literature, the "natural resource" of indigenous folklore seems to have been often exploited by the "otherwise" – for example, the legend of the Algonquian spirit Wendigo,[1] an entity depicted as a cannibalistic monster with an icy heart, eyes rolling in blood and blackened, frayed lips, described by Vatnsdal as "as frightening as any Old World vampire myth" (2004, 22). Northrop Frye tells us that "a writer who is or who feels removed from his literary tradition tends rather to take over forms already in existence" (Frye 1971, 232), and for white writers, the Wendigo seems to be a favourite form to take over. The Wendigo also appears in American film as far back as 1914 with *The Lure of the Windigo*[2] as well as more recently in the horror film *Wendigo* (2001, Larry Fessenden) and the satire *Ravenous* (1999, Antonia Bird). Continually associated with stories of relational and racialized boundary-crossings, the ravening spirit stomps through the wilderness-themed horror story of nineteenth-century Englishman Algernon Blackwood (1910) and possesses family members in

American horror icon Stephen King's novel *Pet Sematary* (1983), as well as appearing in the much lesser-known novel *Winter Hunger* (1990) by Ann Tracy, described by Margaret Atwood as a Canadian "female Wendigo" story associated with the liminal state that Barbara Creed calls "the monstrous feminine."[3] Atwood (1995, 109–14) summarizes *Winter Hunger* by arguing that the Wendigo is "used by the author for subversive and often hilarious purposes," turning a "terrifying male monster and ravenous personification of winter and of scarcity" inside out to become "an enormous and ravenous female body part."[4]

The Wendigo is therefore continually pressed into the service of gendered and racialized political subversion, a role it often seems to play in the more contemporary films in which it has appeared. In the context of a move away from the politics of establishing a national or "Canadian" identity towards what Alan Lawson calls "examinations of representations of the nation's Other ... the Indigene" (Lawson 2004, 160), the Wendigo seems to occupy a privileged representational space. In this chapter, I will discuss the Wendigo as an indigenous cultural form that has been appropriated, repackaged, and retold as a type of *indigenization horror*, producing narratives that effectively leave settlers *unsettled*, as all good horror stories ought to do.[5] I raise here the question of how indigenization horror might serve or potentially challenge national myth making, particularly when monstrous genders are also invoked.

Sunnie Rothenburger has convincingly argued that the Canadian feminist werewolf *Ginger Snaps* films and particularly *Ginger Snaps Back: The Beginning* subordinate race to gender in order to reproduce the dominant discourse of settler culture in the context of what Daniel Francis describes as "ubiquitous" attempts to appropriate indigenous mythology into "a more general mythology of relevance to all Canadians" (Francis 1992, 187). Such analysis, while valuable, does not necessarily do justice to all the unsettling implications of indigenization horror, as I intend to show. I focus here on how *Ginger Snaps Back* portrays the desire for indigenous identity, briefly comparing the Wendigo/werewolves in this film with the portrayal of Arthur in Ryszard Bugajski's film *Clearcut* (1991) – an environmental horror film distinguished by, as Gina Freitag and Peter Thompson point out in their respective chapters on eco-horror in this volume, boundary transgressions between nature and the human. Thompson in particular remarks that "the 'spectral presence' of North America's indigenous population is jarring to audiences who would prefer to deny the continent's colonial history and throws the bounded and unified notion of the Canadian state into question."[6]

Indigenization horror foregrounds such a presence, complicating the relationship between settler and indigene. Here, I consider monstrous masculinities linked with indigenous or Othered men that present an alternative to patriarchal white supremacy as part of indigenization horror.

It is instructive to compare the use of mythical creatures such as the Wendigo in indigenization horror with Isabel Cristina Pinedo's concept of race horror, which she describes as being predominantly relegated to urban settings where racialized minorities are concentrated, rather than the wilderness settings of indigenous encounters. Pinedo remarks on the continual surfacing of magic in narratives of race horror, including *Candyman* (1992, Bernard Rose), which she analyzes in depth: "Magic ... operates as a critical signifier of racially specific power and racially specific evil. Anthropologist Michael Taussig ... argues that the attribution of magical powers to oppressed peoples of color is a colonial construct. Though shamanism predates European colonization, historically it developed in relation to white imperialist power ... the colonial construction of magic aligns white colonial power with civilization and nonwhite colonized people with savagery" (Pinedo 1997, 119).

The Wendigo, and indigenous folklore in general, has long been mined in order to create particular types of quasi-magical representations infused with the sensibility that Terry Goldie names "indigenization" or "the impossible necessity of becoming indigenous" (Goldie 1989, 26). Goldie describes the psychological dynamic of indigenization as founded on the settler's gaze, perpetually trying to solve a riddle of occupation: "The white Canadian looks at the Indian. The Indian is Other and therefore alien. But the Indian is indigenous and therefore cannot be alien. So the Canadian must be alien. But how can the Canadian be alien within Canada?" (1989, 25). Goldie's concept is helpful for understanding horror narratives that are already heavily bound up with the implications of the gaze.[7] In "When the Woman Looks," for example, Linda Williams describes the "woman's terrified look at the horrible body of the monster" as containing also a germ of possible kinship: "a surprising (and at times subversive) affinity between monster and woman, the sense in which her look at the monster recognizes their similar status within patriarchal structures of seeing" (Williams 1996, 18).[8] Whereas the indigenizing gaze seeks affinity, the subject of horror finds it frequently in the monstrously rendered landscape of Canadian wilderness.

The very question of a "Canadian" identity is founded upon settler cultures that have persistently represented indigenous people as
hauntingly Other, whether monstrous or desirable (or both simultaneously). According to Francis, "The Indian is the invention of the European" (Francis 1992, 4), a mythical figure that "began as a White man's
mistake, and became a White man's fantasy ... anything non-Natives
wanted them to be" (1992, 5).[9] Or, as Goldie puts it, "The indigene is
a semiotic pawn on a chess board under the control of the white sign-
maker" (1992, 23). Alan Lawson's theory of "Second World" cultural
production is also useful to consider, the "Second World" in question
referring to "that part of colonial space occupied by so-called settler
cultures" such as Canada. In the "Second World," "mimicry is a necessary and unavoidable part of the repertoire of the settler ... the settler
mimics, appropriates and desires the authority of the Indigene." Second World narratives enact the "tripled dreams of the settler situation":
first, the myth of the vanishing tribe; second, the recovery of "authentic" Aboriginal art to efface the history of invasion; third, "the desire
to inherit the Natives' spiritual 'rites' to the land" (Lawson 2004, 156).

Atwood's classic *Survival* (1972), echoing Northrop Frye, connects
the question of Canadian identity to the question of land – "Where
is here?" – a query that Scott Birdwise takes up in his contribution
to this anthology. Atwood remarks that "'Who am I?' is a question
appropriate in countries where the environment, the 'here,' is already
well defined": "'Where is here?'" on the other hand, "is a different kind
of question. It is what a man asks when he finds himself in unknown
territory" and may or may not survive (Atwood 1972, 17). Atwood
traces a "preoccupation with the obstacles to that survival" (1972, 33)
through the Canadian imaginary, arguing that "the Canadian gloom is
more unrelieved than most and the death and failure toll out of pro-
portion" (1972, 35). In her earlier work, Atwood relates this grimness
to the idea that Canada as a colony is a "collective victim" and fits
the fictions she surveys into different "Basic Victim Positions," ranging
from denial to being a "creative non-victim" (1972, 36–8). Her reading
of the Earle Birney poem "David" emphasizes how the "landscape has
come alive; it is no longer an ocean but a body, the body of a vampire or
cannibal or ghoul, with its fangs and bloodthirsty lichens and its stench of
decay ... a destructive and hideous monster" (1972, 58). This "monstro-
phomorphism" of the wilderness, Atwood argued in the 1970s, reveals
the weakness of blaming victimhood on some "large powerful idea"
(1972, 63).

Since then, Atwood has moved significantly away from the conclud-ing summons of *Survival* for Canadian culture to make explicit "the real causes of victimization" (1972, 241) to the gleeful recognition and celebration of Canadian monstrosities, dramatizing Lawson's point referred to earlier about examining representations of the Other once the idea, however ephemeral, of a national identity exists. Atwood's *Strange Things: The Malevolent North in Canadian Literature* (1995) forms an interesting contrast with *Survival* – a radical shift from classifying the more macabre images in Canadian culture as indicative of a disem-powered victim position to acknowledging the "imaginative power" that such images might hold. Atwood, like Grey Owl before her, decks herself out in fringed jackets and ivory earrings to perform a type of Canadian/indigene hybridity for "real scholars from England," recall-ing Judith Halberstam's argument that the monster "always represents the disruption of categories, the destruction of boundaries, and the presence of impurities and so we need monsters and we need to recog-nize and celebrate our own monstrosities" (Halberstam 1995, 27).

Indigenization can thus be compared to Halberstam's "skin shows," celebrating and impersonating the racialized Other where "the ambiva-lent aspect of the stereotype [or Atwood's "cliché-image"] is … a func-tion of the possible simultaneity of fear and desire within represen-tations of otherness" (1995, 80–1). In the same way in which, as Hal-berstam argues, *Silence of the Lambs* monster "Buffalo Bill" illustrates how "gender is always posthuman, always a sewing job which stitches identity into a body bag" (1995, 176), indigenization horror signifies the covetousness of the white stranger or "ghost" who, through "desperate longing" for a presence on the land, claims kinship with the indigene in a postcolonial present (Atwood 1995, 60). In contrast to non-horrific narratives, however, the horrific aspect of a "national" identification with Indigenous monsters seems to register a great and terrible ambiva-lence about that longing or desire.

The Wendigo's appearance marks "that imaginative frontier, where the imported European imagination meets and crosses with the Native indigenous one" (1995, 64). It is at this juncture, Atwood tells us, that monsters become a topographic feature of the Canadian imaginative landscape for the settler looking at indigenous culture: "For indigenous peoples the wilderness was not empty but full and one of the things it was full of was monsters" (1995, 64). What is overlooked in Atwood's description is that monstrosity itself as an invocation of fear or hor-ror appears to be very much in the eye of the beholder of indigenous peoples, preoccupied above all with his or her own lack of place. Goldie's process of indigenization mirrors the gaze of white Canadians towards the Indigene, mediated by perceptions of monstrosity and haunted by genocidal guilt.[10]

Halberstam contends that horror produces national identity according to "imagined communities which are 'conceived in language not in blood'" (Halberstam 1995, 14). For example, "the racism that seems to inhere to the nineteenth-century Gothic monster … may be drawn from imperialistic or colonialist fantasies of other lands and peoples, but it concentrates its imaginative force upon the other peoples in 'our' lands, the monsters at home" (1995, 15). We might also recall Robin Wood's formula for horror as containing the three variables: "normality, the Monster, and, crucially, the relationship between the two" (Wood 1979, 14). Drawing on these ideas, we could say that, in Canadian horror, the settler is confronted in a variety of ways with the presence of the Indigene, the relationship calling into question his or her complacent sense of ownership over the land and his or her privileged position as the "normality" by which the Monster is defined. Horror therefore produces an *unsettled* Canadian identity, one in which the boundary between monstrous wilderness and brutish "civilization" becomes blurred with violence, death, and atrocity. As such, indigenization horror in Frye's bush garden is conceived not in language but in blood.

Werewolves and Wendigoes: *Ginger Snaps Back*

Indigenized monsters thus become enmeshed in a discourse of white settlers facing – and often embracing – indigenization as part of their discovery of self. One such narrative is the horror film *Ginger Snaps Back: The Beginning*, framed as a "prequel" to the cult feminist werewolf hit *Ginger Snaps* and its sequel *Ginger Snaps: Unleashed* where two suburban teenage "misfit sisters"[11] Ginger (Katharine Isabelle) and Brigitte (Emily Perkins) rebel against sexism by combining the curse of the werewolf with the onset of menstruation. *Ginger Snaps Back* features the same protagonists in period garb in 1815. While the opening credits roll, Brigitte's voice recounts the foundational story of the werewolf curse as an oral indigenous myth "passed down through the blood of generations" as "legends of the Wendigo" and "the coming of the Red and Black," a reference to the respective hair colours of the sisters. In an apocalyptic "Day of Reckoning," Ginger and Brigitte will determine whether the curse will linger "through generations to come," ultimately to be settled in the time of the first film by Brigitte's slaying of the were-wolf Ginger. Brigitte's voice, however, seems to contradict this inter-textual knowledge by continuing with the affirmation: "But ours was a story of survival, of two sisters bound by blood, a bond that would not be broken. That was our promise, above all – above men, above God, above Fate – it was in our blood. Together forever." The mystical oral-ity conveyed by this voiceover "becomes land, becomes presence," as Goldie describes, a signpost to a very different episteme and semiotic system, where indigenous oral tradition is set against White written history (Goldie 2004, 199).

Ginger Snaps Back can also be read as Atwood's "women writing wil-derness" with its opening scenes of the girls moving through snowy forests. The opening sequence, in fact, seems to encapsulate Lawson's theory of Second World narrative. Ginger and Brigitte first encounter an Elder (Edna Rain) at the site of an apparent massacre, who replies to their "What happened here?" with "My sister … gone" while handing them matching bird-skull necklaces, the meaning of which might be interpreted as either gift or curse, as Ginger's doubtful "Thank you" implies. Thus, the girls participate in the myths of a vanishing tribe and the recovery of "authentic" Aboriginal artefacts that Lawson notes as characteristic of Second World narratives. As soon as they don the neck-laces, the third settler dream of indigenous spirituality is invoked; their horse rears and panics, and the woman tells them, "Kill the boy or one sister kills the other," and Ginger begins to have a recurring hallucina-tory vision of Brigitte lying bloodied and dead. Chasing their horse, Bri-gitte subsequently gets caught in a leg trap from which she is rescued by the Indigenous Hunter (Nathaniel Arcand), figured as a menacing presence who has been stalking her from the woods, accompanied by howls and the appearance of a fierce, wolfish dog.

Advancing towards the trapped Brigitte with an axe, the Hunter is attacked by Ginger, but it soon becomes clear that his intent was to free Brigitte. The Hunter, therefore, is a complex character – simultaneously the compelling "monster" with whom Brigitte continually exchanges lingering looks of affinity as well as her rescuer who gently staunches her wound, mirroring what Caroline Podruchny tells us in her research on the oral histories of the fur traders, that "stories implicitly instructed voyageurs to cultivate relationships with Aboriginal people as a means of survival" (Podruchny 2004, 693). At the same time, the Hunter may or may not be "the boy" whom the girls are instructed to kill; instead it may also be the little boy Geoffrey (Stevie Mitchell) whose bite eventually "turns" Ginger.

The association of the werewolves with the indigenous characters thus at first seems straightforward. Goldie mentions the frequently recurring Canadian trope of "Indian wolves" (Goldie 1989, 37) and also the stereotypes of animalistic "Indians" in schoolbooks: "Indians prowl the pages of these schoolbooks like wild animals prowling the forest. Much is made of their highly-developed senses ... Their always crowded, dirty lodges are no better than animal dens. Their ferocity, too, is compared to that of wild beasts" (1989, 162). Ginger's transformation can be read as the "myth of transformation" that "lies at the heart of Canadian culture: Canadians need to transform themselves into Indians" (1989, 223). The werewolf transformations in the *Ginger Snaps* series might also be read as literal, monstrous embodiments of indigenization, turning white settlers in suburbs into that which they both fear and desire. This is the interpretation that Rothenburger favours, arguing that each *Ginger Snaps* film and this one in particular "engages with and critiques colonial history, only to then stereotype and negate Native peoples" (Rothenburger 2010, 106), ultimately subordinating issues of racialization to issues of gender. While I am mostly in accord with Rothenburger, I think a closer reading will lend some nuance to this argument.

The girls follow the Hunter to Fort Bailey, a remote fur trading outpost of the "Northern Legion Trading Company," easily recognizable for those familiar with the basic Canadian history of the Hudson's Bay Company. The garrison is, we soon learn, besieged by werewolves; the men in it are ragged, wary, and sullen. "Welcome to civilization," Ginger sniffs as she enters the fort and boldly surveys the men, foreshadowing her boundary-disrupting act of flinging open its doors and letting the werewolves in. The figure of the Wendigo lurks behind the werewolf attacks as a curse associated not only with indigenous traditions, but with the white colonialists' dubious "civilization." This ironic narrative strand, along with the deaths of all the indigenous characters in the film, seems to reinforce, as Rothenburger points out, the stereotype of the "vanishing Indian," for whom "contact was a curse, a sentence of death" (Francis 1992, 57). Similarly, the prehistorical setting of *Ginger Snaps Back*, "a story before story" (Goldie 1989, 151), recalls Frye's reminder that "Indians, like the rest of the country, were seen as nineteenth-century literary conventions" (Frye 1971, 233), impossible for settlers to envision as a part of contemporary life. At the same time, the fact that the film is actually a prequel, rather than a precursor, to *Ginger Snaps* takes the irony a step further, complicating matters by implying that the werewolf in the first two *Ginger Snaps* films may be a Wendigo, laying siege to the suburbs and institutions of contemporary white settler society.

The film also directly invokes the historical horrors of colonialism with its depictions of slaughter and open racism. For example, take the scene, shot from above, of werewolves entering the beleaguered fort, ushered in by a black-cloaked Ginger, who is rapidly transforming into a monster, as well as our first look at the clawed, blood-stained crucifix-laden doors of the garrison, recalling the following appalling account from the historical record: "At Fort Pitt on the North Saskatchewan River, dozens of Cree had died outside the post, their corpses devoured by wolves. The Natives believed they could rid themselves of the disease by transferring it back to the Whites and they crowded around the stockade, touching their pustules to the walls and spitting on the door handles" (Goldie 1989, 48). Similarly, when the girls stumble upon the smoking remnants of the Aboriginal camp at the beginning of the film, Ginger's question "What happened here?" is never really answered. Was it werewolves or white men who ravaged the camp and destroyed the Elder's sister? Colonialism is thus the real monster that lurks in the background.

These ambiguities are lost in Rothenburger's essay, which focuses on the binary opposition of race and gender; thus, the Elder woman's cave and ceremony in the film represent "an alternative to the fort and its military rituals," and her interpretation of the werewolf Wendigo mythology of the film is as follows: "It is as though the girls have used Native mysticism to facilitate the 'return of the repressed,'" accessing the power of the animalism that the colonial paradigm has denied (Rothenburger 2010, 107). The Hunter's death as well as that of the other indigenous characters in the film confirms, for Rothenburger, a triumphal colonialism, "the sisters' ownership of the land" (2010, 109). Rothenburger thus argues that "the films, from a certain perspective, offer little that is new in relation to a critique of colonialism in Canada in that the end of the trilogy leaves the land in the hands of Anglo-Canadians, even if in this case they are female." As such, Rothenburger justly accuses the films of "attempting to achieve 'indigenization' for their White, female protagonists" at the expense of the film's indigenous characters (2010, 99). However, Rothenburger ignores the hybridities of the *Ginger Snaps* films, resulting in a black-and-white analysis that leaves out much of the details.

The commander of the garrison, Chief Factor Rowlands (Tom McCamus), for example, far from enacting "military rituals," is in mourning for his indigenous wife, shown wearing European dress in a family portrait. It is revealed that she has been killed by werewolves; it may not be completely far-fetched to speculate that she may even be the sister spoken of by the Elder the girls meet at the beginning of the film. Rothenburger claims that Rowland's shot and shout of "I'm in charge here!" "explicitly link violence with patriarchal and governmental authority," disregarding his previous attempts to avoid violence, his concern for the wounded Brigitte, and his confrontations with the far more aggressively patriarchal figure of Reverend Gilbert (Hugh Dillon), the fanatical priest who snarls at Rowlands that the "plague has come because of your love of your savage wife!" and who attempts to burn Brigitte alive. Thus, for Rothenburger, "Gilbert blames the existence of the werewolves on the European men's sexual and romantic involvement with Native women, a punishment for the 'sin' of miscegenation" (2010, 107), but at the same time, Rothenburger evades drawing attention to the demasculinizing and humanizing effect that such romantic involvement produces on Rowland's character. This avoidance illustrates what Goldie terms "the unacceptability of interracial love," where "the problem is erased by the death of the indigene woman" (Goldie 1989, 70), with both priest and critic condemning or shunning such mingling. Lawson also disapprovingly mentions the "sentimentalization of the mixed-race figure that enacts a slippage between the white desire and the Native right, white 'civilization' and Native 'elemental energy'": "There is also a complex chain of signification between desire for indigenized identity, spirituality and land and desire for Aboriginal women … The settler's desire to stand in for the Indian produces the inadmissible desire for miscegenation, what is often known in South Africa as 'the taint'" (Lawson 2004, 157).

It is Rowlands's half-son Geoffrey, a vulnerable child rather than the predatory male werewolves of the first two films, who is the disseminator of the lycanthrope "taint" in *Ginger Snaps Back*, biting Ginger on the shoulder when she responds to his crying, and gradually becoming more animalistic and uncontrollable. Goldie notes that "at the centre of the blending of white and indigenous violence is the male character of mixed race" (Goldie 1989, 118). The hybridity of Geoffrey sets in motion the events of the film, but rather than supporting Gilbert's fire-and-brimstone rants about "stinking whore" and "dusky heathen bitch," the monstrousness of Geoffrey turns masculinity itself on its head.

In Canada, indigenous women who married non-indigenous men have historically been stripped of their status, and it is this dispossession and erasure that the werewolf Geoffrey seems to continually protest through his monstrous transformation. The only time we see Geoffrey as a human child, free of his deformity, is when he tells Ginger he is searching for his mother. Despite his hideousness, his father treats the child with a tenderness that is elided by Rothenburger's characterization of Rowland's shooting of his son, when all his attempts to shelter and protect him have failed and Geoffrey finally lunges at his father.

The shooting of Geoffrey recalls the choice Brigitte is forced to make at the conclusion of the first *Ginger Snaps* when she holds out a knife in one hand and a healing syringe in the other to the werewolf Ginger, who responds by attacking her and leaping on the knife. Yet another parallel with Brigitte's situation is drawn with the French-Canadian Claude (David La Haye), who, grieving for his brother Jean-Pierre, tells Ginger about hearing of the loup-garou in their boyhood in France: "But my brother said, 'Don't worry, Claude. If it bites you, you won't become one. Because I will help you catch it, so you can kill it before you turn, and the spell will be broken.'" Doc Murphy (Matthew Walker) must similarly shoot Finn (Brendan Fletcher), who has been bitten; the boy's pitiful plea "I just want to go home" reminds us that "Where is here?" is a question for settlers from more than one singular place. Most of the garrison's male characters, in fact, fail dismally at patriarchal white supremacy in their role as colonizers and embody instead a range of potential masculinities.

Contrasts with the aggressive, domineering, and misogynistic masculinity personified by Gilbert and the swaggering, racist sergeant major James (JR Bourne) abound in Fort Bailey, from the boyish, bespectacled Finn to the stoic Doc Murphy to the young guide Milo (Fabien Bird), who may be another mixed-blood Indigene, possibly connected to Seamus (Adrien Dorval); Gilbert calls him a "whelp" and a "mongrel," and Claude and James – the French and the English – gang up, as they do with the Hunter to expel him from the fort. The Hunter personifies yet another masculinity, one allied with the sisters. This stiflingly male-dominated world of the garrison, first penetrated then turned inside out by Ginger and Brigitte, therefore reveals not a flat and monolithic but a striated and porous patriarchal web, where the flimsiness of James's swagger and Gilbert's Scripture become all too apparent under the pressure of the girls' presence and the werewolves' raids. Ginger and Brigitte, too, are differentiated in their perceived degree of banally constructed femininity; while the Hunter exchanges intense and knowing looks with Brigitte, as Sam does in the first film, he regards the ultra-feminized and hyper-sexualized Ginger, as Sam does too, with little more than contempt.

In "Werewolves and Windigos: Narratives of Cannibal Monsters in French-Canadian Voyageur Oral Tradition," Podruchny notes that "voyageurs' tales of cannibal monsters most closely connect to stories about werewolves" and finds a "genuine cultural mingling in the meeting of these two sets of stories. Werewolf stories provided a framework for voyageurs to understand windigos [sic]" (Podruchny 2004, 681). Using Whitehead's idea of mimesis as "the active attempt to seek convergences in meanings and the conscious incorporation of symbolic similarities in cultural repertoire," Podruchny argues that "recognitions of commonalities across cultures ... may be the pattern with windigos and werewolves" (2004, 684):

> Voyageurs could access cultural similarities of Algonquian-speaking peoples through the monster stories. In this case of cross-cultural encounters between French-Canadian indentured servants in the fur trade and the Algonquian-speaking communities with whom they traded, cannibalism was not a symbol of alterity but, rather, one of sameness ... (a story of Wendigos) could be interpreted as an example of Europeans demonizing Aboriginal people as the other, yet the more interesting point is that Europeans could fall victim to Aboriginal classifications of demons. (2004, 685)

Podruchny's suggestion that stories are "not fixed things" and that "cross-cultural interaction and exchange" demonstrated by "entangled motifs of windigos and werewolves" are indeed possible works against narrower, more literalist views. (2004, 694)

Clearcut and Colonial Encounters

Ryszard Bugajski's Clearcut (1991) is another interesting example of cross-culturally colliding masculinities that plays with indigenization horror. Like its literary source, M.T. Kelly's A Dream Like Mine, as J.A. Wainwright has observed of the novel, the film strongly resists Francis's "imaginary Indian" created by European settler culture. For Wainwright, Kelly shows "more clearly and starkly than most of his non-Native colleagues, the methodologies and rationalizations used by colonizing peoples to construct the imaginary Indian" (Wainwright 1999, 256). The

unforgettable indigenous character Arthur (Graham Greene) continually plays with the expectation that he represents spirituality; he is
first depicted as rising up out of the water and eventually returns to
it when his body drops beneath the waves. The film is punctuated
by shots of water – motel pools, lakes, waterfalls, the "V" of the boat
carrying the main characters and the rivulet trickling from between
the thighs of the pictographic Earth Mother during the final part of
Arthur's ceremony. When asked where he is from, Arthur replies teas-
ingly "Recently?" and trails his hands in the water, flicking it into his
interlocutor's face. His emergence in the film, like that of the Hunter
in *Ginger Snaps Back*, becomes a version of the "monster cam," as the
camera tracks through water, grass, and over rocks, accompanied by
eerie sounds of screaming and wailing. This "water spirit" perspective could also be identified with Polly, the little girl who greets the
idealistic lawyer Peter Maguire (Ron Lea) when he is dropped off by
bush plane to the community for whom he has just lost a court battle
to prevent clearcut logging.[12]

   In the book, Arthur is described as Métis, like Geoffrey Rowland
"a hybrid figure of intercultural potential" (Kelly 1987, 258). Goldie,
suspicious of the hybrid, calls Arthur a "degraded Métis" and the
novel an example of a "pessimistic ideology" of the "defeat of nature."
Elsewhere, he writes that Arthur "has a clear political agenda but his
behaviour, and particularly his suicide, suggests not revolution but
psychosis" (Goldie 1989, 104). However, Wainwright takes issue with
this reading, arguing that "Kelly does not facilitate a *sauvage diabolique*
reading of this character because he consistently contextualizes and
so complicates the book's first-person narration of Arthur's deeds"
(Wainwright 1999, 256). Like the confrontations of the Mohawks at
Oka, Arthur "demands that we consider the inevitable and vital confla-
tion of cultural and violent resistance to racist stereotypes and power-
based inequities" (1999, 257). Culturally aligned with the explorers and
artists who depicted "vanishing tribes," the journalist narrator of the
novel becomes Maguire in Bugajski's film. Much as the opening shot
of *Ginger Snaps Back* has the girls wandering through the woods, the
settler's question – "Where is here?"– is instantly evoked by Maguire's
"You know" to the bush pilot when he asks "Whereabouts in particular?" Then Maguire, once landed, asks less confidently, "Are we in the
right place?" whereupon the film cuts to the "monster cam" accompanied by the eerie sounds, implying that the presence draws closer to
Maguire.

Maguire's complacent assumptions collide roughly with the larger-than-life presence of Arthur, who is, as Wainwright maintains, empowered "with the ability to unsettle and undermine the narrator's certainties about Native life" (1999, 257). Part of this unsettling involves the erosion of the white characters' certainties about what is being seen and experienced. The settler society's exclusive control of the narrative is swiftly repudiated at the beginning of the film when Polly leads Maguire to a scene of intense struggle as her band blockades the logging site while the police attempt to move them and loggers sitting in bulldozers rev their engines and chainsaws. A cameraman and Louise, a reporter (Rebecca Jenkins), run up to one of the fighters as he protects his head from blows from a police truncheon and start badgering him – the cameraman wheedling "Hey pal, say cheese" and the reporter asking "What does this mean for your people – what's next?" In response, when the young man sees Maguire on his other side, he explodes with fury at Maguire's "white mouth" and screams at them all to "Get out of here!" to which the cameraman replies jocularly, "Thanks pal," and leaves him screaming in frustration, a cry which foreshadows the anger and violence to come.

As obnoxious as the media people are in this scene, their presence as the sole media representatives at the protest is contrasted with the obsequious circle of journalists hanging onto the words of the "filthy industrialist," pulp mill owner Bud Ricketts (Michael Hogan). Both scenes underscore the surreality of the settler society's utter lack of connection with the seriousness of environmental destruction and the fury of the people forced to bear it. The film also establishes in this way the possibility of alternative means of storytelling by destabilizing "official" accounts – later, Arthur breaks into the motel room where Louise and her colleagues are making a noise and silences them by duct taping their bodies, eyes, and mouths.

Watching his clients being dragged away by the police as the loggers prepare to move in, Maguire first notices Arthur standing next to him, wearing a distinct necklace and heralded by the same eerie noises as accompanied the stealthy tracking camera at the beginning; Arthur also makes a fleeting appearance at the pulp mill just before Maguire confronts Ricketts. While Maguire exhorts the band's chief Wilf (Floyd "Red Crow" Westerman) to refrain from "violence," Arthur freely adopts violence as an effective way to deal with the issue – a violence that, it is suggested, also simmers beneath Maguire's own yuppie pacifist exterior. In the novel, Arthur is described as "like a ghoul in a horror movie or a madman in a child's campfire scare story," but the simulta-neous assertion is made that "This had nothing to do with images of the devil" (Kelly 1987, 92).

Such passages, simultaneously invoking but rejecting the indigenized spectre of the Wendigo as "a campfire scare story," mean that, as Wain-wright observes, Arthur "won't stay still long enough to be imagined" (Wainwright 1999, 259). Like the hybrid Aboriginal characters of *Ginger Snaps*, his relationship to monstrosity is obscured, reflecting the settler back at himself. The film's hallucinogenic quality is greatly enhanced by Maguire's continual air of incredulity at what he is seeing and expe-riencing at Arthur's hands. Another example of losing control of the narrative is when, following the kidnapping, Maguire and Ricketts see American hunters and, assuming they are saved, Maguire pleads with the hunters to take them out of there, showing his business card and yelling "There's two of us, we've been kidnapped!" Arthur's counter-narrative holds sway, however, as he calmly tells the startled hunters, "This is Indian land … We're doing a ceremony … it's confusing." Another conventional "rescue" fails when the police show up and Arthur kills them both, saying "It's the Indian guy that's supposed to be dead. That's what you think, isn't it?" Wilf appears in this sequence, but it is not clear where he came from or what he knows. He tells Maguire, spattered with the cops' blood: "Somebody had to pay … You dreamed anger and your anger is real."

Maguire's text-based knowledge of indigenous people is shock-ingly transformed by Arthur's violence. For example, Arthur laughs at Maguire's claim to know Native culture through "books," asking him if he knows about "oral tradition." He then, astonishingly, produces a small snake from his bag and bites its head off, saying "That's oral tradition." Such an outlandish act, as Wainwright suggests, "begins the rewriting of the text" (1999, 258) as Arthur – author – inscribes himself irrevocably on the bodies and minds of both Maguire and Ricketts through ritual acts of violence such as the flaying of Ricketts's leg – which Arthur calls "debarking" – and Arthur's severing of his own fingers in a sweat lodge ceremony, viewed unflinchingly by the camera. Arthur's rituals evoke the outlawed Sun Dance ceremonies described by Francis as susceptible to lurid accounts penned by colo-nists as horror stories: "Whites … were horrified at the self-mutilation involved, which did not stop them from describing in great detail the tearing flesh … Readers were meant to experience a real thrill of hor-ror before they were asked to condemn the practice as 'debasing and cruel,' 'revolting' and 'barbarous.' No White writer attempted to put the ceremony into the context of Indian religious beliefs" (Francis 1992, 66).[13]

In *Clearcut*, indigenization horror consistently unsettles and overturns stereotypical notions and clearcut identities, demanding closer attention be paid to its concerns. For example, the popular figure of the romantic "Mountie movie" (1992, 78–9) is transformed: the RCMP are sinister and brutal lackeys of an unjust system who beat up Elders in the middle of the night and who die ignominiously and messily. Tom Starblanket (Tom Jackson) tells Maguire: "All police are Mounties." Their importance in the myth of Canadian national identity, undermined by their role in *Clearcut* as oppressors, is described by Francis: "Canadians believed that they treated their Natives justly. They negotiated treaties before they occupied the land ... The story of the Mounted Police had a powerful influence on the way Canadians felt themselves to be distinct from, and morally superior to, the United States" (1992, 69).

Ultimately, Arthur clearly mirrors the fears and longings of the white narrator, desiring to make painless amends for colonialism's nightmares without realizing (or avoiding) the impossibility of such a task. As the little girl, Polly, smoking her cigarette, points out to Maguire, "You're the man who talks for us." In despair, Maguire mutters early in the film, in Wilf's house, "the world is turning to shit ... I feel like somebody has to pay ... somebody has to hurt." In Wilf's look of concern at Arthur's anger, a shadow of the Wendigo appears. However, this, too, is destabilized when Wilf asks Maguire, "Who do you feel bad for, us or yourself?" when he says "People like me have done you no good." Prior to Maguire's first sweat ceremony, he is told "don't be afraid ... of yourself"; he then has a vision of blood running in thick rivulets over the stones and sees Arthur's face as well as the stick structure on the island where he ends up with Arthur. Arthur then comes to talk to him, beginning their journey together. It is Maguire, during this initial conversation with Arthur, who suggests, jokingly "tying the mill owner up and skinning him alive" – a suggestion which Arthur puts into practice. Thus, Maguire's own identity is constantly called into question, even though Wilf frequently and half-humourously calls him "white man." During their ordeal, Bud tells Maguire, "You're starting to look like one of them," although earlier he mocks Maguire for his in-between position. As Goldie puts it, "individuation is often joined by indigenization. The character gains a new awareness of self and of nationality through an excursion into the wilderness" (Goldie 1989, 59).

In *Clearcut*, a strong gendered element also becomes apparent: Wilf, as a sort of mentor to Maguire, displays an alternative masculinity to that of Bud Ricketts and the Mounties. Arthur repeatedly performs masculinity for Maguire, who is afraid to tell loud neighbours – the media representatives from the protest – to shut up and who bruises his knuckles throwing a feeble punch at the wall. Later, he runs up behind Arthur with a club, but cannot bring himself to strike; much later, Arthur challenges him to strike with his knife, instructing him to place it between his ribs. Instead, Maguire drives the knife into a log, letting trickles of sap run down instead of blood. Arthur's violence is contrasted with Maguire's pacifism as a "cruel" but necessary act. Striking Maguire, Arthur tells him: "You think I give a fuck what you say? Your words, your papers, your limp white dick? You think you know what I think."

Regardless, Arthur's use of violence as a product of Maguire's wistful thinking reflects the dark mirror of indigenization horror at work. Dragging Bud Rickett, gagged with duct tape, from his truck, Arthur says to him and to Maguire: "I'm going to scalp him. I could scalp him and be a real Indian. I should be a real Indian, shouldn't I? Shouldn't I?" The question hangs, undermining the very idea of authenticity upon which indigenization depends. Maguire must ultimately stop Arthur by becoming him, creeping up on him stealthily with the tracking camera, hitting him with a rock, and finally seizing a log and battling with him over the sacred pictographs.

At the end of the film, Arthur walks back into the water and sinks back under the waves. It is implied that Maguire has undergone a rite of passage towards full manhood – he is hauled off to jail, grim and silent. However, in a tempering of the masculinity of this ending, it is the young girl Polly who keeps Maguire's briefcase, which she stuffs with relics from the forest. She is shown wearing Arthur's necklace at the end of the film; like the necklace in the *Ginger Snaps* trilogy, it is a token of the enduring survival of indigenous presence, with which so much still remains to be settled.

In this chapter, I have attempted to trace some of the workings of indigenization horror, signified by encounters with indigenous spirits and folklore, but also, as we have seen, deeply entrenched in the consciousness of a history of colonialism at its points of intersection with the colonized. As Goldie puts it: "The guiding adjective, 'bloody' … is also the definition of the violence produced by miscegenation … The history of white invasion … provides a clear source of blood, but in the image of the indigene the blood of the Other is passion and the blood of the white is a product of that passion" (1989, 106). The blood in the bush garden of Canadian indigenization horror tends to belie Frye's ideal of the Canadian imaginary as a "quest for the peaceable kingdom." As our nightmares so repeatedly show us, there can be no peace without justice for indigenous people.

NOTES

The author wishes to thank the reviewers, editors, and Brian Johnson of the Department of English Language and Literature at Carleton University for their valuable feedback on earlier drafts of this essay.

1 Variously spelled "Wendigo," "Windigo," and otherwise. This chapter uses "Wendigo" but also uses the spellings of the source texts wherever referenced.
2 The film is summarized as follows: "A young woman in the Canadian wilderness, seduced and then abandoned by her Canadian Mountie lover, turns for help to her old Indian friend" (IMDB), http://www.imdb.com/title/tt0004274/.
3 Creed bases her idea of the monstrous-feminine on Kristeva's theory of abjection as the ritual rejection of the mother's body, associated with polluting substances – sweat, tears, blood. According to Creed, the "central ideological project" of the horror film is the "purification of the abject through a descent into the foundations of the symbolic construct." Barbara Creed, "Horror and the Monstrous-Feminine: An Imaginary Abjection," in Mark Jancovich, ed., *Horror: The Film Reader* (London: Routledge, 2002), 75.
4 Margaret Atwood, *Strange Things: The Malevolent North in Canadian Literature* (Oxford: Clarendon Press, 1995), 109–14. Atwood situates the grim humour of *Winter Hunger*, with its Wendigo-possessed heroine Diana, who concludes the novel by stewing her baby and slaughtering her husband, firmly within the context of women "rewriting wilderness": that is, adapting "mainly manly Northern icons" for the purpose (at least since the mid-twentieth century) of "renewal," which has "something to do with the absence of men from the scene": "In the later 1970s and 1980s, the patter of female feet heading for the hills, not to mention the valleys, islands, forests, and plains, becomes a small stampede." This rewriting of the wilderness as woman is embodied in the *vagina dentata*, which is also the symbol of the Wendigo in *Winter Hunger* as repeatedly sketched by the

indigenous artist character Proxene Ratfat. However, an alternative version of masculinity has also been implicated with wilderness and "going Native," as Francis observes of Ernest Thompson Seton's influence on the contemporary (white) men's movement.

5 Since the publication of *They Came from Within*, several films produced by indigenous filmmakers have drawn heavily on the figure of the Wendigo, such as Kris Happyjack-McKenzie's *Windigo* (2009), Armand Garnet Ruffo's *A Windigo Tale* (2009), and Jeremy Torrie's slasher film *A Flesh Offering* (2010). The realism of Ruffo's film in particular contrasts with fantasy-horror versions of the Wendigo such as *Pet Sematary*. Robin Wood has argued that horror as the return of the repressed signifies the presence of the oppressed Other under white supremacist capitalist patriarchy because "what escapes *re*pression has to be dealt with by *op*pression": horror can therefore be evaluated ideologically in terms of what it renders monstrous. A "reactionary" horror film reaffirms the dominant discourse of patriarchal and capitalist values by depicting the monster as simply evil, as it is in King's novel. The appearance of Ruffo's Wendigo, on the other hand, as an abusive stepfather returning to possess the body of an indigenous artist's white boyfriend, is linked to the tribulations undergone by a family attempting to cope with the traumatic legacy of cultural genocide perpetrated by the residential school system. Here, however, I will largely refrain from discussing *A Windigo Tale* and the other indigenous productions as I wish to avoid appropriative criticism by subordinating these films to a white-dominated discourse of horror.

6 See Peter Thompson's article "Eco-Horror and Boundary Transgressions in Orca" page 165 in this volume.

7 The male gaze was first famously conceptualized by Laura Mulvey in her classic essay "Visual Pleasure and Narrative Cinema," *Screen* 16, no. 3 (Autumn 1975). Mulvey argues that traditional cinema reflects men's status as "bearer of the look": "cinematic codes create a gaze, a world, and an object, thereby producing an illusion cut to the measure of desire." Since writing "Visual Pleasure," Mulvey's perspective has shifted more recently away from the simple binary opposition of spectacle/gaze to incorporate considerations of audience, spectatorship, and consumerism. See her essay "Unmasking the Gaze: Feminist Film Theory, History and Film Studies" in Vicki Callahan, ed., *Reclaiming the Archive: Feminism and Film History* (Detroit: Wayne State University Press, 2010), 17–31.

8 See also Williams's earlier essay, "Film Bodies: Gender, Genre, Excess," in *Film Quarterly* 44, no. 4 (Summer 1991), 2–13, for further gendered analysis of spectacle in horror film. See also Carol Clover's chapter on looking at

horror and the role of the "assaultive gaze" in "The Eye of Horror" in *Men, Women and Chainsaws* (Princeton: Princeton University Press, 1993).

9 Francis points out that the figure of the Imaginary Indian has fluctuated according to the political needs of colonialism, nation building, and the disposition of the colonizers to view either America as "a Garden of Eden" with "blessed innocents" or "an alien place" full of "frightful and bloodthirsty" natives.

10 The figure of Grey Owl/Archie Belaney, for example, is described by Atwood (1995, 60) as rife with the anxiety of "going Indian," which she contrasts with the "historical reality" of cultural genocide. Belaney's propensity for indigenous drag, according to Atwood, symbolizes the larger settler fear "of being alien, of being shut out." See also Ward Churchill's *Fantasies of the Master Race: Literature, Cinema and the Colonization of American Indians* (New York: City Lights Books, 1998).

11 See Sue Short, *Misfit Sisters: Screen Horror as Female Rites of Passage* (New York: Palgrave Macmillan, 2006).

12 The events of both novel and film likely reflect the massive protests at the logging of Clayoquot Sound, British Columbia, in the 1980s and 1990s. The film, however, was shot near Thunder Bay, Ontario.

13 Later, Francis (1992) writes: "On the Prairies the government took similar steps to outlaw traditional Native dancing, especially the Blackfoot sun dance and the Cree thirst dance. Initially, missionaries and government officials feared the potential these ceremonies had for inciting warriors to acts of violence. In the excitement of the moment, it was argued, young men might decide to return to the warlike days of old (as described in dime novels and Mountie histories). As the threat of violence faded, the dances, which sometimes featured self-mutilation, came to be seen as relics of barbarism, impediments to the assimilation of the Natives" (100).

4 Pure Laine Evil: The Horrifying Normality of Quebec's Ordinary Hell in the Film Adaptations of Patrick Senécal's "Romans d'épouvante"

ANDRÉ LOISELLE

He has a small brown mustache and curly brown hair that make him look rather tacky ...
a typical suburbanite.[1]

Patrick Senécal, 5150, rue des ormes

This is how Yannick Bérubé, a college student on a bike ride gone awry, describes Jacques Beaulieu when he initially meets him at the beginning of popular author Patrick Senécal's first horror novel, *5150, rue des ormes* (*5150 Elms Way*), published in 1994. Little does Yannick know, at this early point in the story, that this rather tacky, typical suburbanite is about to point a shotgun at him, lock him up in a small room, and hold him captive for several months. Throughout the novel, as in the film adaptation directed by Éric Tessier in 2009, Yannick is understandably disconcerted by his terrifying circumstances. But what is most disturbing to the student is the radical disconnect between the insanely malicious actions of the monster who keeps him trapped in his house, and the bewildering ordinariness of this middle-aged, middle-class man and his typical French-Canadian family. When Yannick first learns the name of his captor, he writes in his journal: "This name is just too banal; totally incongruous for such a demented man. I imagined he'd have some bizarre name with a bunch of Xs and Ys. Jacques Beaulieu. It's horrifyingly normal!"[2]

This horrifying normality, this "enfer ordinaire" as filmmaker Tessier puts it,[3] not only is at the centre of *5150, rue des ormes*, but also characterizes all three of Senécal's "romans d'épouvante" that have been brought to the screen over the past decade: *5150, rue des ormes, Sur le seuil* (novel 1998; film 2003, Éric Tessier, aka *Evil Words*), and *Les sept jours du talion* (novel, 2002; film 2010, Daniel Grou-Podz, aka *7 Days*) (and a fourth adaptation on the way: *Hell.Com* [novel, 2009; film to be directed by Daniel Roby]).[4] The three narratives do not share obvious stylistic similarities and thematic concerns. While *Sur le seuil* involves a strong dose of the supernatural, *Les sept jours du talion* and *5150, rue des ormes* are tales of terror exclusively concerned with the iniquities of human villainy. Furthermore, *Sur le seuil* and *5150, rue des ormes* adopt a comparable first-person narrative form, but *Les sept jours du talion* uses a conventional omniscient narration. The one element that recurs in all three novels, and which is foregrounded in the film versions, is the centrality of a male subject who is confronted with a villain whose monstrosity is marked by such banal ordinariness that it calls into question the hero's own sense of his "normal" self. These banal monsters have little to do with the mythical Wendigo that Aalya Ahmad discusses in the previous chapter. They are just average men who choose to drag other average men into their ordinary hell.

Evil and the Ordinary Québécois

College student Yannick in *5150, rue des ormes*, psychiatrist Paul in *Sur le seuil*, and surgeon Bruno in *Les sept jours du talion* are all men who comfortably belong in the cultural elite and (certainly in the case of Paul and Bruno, if less obviously for Yannick) economic elite of Quebec society. When they are thrown in the middle of horrific circumstances, their otherwise solid bourgeois values are shaken to the core and their sense of self is deeply undermined. But one particular aspect of their terrifying experience threatens them more than anything else: the alarming familiarity and troubling casualness with which they encounter their respective demons. The ordinary Québécois men at the centre of each text are faced with the incomprehensible evidence that their nemesis – a satanic novelist in *Sur le seuil*, a murderous vigilante in *5150*, and a sadistic pedophile in *Les sept jours* – are themselves ordinary Québécois men. Horror in these novels and films is not caused by some heretic "Other" from some foreign land. Rather, both heroes and villains are "Canadien français pure laine," old-stock French Canadians, who share cultural values and historical heritage. In these texts, fear emerges from the inconceivable personal and cultural affinity between protagonists and antagonists. What horrifies Yannick, Paul, and Bruno is that monstrosity exists in such mundane people – "pure laine" French Canadian men who, in many ways, are so much like them.

The idea that ordinary French Canadians might commit extraordinary acts of violence is certainly not new in Quebec cinema. While there have been relatively few horror films produced in Quebec,[5] there is a long tradition of violence in French-Canadian films where the perpetrators and the victims belong to the same familiar culture. From the classic 1950s melodrama *La petite Aurore, l'enfant martyre* (1952, Jean-Yves Bigras), in which a nine-year girl is tortured to death by her father and stepmother, to Denys Arcand's 1970s rape-revenge movie, *Gina* (1975), in which a stripper and her thugs eliminate one by one the men who savagely assaulted her, including shoving one of them in a giant snow blower, there has been no lack of Québécois-on-Québécois brutality in French-Canadian cinema. However, in these and many other films produced over the past sixty years, there is generally a clear distinction between the aggressor and the prey. Most significantly, vile cruelty tends to be divided along gender lines. From Anne Claire Poirier's devastatingly realistic exploration of violence against women, *Mourir à tue-tête* (1979), to Denis Villeneuve's sombre fictionalization of the factual cold-blooded shooting of fourteen female students by a lone male assassin at Université de Montréal in 1989, *Polytechnique* (2009), Quebec cinema has often denounced the atrocity of spiteful misogyny.

But in the works considered here, the typical gender distinction is patently absent. French-Canadian men abuse and torture other French-Canadian men in a fratricidal conflict that suggests a perplexing, self-destructive drive. These internecine struggles reflect an intense anxiety about Quebec's increasingly untenable myth of the homogeneous nation. If it ever existed, the homogeneous nation has definitely started to experience profound fragmentation: the acrimonious debates around reasonable accommodations for immigrants, which have pitted multicultural cities against more conservative rural regions; the fierce tensions between students, the government, and the general population during the 2012 university and college strikes; the split in the separatist movement, with no less than three political parties in the province claiming to represent the only viable option to achieve sovereignty (Parti Québécois, Québec Solidaire, and Option Nationale). All these, and other similar recent phenomena, manifest internal conflicts that are tearing to pieces the cohesive nation. It is not surprising that these horror films would emerge at this time to echo the disintegration of traditional notions about Quebec society, for horror is a genre gleefully fixated on disastrous dismemberment.[6]

Moreover, the fact that both protagonists and antagonists are men also encourages an interpretation of the texts as analogies for masculine insecurities within the Quebec nationalist project, in which the French-Canadian man is always doomed to failure. The nationalist project, Jeffery Vacante argues, was an attempt at "masculine emancipation." He writes: "Many Québec nationalists have also defined their own heterosexual virility according to their ability to lead the province out of its figurative state of homosexual weakness and dependence within Canadian federalism ... In addition to reversing almost two centuries of humiliation and subservience within the 'colonial' shackles of the federal state, then, the push for 'decolonization' and subsequent calls for independence came to be seen as necessary steppingstones to achieving full manhood" (Vacante 2006, 98). As such, the failure of the nationalist ideal (evidenced by two failed separatist referenda) corresponds to a failure of Quebec men, who remain trapped in shackles imposed by other men who are, themselves, prisoners of their own impotence.

Such cultural hermeneutics might appear somewhat suspicious. Indeed, suggesting that the ethos of an entire nation can be determined through an analysis of three novels and their film versions seems rather dubious. Yet in this case, there might be something to it. If nothing else, commercial success indicates that Quebec readers and spectators do recognize something of themselves in these tales of terror.

As early as 1998, with the publication of his second novel, *Sur le seuil*, Senécal was already starting to get some recognition as "le maître du roman d'horreur québécois" (Francoeur 1998, 7). Within a few years, the CEGEP teacher had become one of the top-selling authors of Éditions Alire, Quebec's foremost publisher of science fiction, crime, spy, and horror novels (Chevrier 2003, 5). As Senécal's novels were starting to sell in increasingly considerable numbers, his fame reached new heights thanks to cinema. Éric Tessier's screen version of *Sur le seuil* ranked among the five top-grossing Quebec films of 2003 (Loiselle and McSorley 2006, 321–2), an achievement repeated in 2010 by Daniel Grou-Podz's adaptation of *Les sept jours du talion* ("L'année 2010 ..." 2010). As for Tessier's *5150, rue des ormes*, it ranked a respectable seventh among the Quebec box-office hits of 2009 (Tremblay 2009, B8). Given that the horror film is something of a niche genre (as I have said elsewhere, some people will never go to see horror films),[7] such results are nothing short of remarkable. Clearly Quebeckers find something in these horror books and films that strikes a chord, and an argument could be made that what makes this chord resonate are the horrific affinities between the hero and the villain, which imply that *le monstre, c'est nous* (Vax 1960, 11).

This choice of words – "horrific affinities" – owes something to my co-editor, Gina Freitag, who developed the idea of the "shock of similarity" in her brilliant thesis on female characters in contemporary Canadian horror films. Freitag argues that in horror films such as the Canadian co-production *Orphan* (Jaume Collet-Serra, 2009), female protagonists encounter female antagonists in a "shock of similarity." This "shock of similarity" occurs at

> a moment of recognition between the two characters as they come to understand one another's positions, not simply as victims of patriarchal "otherness" but as liminal figures … [It is] a shared sense of connection with another, clear and distinct being, who also embodies the capacity for both good *and* evil. This moment brackets them within the narrative realm, highlighting their fragmentation from some collective (family, traditional notions of femininity, and so on). Horror is not necessarily inherent in the moment; rather, this moment acts as a catalyst for the horror which erupts as a result of it. (Freitag 2011, 65)

Freitag's concept of the "shock of similarity" opens up possibilities beyond Linda Williams's conventional model of shared victimization between the woman and the monster.[8] Aside from shared victimization, there can also be shared villainy, shared violence, aggressive selfishness, and emotional greed. What is shocking in this recognition is that the heroine discovers in the female monster a sign of her own sadistic potential.

5150, rue des ormes and the Horror of Suburbanite Self-Righteousness

Like the flawed mother Kate in *Orphan*, who recognizes her own destructive potential in her murderous adopted daughter Esther, Yannick recognizes himself in his tacky captor Beaulieu. But unlike the "shock of similarity," which can be quite empowering for the woman who comes to appreciate her potential for violence and cruelty, the affinity between Bérubé and Beaulieu is paralysing. And less than a sudden shock, as in *Orphan*, the recognition of affinity in *5150* is a maddeningly slow and neurotically incremental process of discovery which leads to an abyss of subjective futility and obsessive self-absorption.

Throughout *5150, the novel,* Yannick writes journal entries as his captivity persists. As the narrative unfolds Bérubé becomes increasingly captivated by his captor, Beaulieu. He becomes fascinated with the astounding coherence and delirious logic of Jacques's insanity (Senécal 2001, 140). He "masochistically tries to relive the sensation of terror" (2001, 70) he experienced when an angry Beaulieu almost strangled him to death after a failed escape attempt. Yannick's fixation on Beaulieu becomes so intense, in fact, that near the end of the novel, after he has managed to escape the Beaulieu house, he actually chooses to walk back to the site of his confinement to play a final game of chess with Jacques (2001, 287–8). Similarly, near the end of the film, Yannick refuses to leave when Beaulieu's wife, Maude, allows him to, and prefers instead to stay in the house at 5150 Elm's Way to wait for his chess opponent. This is in drastic contrast with the first part of the narrative, during which the young man desperately tries to escape and fantasizes about killing Beaulieu by stabbing him in the neck (2001, 93–4).

The tacky suburbanite that Yannick initially approaches to ask for help when his bicycle breaks down very quickly reveals his monstrosity. As Yannick first enters Beaulieu's house, he hears someone screaming for help. Curious, he climbs upstairs and finds a bleeding man, chained to a wall in an empty bedroom. As he quickly finds out, this is one of Beaulieu's many victims, one of the "sinners" whom the monstrously self-righteous suburbanite kidnapped and tortured in punishment for their guilty actions. Having been found out, Beaulieu abducts Yannick. But as the readers and spectators soon learn, Beaulieu cannot, in "good conscience," kill Yannick for the young man is not guilty of anything (2001, 16). He was only at the wrong place at the wrong time. So while the college student knows from the beginning that Beaulieu is a kidnapper, a killer, and, basically, a madman, he is also confronted with a tacky suburbanite who tries to be friendly under the circumstances and behave like a "good host." He invites Yannick to eat with him and his family and encourages him to play chess to pass the time. This pastime soon becomes an obsession for both men.

At first Yannick is appalled at the sense of incongruous normality that surrounds his dire circumstances: "There's a man locked up on the second floor of their house and this traditional little family eats dinner like any other day!" (2001, 49).[9] He witnesses Maude "doing her work like a good little housewife. Surreal. Absurd" (2001, 53);[10] and he sits in disbelief before a radiant Beaulieu, who looks like a genuinely delighted nice guy when Yannick eventually accepts to play chess with him (2001, 102). Yet, the normality that Maude and Jacques project clashes with the strange-ness of Beaulieu's children. Anne, a ten-year-old girl (visibly younger in the film), is forever silent, and her vacuous, mindless gaze is oddly menacing. Michelle, the sixteen-year-old *nymph fatale,* is as seductive as she is ferociously violent. In one of the most intense scenes of the film, which reflects a similar moment in the novel (2001, 110–11), Michelle viciously strikes Yannick on the shin with a baseball bat as he tries to escape, and repeatedly kicks and strikes him as he lies on the ground in excruciating pain. What renders this scene all the more disconcerting is the sunny suburban sky that shines over the inconspicuous back-yard where the violence occurs. Michelle resembles her father, whose bouts of rage whenever the young man challenges him are terrifying. But while Jacques can switch back to perfect normality moments after a burst of fury, Michelle remains a constant threat. Yet Yannick starts to develop a fixation on this cruelly sensual teenager, which parallels his growing fixation on Beaulieu and his daily chess games. In the novel, Yannick dreams of Jacques and Michelle, the former playing chess, the latter seductively enticing the young man to hurt her (2001, 114). The crux of the narrative is Jacques's claim that, because he is righteous and punishes only unrighteous sinners, he can never lose at chess – the white pieces that he always uses symbolize his just cause (2001, 141). And by all accounts, Beaulieu is indeed a remarkable chess player, the undisputable champion of his local chess club whose incredible win-ning streak leads some of his peers at the club to speculate that he's made a deal with the devil (2001, 117). But Yannick does not believe that Jacques is unbeatable and therefore endeavours to win against him, at least once, to disprove his self-righteous theory. The novel elaborates at great length on Yannick's incredulity regarding Beaulieu's invincibility. No need to review the entire canon of adaptation theory to understand that the film has to be far more concise than the literary text in its evoca-tion of the young man's suspicion. Rather than relying on an awkward voice-over to reproduce the journal entries, Tessier wisely chooses to use a simple but very effective visual device to bring to mind Yannick's dis-belief. The director includes one brief shot that sows the seed of doubt in Yannick's mind. The first time Yannick is invited to eat super with the Beaulieus, about twenty minutes into the film, he sits in the dining room and notices all the plaques that commemorate Jacques's victories at the chess club. One wall is covered in such mementos of invincibil-ity, except one spot: an absence that conspicuously breaks the chain of triumphant signifiers. Tessier does not foreground this (seemingly) missing trophy at the time. But the shot in the dining room is quickly repeated later in the film when Jacques reasserts that he has never lost a game. This small empty space on the wall might go unnoticed on both occasions when the image appears on screen. But it is definitely visible. And it is this interval, this visual hiatus in the winning streak that gives rise to Yannick's obsessive certitude that he *can* beat Jacques – for he must have lost at least once, hence the one missing trophy.

The idea of a small spot on the wall that becomes the locus of obsession is rendered manifest through a somewhat typical but nevertheless effective device of the horror genre[11] as a blotch of blood in Yannick's prison room inexplicably grows until a pool of blood overwhelms the domestic cell. Like this small red mark, which eventually becomes omnipresent, the space of absence on the dining-room wall engenders Yannick's all-pervading obsession with winning against Beaulieu. Soon Yannick's room becomes something of a chessboard, both visually as the student covers the walls with chess graffiti, and narratively as Yannick increasingly identifies Beaulieu as the subject who dictates his every move.

Interspersed with distorted shots of the walls around him, images of Yannick's own abusive father, stunning nightmarish hallucinations in which Jacques bleeds ink as he beats his young opponent yet again, the captive student's intensifying obsession with Beaulieu and chess is counterpointed by segments of banal normality: Maude's mundane religiosity; typical tensions between a strict father and his insecure, rebellious teenage daughter; commonplace domestic violence. These are all markers of an unpleasant reality. But it is hardly the stuff of a horrifying descent into the bleeding bowels of hell. Even Jacques's righteous struggle against the unrighteous is rather unremarkable. The scene in which Jacques kills a reprobate with Michelle, as part of her "initiation" into her father's self-righteous operation, reveals the victim's sin as sexual deviancy: vague pedophilia, barely hinted at through mildly creepy behaviour. Again, hardly the stuff of an epic battle between good and evil. Similarly, Michelle's initiation scene in the novel involves a victim whose sin is racism (2001, 256); again, unpleasant, but not the stuff of Greek tragedy.

In the scene where the pedophile is killed the most powerful moment is not Jacques's self-righteous punishing of the sinner, but rather Michelle's incensed kicking and stabbing of the victim. While her father disapproves of this "unnecessary violence," the spectator is most enthralled by this sensuous outpour of aggression from the diminutive but dangerous body of the teenager. Later in the film, when Michelle's boyfriend discovers Beaulieu's secret after accidentally coming across a videotape that Yannick had managed to record in the early days of his captivity, she does not hesitate to beat him to death using a digital camera. While one could easily read a facile metaphor on the horror film in this lethal use of a camera, what is most arresting about the scene is Michelle's ferocious violence against someone of whom she seemed to be rather fond just moments before.

In her extraordinary capacity for gruesome violence, Michelle is clearly the most dazzling presence in *5150, rue des ormes*. Not surprisingly, Senécal has further developed her character in the eight-episode web series, *La reine rouge*[12] (Senécal et al., 2011) in which Beaulieu's daughter moves on after her father's arrest to cause more chaos and mayhem. But as strangely attractive as she might be, Michelle remains marginal in *5150*. She is merely the sensual, irrational, passionate mirror image of her father's manic logic. Similarly, Maude, with whom the young man develops an awkward friendship,[13] is merely an appendage to Jacques. While Yannick helps her understand that her traditional religious submissiveness has enabled Beaulieu to commit his crimes, when she is finally ready to leave her own oppressive prison, the student is unwilling to help her escape, fixated as he is on playing one more game of chess against the local champion. Even after witnessing Maude's suicide, he runs to work on a strategy to beat his chess opponent.

When Beaulieu discovers his wife hanged in the closet, he and Yannick mutually accuse each other of being the unrighteous man responsible for her death. To solve the question, they decide to play a final game with Beaulieu's special chess set: a human-size set where the pieces are incarnated by all of Jacques's victims whom he painstakingly preserved as trophies like stuffed animals and the recently deceased Maude has just been crowned White Queen. Now sharing Beaulieu's insanity, Yannick readily accepts to play the game. As Yannick is on the verge of victory, Anne, the silent child with the sinister gaze, enters the scene. As she recognizes her dead mother in the middle of the giant chessboard, she puts an end to the demented competition by screaming and attacking her father. Terrified by this little monster, Jacques frantically grabs his shotgun and kills the girl. Incredibly, Yannick begs Beaulieu to finish the game, in vain. Having killed an innocent child, Beaulieu has all of a sudden invalidated his self-righteous theory. In his own mind, Beaulieu has irrevocably lost the game. Henceforth, he will remain silent and does not resist arrest when the police arrive on the premises.

Months later, back to his "normal" life, Yannick remains obsessed with the chess game he never finished. Unable to communicate with others, including his girlfriend, he has withdrawn into an imaginary world where he and Beaulieu sit at a table, on the verge of playing chess. The film's final scene is highly theatrical, comprised of a brilliantly nightmarish decor where banal suburban houses surrounded by gothic trees and fog engulf the players in a bleached-out environment of lunacy. The clash between theatricality and realism – "le choc entre la folie totale et la normalité," which first attracted Tessier to the novel (Laurin 2009, 68) – echoes the typical composition of Senécal's "romans d'épouvante," in which the mundane and the monstrous coexist to evoke a world where normality and aberration are intertwined.

Les sept jours du talion and the Dread of Ubiquitous Pedophilia

The ordinariness of violent insanity is even more explicitly highlighted in *Les sept jours du talion*. Something of a mirror image of Senécal's first novel, *Les sept jours* also deals with self-righteous punishment. But this time the "hero" is the vigilante, seeking retribution for the rape and murder of his daughter Jasmine. As the novel opens, Jasmine's body has already been found in a field near her school; her murderer has already been arrested; and Bruno's elaborate plan to kidnap, torture, and eventually kill the culprit has already been set in motion.

Like Beaulieu, an average Joe whose fifteen-year killing spree began when he slaughtered the incompetent physician responsible for the death of his stillborn son,[14] Bruno is an ordinary man who, presented with the horrific death of his child, is pushed over the edge of sanity. With *Les sept jours*, as with *5150, rue des ormes*, Senécal productively taps into the pedophilic mentality that has dominated not only Quebec, but all of North America over the past several years. "Pedophilia," in its etymological sense of "love of children," has indeed become an omnipresent credo, verging on dogma, in our society. It is everywhere to be seen in contemporary culture – from Oprah Winfrey's heartwarming stories about special kids and John Gray's self-help parenting bestseller saccharinely entitled *Children Are from Heaven* (1999) to Pitt-Jolie style adoption extravaganzas and reality shows such as *Toddlers and Tiaras* and *Here Comes Honey Boo Boo*. It is not surprising then that in a society so fixated on children, pedophiles (in the narrowly pathological sense of the term) would become front-page news and emerge as the villain par excellence in tales of terror. Where Senécal proves most original and daring in his treatment of pedophilia, as a theme much broader than a mere psychiatric disorder, is in his argument that there is a very fine line between a monstrous obsession with prepubescent girls and the intense love that an ordinary man feels towards his daughter. What lies at the core of *Les sept jours du talion* is precisely a demonstration that the ordinary man in his obsession with his deceased child can become as monstrous as the murderer himself.

The intense bond between Bruno and Jasmine in the film is represented through a few stereotypical moments that immediately signal that father and daughter have a special relationship. The girl is heard insisting that her dad, rather than her mom, should spend time with her. He insists on getting a kiss as his "dessert" before the daughter leaves and carefully ties a bow in her hair. In a brief but noteworthy scene, Bruno and Jasmine are espied in the distance walking on the sidewalk and heard chatting playfully. Significantly, another father-daughter pair is also seen in this long shot. The pairs are so similar that, given the distance, it is difficult to know which one is overheard on the soundtrack. The "doubling" effect suggests that while very intense, Bruno and Jasmine's relationship is not uncommon: any "ordinary man" blessed with a charming daughter would love her as intensely as Bruno loves Jasmine.

Throughout the novel, the omniscient narrator often comments on Bruno's ordinariness: while as a surgeon he is comfortably wealthy, he lives a normal, uneventful life. His house is sober (Senécal 2002, 90), decorated in a simple, tasteful, but non-ostentatious manner (2002, 108). Bruno and his wife Sylvie drive ordinary cars and own a small, ordinary cabin.[15] Bruno himself looks quite ordinary: he is described in the novel as a balding, slim, aging thirty-eight-year-old with brown eyes.[16] As is to be expected, the film version is much more limited in its ability to convey the concept of "ordinariness" – again, it would be awkward to have a voice-over narration waxing poetic over the banality of Bruno's life. Rather, director Grou-Podz chooses to evoke the ordinariness of the surgeon indirectly by emphasizing the analogy between him and the detective in charge of investigating his case, Hervé Mercure.

As in the novel, Mercure's wife in the film was murdered, and he is experiencing great difficulty in mourning his loss (2002, 107). But while this information is gradually introduced in the novel, it appears at the very beginning of the film. Even before spectators encounter Bruno, we have already seen the dejected Mercure, living a life of banal routine interrupted only by his obsessive review of the surveillance tape that recorded his wife's random execution during a convenience-store robbery. The darkness and dreariness of his house, the fact that he sleeps on the couch, the boarded-up bedroom door, his slow, heavy movements through his morose domestic space, and, of course, his repeated viewing of the shooting, all create the impression of a heartbroken individual who tries to cope as best he can. This is how an ordinary man deals with tragedy.

A similar moroseness and silent introspection characterize the few scenes that show Bruno and Sylvie after the discovery of Jasmine's body. But as the grieving father starts plotting his revenge, the surface resemblance between the cop and the surgeon is replaced by a deeper analogy. This similarity is constructed according to the well-established crime-thriller convention of a complex parallel between the troubled cop and the tormented suspect he is pursuing. Matching close-ups and voice-image overlaps are used to connect the angst-ridden criminal and the suffering police officer. As the parallel unfolds there emerges a sense of both "ordinariness" and "aberration." The ordinariness of the detective's difficult mourning serves as a point of reference from which we can imagine an alternative to Bruno's radical actions. They are two ordinary men, but while one chooses routine bereavement, the other follows the path of horrifying atrocity.

Like Jacques Beaulieu, Bruno Hamel is initially convinced that he is doing the right thing and sees in the succession of coincidences that aid his vengeful project clear indications that his cause is just (2002, 24–5, 31). But as the narrative unfolds, the self-righteous vigilante becomes increasingly monstrous, increasingly similar to the murderous pedophile, to whom Hamel always refers in the novel as "le monstre." Having kidnapped "le monstre" and sequestered him in an isolated country house for a seven-day nightmare of horrific tortures, Bruno begins with brute physical assaults on the rapist-murderer. His first act of violence, both in the film and in the novel, is to unceremoniously crush the captive's right knee with a sledgehammer (2002, 95). In the novel, Bruno eventually moves on from straightforward violence to performative torment, in which spectacle becomes a strategy of fear inducement. Bruno "runs towards the monster, wielding the sledgehammer and grimacing theatrically. His prisoner screams in terror and covers his face as Bruno lowers the sledgehammer and starts to laugh."[17] From this moment in the novel, when Bruno performs terrifying threats rather than merely inflicting pain, his actions bring him increasingly close to the realm of

4.1. Video capture from *Les sept jours du talion*. Courtesy of Go Films.

monstrosity. As I have argued elsewhere (Loiselle 2008), the monster is necessarily theatrical and the performance of villainy is intrinsic to the sensation of fear and terror that the horror text seeks to elicit: "The monster's very name, derived from the Latin *monstrare*, connotes the state of being put on display. By definition, the monster is theatrical, for it must be perceived as a menacing spectacle in order to achieve its terrifying impact" (3).

It is no coincidence, therefore, that shortly after Bruno's theatrical performance of villainy in the novel, elements of the narrative establish an increasingly direct link between Bruno and "le monstre." From a legal perspective, one character points out, the crime of abduction, torture, and potentially murder, would earn Bruno the same sentence as the pedophile (2002, 107). By day three of the ordeal, Mercure describes the vigilante as someone who no longer has "anything in common with the happy and sociable family man" he used to be, "nothing in common with the man who has Amnesty International posters in his home office."[18] "Has Hamel become a monster?" Mercure later asks in the novel.[19] As the tortures become gradually more vicious and insane, the captive rapist starts seeing a terrifying streak of madness and inhumanity in his captor's eyes (2002, 165). More importantly, Bruno himself starts recognizing his own monstrosity. He has visions of blood and gore in which he performs unspeakable acts of violence: "Gruesome images popped in his head. He saw himself chopping off the monster's arms, scalping him, sewing his testicles to his eyes. And these images turned him on as much as they annoyed him."[20] In another nightmare he literally sees himself as a monster: half-beast, half-human, with horns and hoofs (2002, 258), reminiscent of medieval depictions of the devil.

Of course, the film cannot use lengthy explanatory passages to expose the theatrical nature of Bruno's monstrosity. Instead, it must use concise audiovisual precepts to suggest that Bruno is no longer an ordinary man but has rather become an ostentatious villain. Not surprisingly, therefore, Bruno's monstrous theatricality takes the form of overacting on the part of Claude Legault in the role of the vigilante. While generally stoic, Legault's Bruno becomes increasingly histrionic in his hysterical phone calls to his wife, his demented fits of rage as he realizes that torturing "le monstre" brings him no satisfaction, and his abject facial expressions as "le monstre," in his maimed delirium, starts tormenting the father with obscene references to his daughter. But in both the film and the novel, the final step in Bruno's progression from ordinary man to monster is when he is eventually accused of having killed his own daughter.

Watching TV in his chamber of torture in the middle of the forest, Bruno sees a report on a woman whose own child had been killed by "le monstre" but who refuses to hold the same violent grudge as Hamel. In a vain attempt to convince himself that he is still doing the right thing, Bruno manages to find out where the woman lives, kidnaps her, and brings her to the cabin where she can see the tortures he has inflicted on her daughter's murderer. But in spite of her fear of Bruno and her hatred of "le monstre," the woman refuses to grant the vigilante the approval he now desperately needs. Rather, by showing her the killer, whom she has struggled to forget since the death of her daughter, Bruno has reignited the pain and suffering she had managed to repress over time. "When I saw this man," she tells her kidnapper in both the novel and the film, "I felt that my daughter died again. But this time, it is your fault. *You have killed my daughter a second time* ... and each time you have tortured this man over the past week, *you have killed your own daughter*, over and over again."[21] Bruno then violently strikes the grieving mother – a gesture that clearly makes him inexcusably monstrous, especially within the Quebec film tradition of gendered violence referred to previously. Bruno's vengeful plan, which might have once seemed like a normal reaction from a father devastated by his child's murder, now comes across as the horrid machination of a criminally deranged psychopath. Accordingly, when Bruno finally surrenders to the cops surrounding the cabin, police officers are petrified at the sight of Bruno's horrifying visage; he has become a "spectre effrayant" (2002, 328 and 330), an unrecognizably ordinary monster whose terrifying actions proved aberrantly normal.

Sur le seuil and the Terror of the Jaded Soul

The ordinary man who becomes a monster is also at the core of Senécal's most accomplished novel and, in my opinion, the best horror film ever made in Quebec: *Sur le seuil*. Decades ago, Father Pivot was a friendly and kind young priest in a small Quebec town (Senécal 1998, 355). As in the case of Bruno Hamel and Jacques Beaulieu, a traumatic tragedy – the death of a beloved family member – transformed the pleasant, ordinary priest into a monster who worships "the power of evil" (1998, 359). Pivot took over a village church and recruited a clan of devil worshippers, who proceeded to tear each other to pieces during a demonic orgy of blood and gore. Pivot's turn from ordinariness to malevolence is the historical backdrop that explains the contemporary case of pure laine evil that forms the story's present tense. *Sur le seuil* focuses on Paul Lacasse, a jaded psychiatrist who tries to cure a deranged horror novelist, Thomas Roy. Roy has cut off his fingers and tried to commit suicide so he will no longer write the tales of terror that inevitably become ghastly reality.

Significantly, Doctor Lacasse is initially indifferent to Roy's case (1998, 49), which he considers to be ordinary; and when a journalist, Charles Monette, shows him evidence that Roy has supernatural powers, Lacasse dismisses his argument as absurd (1998, 107). Even when the accumulation of strange and morbid coincidences incites Lacasse to drive to a remote village and the church that might hold the key to this bizarre case, what he finds is merely "une église bien banale" (1998, 341).

Banality and ordinariness are central to Lacasse's jaded experience of the whole affair. Yet, nagging oddities distress him. The church is banal, but its location is strange. While he has treated innumerable psychopaths, this case gives him irritating stomach aches (1998, 139) and disturbing nightmares (1998, 155). And in spite of his rational, scientific mind, he constantly feels that he is on the edge – "sur le seuil" – of something frighteningly incomprehensible (1998, 286). Lacasse's response to Roy's case is thus profoundly uncanny. As Freud writes:

> We – or our primitive forefathers – once believed in the possibility of these things and were convinced that they really happened. Nowadays we no longer believe in them, we have surmounted such ways of thought; but we do not feel quite sure of our new set of beliefs, and the old ones still exist within us ready to seize upon any confirmation. As soon as something actually happens in our lives which seems to support the old, discarded beliefs, we get a feeling of the uncanny. (Freud 1953/1974, 247–8)

As a psychiatrist who no longer fully believes that his science can help anyone, Paul is a prime candidate for an uncanny experience. The thin veneer of comfortable boredom hides the dread of unimaginably familiar terror.

As is the case for the other adaptations of Senécal's work, Tessier's film version of *Sur le seuil* is more limited than the original novel in its ability to convey the inner thoughts and emotions of the main character. However, the audiovisual material still manages to evoke effectively the terrifying underpinnings of the banal and the ordinary. The film opens with a television report of eleven children having been shot to death by an otherwise "normal and stable" police officer. Lacasse is then observed watching the TV report with an inscrutable facial expression that seems to blend indifference and rage. As such, Lacasse immediately appears as a liminal character who seems calm and able to respond with rationality to violence and madness, but also has the potential to engage with the deep "terror of the soul" that lies beneath the banality of the everyday.

The following sequence then constructs a sense of the dull routine of Dr Lacasse's daily hospital rounds. Even when his colleague Dr Jeanne Marcoux announces that famous author Thomas Roy has been brought to the psychiatric ward after he tried to commit suicide, Lacasse remains unimpressed. This brief succession of shots, which show his tediously repetitive morning visits, creates a sense of dull comfort, with actor Michel Côté as Dr Lacasse generally presented in medium close-ups uninterestedly listening to his patients sitting in their plain but clean and cozy hospital rooms. Lacasse's first visit to Roy's room interrupts this tone of comfortable boredom. But it is not a radical break with the ordinary. The first scene with Roy is just peculiar enough to evoke strangeness. Rather than routine medium close-ups, we are introduced to Roy through a low-angle medium-long shot that displays an odd-looking room, with a peculiar combination of mauve curtains, lavender walls, and greenish-blue bedding. The first close-up on Patrick Huard as Thomas Roy emphasizes the feeling of strangeness. He is not menacing, only creepy: he has one blue eye and one brown; dark facial stubble and bleached blond hair; and an eerily blank expression.

The typically Canadian sense of comfortable boredom is re-established in a number of subsequent scenes in the first half of the film: when Lacasse discusses the banality of the Roy case with his colleagues in the non-descript hospital boardroom; when Lacasse and Marcoux meet in a pleasant urban bistro to talk about his recent breakup, her current pregnancy, and the "mere coincidences" between Roy and dozens of real-life tragedies; or when Lacasse is seen sitting in his plush home office, listening to classical music and unenthusiastically attempting to write an article on Roy. These scenes do not evoke blissful ignorance unwittingly waiting to be destroyed by alien monstrosity. Rather, they convey a deep awareness of, but surface indifference to, violence, pain, and madness. While the film deploys images of banality that seek to repress terror and dread, bursts of horror sporadically seep through. Flashes of tortured bodies, blood-covered headlines, and distorted Catholic symbols start appearing before the doctor's jaded eyes, and strange voices keep haunting him. The horrifying impact of these visions emerges from their uncanny character: they seem wholly familiar and yet unrecognizably foreign.

As the film unfolds, Lacasse resists the growing "evidence" that Roy has the power to incite people to committee evil deeds. But the more he seeks to repress the uncanny coincidences between fiction and reality, the more (un)recognizable images of rational beings gone mad, and angels turned demonic, perturb the psychiatrist. Uncanny visions become concrete deeds of madness when, almost half-way through the film, the innocuous Madame Héneault, one of Lacasse's many average patients, decides to gouge out her eyes before the good doctor. Madame Héneault's sudden, self-inflicted blindness allows Lacasse to start "seeing." A drawing and a few words scribbled on a page by Roy convince Lacasse that, indeed, the famous author can provoke those around him to commit evil deeds through his writing.

As in the novel, the film culminates in Lacasse's trip to the small village where Roy was born. An aging village priest explains to Lacasse that infant Roy came to life in the middle of a black mass performed by Father Pivot, who turned his back on the Church after his sister's violent death (his niece in the novel) and chose to worship evil. The sequence juxtaposes the quaint kitchen of an old presbytery in the film's present tense and the gruesome flashbacks in which we witness Father Pivot and his flock of devil worshippers indulging in an orgy of mutual torture in an attempt to experience pure evil. The contrast between the appealing simplicity of the presbytery where the old priest reminisces about a pre-Satanist, pastoral time, and the horrors that transpired there thirty-six years ago creates an intense sense of fear routed in the uncanny correlation between pleasant, wistful banality and pure, unadulterated evil. This sequence evokes the nostalgic image of a bygone era in French-Canadian history when priests were the benevolent autocrats of small, self-sufficient agrarian communities that had no interest in the petty, neoliberal concerns of North American modernity – back then, there was "nothing to disturb our daily routine," says the aging cleric. And then, as the old priest recounts, in 1966 all hell broke loose, and this pleasant archaic world came to a crashing end.

Within the setting of the black mass itself, the uncanny resides in the evocative concurrence between the innocent infant and the depraved ritual. As the inoffensive newborn is kissed by the demented thirty-six-year-old Father Pivot at the climax of the Satanist rite, the ordinary baby somehow managed to absorb all the wickedness unleashed in the desecrated church where the black mass took place. At that moment, Roy was granted the supernatural power to write evil into action. While much of the impact of this scene results from the sense of "pastness" of the tale of terror, which injects a strong dose of morbid gothic melancholy into the gory flashbacks, the juxtaposition of malevolent carnage and commonplace innocence also creates fear when it is brought to the present tense of the narrative in the last fifteen minutes of the film. The bloodshed that unfolded in the desecrated church years earlier is now transposed to the contemporary psychiatric ward, at the aptly named Hôpital Ste Croix (Holy Cross Hospital), where Roy's deadly influence has led the other inmates to rape, ravage, and maim one another. Lacasse returns to the hospital just in time to see Roy remove the unborn baby from the womb of a lifeless Dr Jeanne Marcoux, and kiss him as he had been kissed

4.2. Video capture from *Sur le seuil*. Courtesy of Go Films.

thirty-six years before by the thirty-six-year-old Pivot. While Roy is shot by the police the baby is saved.

The epilogue shows Lacasse and Jeanne's spouse Marc a year later, looking after the baby. For Lacasse this "typically charming baby"[22] now incarnates all that is *potentially* wicked. In a final moment of banal familiarity and unspeakable horror, the world-weary psychiatrist intensely stares at the innocent babe sitting on the living-room floor, swearing never to let him out of his sight. That a grown man could be so concerned about the latent malevolence of an infant is as ridiculous as it is frightening. But this is the essence of Senécal's infernal vision: the most normal and inoffensive beings are those who conceal the most monstrous evil.

Conclusion

Senécal's novels and the films they have inspired all share the same concern with the petrifying banality of ordinary terror. Whether this paralysing dread of the common man as monster is something uniquely Québécois or Canadian would be hard to prove. But there is little doubt that these works have struck a chord with local readers and spectators. The texts' reliance on the uncanny and a gnawing distrust of the familiar and the ordinary clearly tap into the deep-rooted fears of a significant portion of the francophone population of Canada. That the ordinary, old-stock French Canadian – *le canadien-français pure laine* – is in fact the most menacing of all fiends is not an easy interpretation to accept; many Quebec nationalist critics would doubtlessly reject this reading of Senécal's corpus. But it is important to keep in mind that the power of the tale of terror is precisely to confront us with disturbing truths and unpleasant realities. Spectators and readers who are looking for comforting stories that will reassure them and provide them with an agreeable vision of Quebec culture should not bother with Senécal's oeuvre. But those of us who are ready to face the unsettling truth about the monstrosity of the everyday will always be mesmerized by the compelling authenticity of these tales of "enfer ordinaire."

NOTES

1 Patrick Senécal, *5150, rue des ormes* (Quebec: Éditions Alire, 2001), 5. My translation. "Il a une petite moustache brune sous le nez et ses cheveux châtains frisés en boule lui donne un air un peu quétaine ... Le banlieusard-type."

2 Ibid. 26. My translation. "Ce nom est trop banal, incongru pour un tel cinglé. Je m'imaginais plutôt un patronyme bizarre avec plusieurs *x* et *y* dedans. Jacques Beaulieu. C'est épouvantablement normal."

3 Tessier, cited in Anabelle Nicoud, "*5150, rue des ormes*: l'enfer ordinaire," 3 October 2009. http://www.lapresse.ca/cinema/nouvelles/201207/17/01-4550499-5150-rue-des-ormes-lenfer-ordinaire.php.

4 The production of this new adaptation was announced in 2011, but has not been completed at the time of writing this chapter. See André Duchesne, "Daniel Roby adaptera Patrick Senécal au cinéma," *La Presse*, 4 July 2011, Arts/Spectacles 8).

5 See my article "Quebecus Horribilis: Theatricality, the 'Moment of Horror' and Quebec's 'Satanist' Cinema" in the online journal *Nouvelles "vues" sur le cinéma québécois* 8 (Winter 2008): 3. http://www.cinema-quebecois.net/pdfs/LoiselleNVCQ8.pdf.

6 For further discussion on these issues, see Gina Freitag and André Loiselle, "Tales of Terror in Québec Popular Cinema: The Rise of the French

Language Horror Film since 2000," *American Review of Canadian Studies* 43, no. 1 (Winter 2013).

7 See my piece, "Popular Genres in Quebec Cinema: The Strange Case of Horror in Film and Television," in Bart Beaty, Derek Briton, Gloria Filax, and Rebecca Sullivan, eds, *How Canadians Communicate III* (Edmonton: Athabasca University Press, 2010), 144.

8 See Linda Williams, "When the Woman Looks," in Barry Keith Grant, ed., *The Dread of Difference: Gender and the Horror Film* (Texas: University of Texas Press, 1996), 22.

9 My translation. "Il y a un homme enfermé dans leur maison, au second, et eux, petite famille traditionnelle, dînent comme tous les jours."

10 My translation. "Elle ... poursuit son travail de bonne petite ménagère. Surréaliste. Absurd."

11 Haunting bloodstains on walls are common in horror tales ranging from Stephen King's *The Shining* (1977) to recent horror films such as *The Messengers* (2007, Danny and Oxide Pang) and *100 Feet* (2008, Eric Red).

12 See the web series at http://www.reinerouge.tv/

13 In addition to Yannicks first-person journal entries, the novel also includes entries from Maude's journal. This device establishes an obvious parallel between the two characters, who, in both the novel and the film, do seem to have certain affinities. However, this structural similarly appears superficial in contrast to the deep connection between Bérubé and Beaulieu. Not surprisingly, when push comes to shove, Yannick betrays Maude and remains true to his doppelgänger, Jacques.

14 Senécal, *5150, rue des ormes*, 182. This information is not provided in the film.

15 Ibid., 21. In the film, Bruno and Sylvie have thought about buying a cabin, but never did.

16 Ibid. 82. The actor playing Bruno in the film, Claude Legault, seems somewhat more handsome than his literary counterpart but still qualifies as "ordinary" looking.

17 Ibid., 103. My translation. "Courir vers le monstre, la mass brandie, grimaçant avec une exagération toute théâtrale. Le prisonier poussa un cri de pure terreur et se couvrit tout le visage des deux mains. Bruno baissa la masse et éclatad'un rire tonitruant."

18 Ibid., 135. My translation. "Rien à voir avec le père de famille heureux et sociable ... Rien à voir avec cet homme qui possédait chez lui des affiches laminées d'Amnistie internationale."

19 Ibid., 176. My translation. "Hamel est donc devenu un monstre?"

20 Ibid., 152. My translation. "Des images sanglantes lui traversèrent l'esprit: il se voyait couper les deux bras du monstre, le scalper à vif, lui coudre les testicules sur les yeux, et chacune de ces images l'excitait autant qu'elle l'agaçait."

21 Ibid., 292. My translation. "J'ai senti que ma fille mourrait à nouveau! Et cette fois par votre faute! *Vous avez tué ma fille une deuxième fois!* ... Et vous, depuis une semaine, à chaque torture que vous infligez à cet homme, vous tuez votre fille. Encore, et encore, et encore."

22 *Sur le seuil*, 428. My translation. "Charmant comme tous les bébés."

PART THREE

A Golden Age of Gore:
The Tax Shelter Slasher

5 (Who's in the) Driver's Seat: The Canadian Brute Unleashed in *Death Weekend*

PAUL CORUPE

The period in Canadian cinema that is often referred to dismissively as the "tax shelter era" is generally considered a shameful episode of our history during which the film industry sold its soul to a crassly commercial and deviously philistine Mephistopheles. From the mid-1970s to the early 1980s – or so the story goes – mercenary producers heartlessly took advantage of the generous tax deductions (the ramifications of which are further discussed in the next chapter by Mark Hasan) offered by the federal government to fund useless pieces of cinematic trash that tarnished the image of Canadian cinema at home and abroad. Doubtlessly, that decade saw a significant shift in film production, away from the realist social dramas that had characterized the late 1960s and early 1970s, towards a more generically inclined output. However, it would be unfair and counterproductive to dismiss every film of the era. Indeed, the second half of the 1970s witnessed the release of a number of memorable features that proved to be much more than mediocre replicas of Hollywood B-movies. In fact, it could be argued that this is the time when Canada first revealed itself to be an exceptional breeding ground for innovative, challenging, and surprisingly *Canadian* horror films, and not only because of David Cronenberg.

One of the most uncompromising horror films of the tax shelter era is director William Fruet's terror classic *Death Weekend* (1976). In this harrowing tale, a woman takes deadly revenge after she is brutally attacked and raped by a gang of hoodlums in the rural backwoods of northern Ontario. Though Fruet was well regarded in Canadian film circles at the time the film was made for his writing contribution to Don Shebib's *Goin' Down the Road* (1970) and his directorial debut *Wedding in White* (1972), *Death Weekend*'s graphic violence did not sit well with critics, who felt the director had turned away from dramatic works earnestly tackling identifiably Canadian themes for more crassly commercial exploitation movies. However, careful examination shows that *Death Weekend* has a familiar focus on gender and class already established in Fruet's earlier works and throughout English-Canadian cinema of the early 1970s.

Featuring characters drawn from the Clowns, Cowards, or Bullies archetypes identified by writer Robert Fothergill's early 1970s exploration of masculinity in English-Canadian films, "Being Canadian Means Always Having to Say You're Sorry," the marginalized male characters in *Death Weekend* are obsessed with re-establishing their bruised masculine egos. However, Fruet's characters exhibit a level of sadistic violence and destruction that goes beyond what was previously seen in Canadian film and Fothergill's own categorizations to introduce a new male character type. Fruet uses the hyper-violent "Brute," an extreme variation on the more familiar Bully character, to depict the way men can use sensationalistic violence and degradation to gain power over women in a way not entirely possible in a dramatic feature. This brutal aggression also spills over into Fruet's take on class and the regional disparities between rural and urban Canada, which the director previously explored in his script for *Goin' Down the Road*.

Fruet's identifiably Canadian depiction of gender and related class issues become especially clear when we compare the male characters of *Death Weekend* with those in the American-made *I Spit on Your Grave* (Meir Zarchi, 1978), one of the definitive rape-revenge movies of the 1970s. The Canadian film and its American counterpart differ notably in their portrayal of the rapists, the techniques they use to feminize the audience, and the way the victim's revenge is portrayed. Released to Canadian theatres in 1976, *Death Weekend* markedly changed the direction of Fruet's career. Throughout the decade, Fruet had regularly received critical acclaim for his writing and directing work. He first made his name by penning the script for Shebib's *Goin' Down the Road*, the story of Nova Scotia dockworkers Pete (Doug McGrath) and Joey (Paul Bradley) who relocate to Toronto on the promise of lucrative jobs, only to struggle to get by. In addition to penning scripts for *Rip-Off* (1971, Don Shebib) and *Slipstream* (1973, David Acomba), Fruet also directed the classic wartime family drama *Wedding in White*. In this film, Jim Dougall (Donald Pleasance) discovers his sixteen-year-old daughter Jeannie (Carol Kane) has become pregnant after being raped by her brother's army buddy Billy (McGrath). All these films but *Rip-Off* won a Canadian Film Award for best feature, establishing Fruet as one of the most respected Canadian writers and directors working at the time.

For his next feature, however, Fruet revisited one of his earlier scripts that drew on his own harrowing experience in rural Alberta. Fruet claims he was out driving with a friend when another car pulled up beside them. They were pelted with beer bottles and verbal abuse as the men in the other car attempted to run their vehicle off the road. This frightening incident reportedly inspired *Death Weekend*, when Fruet wondered what would have happened if it had been a female companion in the car instead of a male friend (Vatnsdal 2004, 103–4). Though the film begins much like Fruet's earlier efforts as a realist drama, *Death Weekend* follows the idea of cravenly violent masculinity to its logical and chilling conclusion. Harry (Chuck Shamata), a dentist, is headed north for a weekend getaway with an attractive fashion model Diane (Brenda Vaccaro). After Diane convinces Harry to let her drive his flashy new Corvette convertible along a country back road, Lep (Don Stroud) and his friends pull up beside them in a muscle car to engage them in a drag race. At first Diane ignores the gang but then unexpectedly veers away in another direction. As he takes off in pursuit, Lep (Don Stroud) exclaims, "Jesus, that broad can drive – that pisses me off!" When Diane forces Lep to swerve off the road, he cannot avoid plunging his car into a small creek. Lep's gang – Runt (Richard Ayres), Frankie (Kyle Edwards) and Stanley (Don Granberry) – are shocked: "Nobody ever did that to Lep before – and it was a chick too!"

The young couple soon arrives at Harry's summer cottage – actually a lakefront estate – filled with expensive furnishings and art. Harry brags about his salary and a deal he got on a piano, claiming he wants "the biggest and the best of everything." Naturally, Harry intends to "possess" Diane too; he only invited her up on the false pretense that he was having a party, but instead plans to seduce her. When Diane discovers the real reason she was asked to Harry's cottage, she demands to be taken home. After angrily packing her belongings, she is confused to find Lep and his buddies sitting in the living room of the house, having spent the last few hours tracking the couple down. Lep demands money to pay for car repairs, and a nervous Harry hands over a wad of cash and implores them to leave. But Lep is not so easily placated and decides to stay for the entire weekend, ostensibly until Harry can get him more money.

As the gang begins to drinking Harry's liquor, Diane becomes increasingly nervous about Lep's motives. Runt, Frankie, and Stanley take

5.1. Video capture from *Death Weekend*. Courtesy of Cinépix.

Harry's motorboat out on the lake and sideswipe another boat, not real-izing they've killed two locals in the process. After they return to shore, Lep chases Diane across the estate and into a rundown cabin, where he attempts to rape her. Initially she fights back violently, but after Lep reveals he is only sexually aroused when she struggles, she stops. But at this point, Lep is unable to continue with his assault and angrily drags Diane back to the house, where his gang begins smashing the house and Harry's possessions with baseball bats and sledgehammers. Harry runs upstairs and grabs a shotgun he keeps hidden in his bedroom, but Lep quickly grabs the gun from Harry's hands. Lep chases Harry out the house's front door and shoots him in the back as he tries to flee.

Meanwhile, Runt drags Diane upstairs and rapes her, but she con-ceals a shard of broken glass in her hand and stabs him in the throat at the precise moment he reaches orgasm. Escaping out the window, she takes refuge in Harry's boathouse. When Frankie and Stanley discover Runt's body, they head off to find Diane. Only Diane is ready for them – she kills Frankie by throwing a flare into the gasoline-soaked boathouse and lets Stanley drown after he falls in a bog while attempting to attack her. As the sun rises, Diane finds a car and hotwires it in an attempt to escape. Lep appears and tries to shoot her, but when that fails he jumps on the car's roof. Diane first shakes Lep loose and then runs him over, killing him, and continues driving until she is outside the gates of the house.

From the beginning of its production, *Death Weekend*'s rape-revenge was dogged by controversy. To finance *Death Weekend*, Fruet approached Cinépix, a Montreal film distributor turned producer. Cinépix began producing films just as the Canadian Film Development Corporation (CFDC) was established to stimulate a feature film industry in the country through a loan fund. *Death Weekend*'s producers, Ivan Reitman and Don Carmody, had just been involved in a debate over Cinépix's first attempt to break into anglophone horror, *Shivers* (1975, David Cronenberg). Funded with public money granted through the CFDC, *Shivers*'s bloody special effects and bold depictions of sex prompted critics to question whether government-funded Canadian genre cinema could reflect nationalist themes. In his often-cited *Saturday Night* article, writer Robert Fulford held up Cronenberg's film as an example of wasted tax dollars, famously claiming "You should know how bad this movie is: after all, you paid for it" (Delaney 1975).

Cinépix quickly responded with a pamphlet entitled "Is There a Place for Horror Films in Canada's Film Industry?" and such questions still lingered when *Death Weekend* was released just under a year later. Also focusing on overt violence and bloodshed, *Death Weekend* was similarly pilloried by Canadian film critics, even those whose publications supported Cinépix's case for *Shivers*. The general consensus was that, like Cronenberg, Fruet's use of established horror elements to appeal to film markets beyond Canada precluded the exploration of any identifiably Canadian themes. In his review for *Cinema Canada* magazine, Clive Denton calls *Death Weekend* "ugly, vicious, downright shitty" and "mean-spirited garbage." Before admitting that it was "adequately" made, he notes that it is hard to understand what the director of *Wedding in White* saw in this material (Denton 1977, 57). Similarly, Gary J. McCallum observes in his review for *Take One* magazine that "in any terms other than the crassest economic, *Death Weekend* is almost a complete write-off" (McCallum 1977, 38). Film critic Gerald Pratley pegs it as "a shoddy tale of rape and violence" (Pratley 1987, 228).

On closer inspection, it is apparent that Fruet does not necessarily sacrifice his interest in home-grown themes with *Death Weekend*. Harry and Lep exhibit characteristics that make them clear variations of the male lead characters seen in Fruet's scripts for *Goin' Down the Road* and *Wedding in White*, as well as other English-Canadian films of the early 1970s, including *The Rowdyman* (1972, Peter Carter) and *Paperback Hero* (1973, Peter Pearson). These films all feature marginalized, ineffective male characters whose insecurity and misguided idealism leads them to a tragic end. Piers Handling partially recognizes *Death Weekend's* relationship to Fruet's past work in a *Cinema Canada* article entitled "Bill Fruet: 2 or 3 Things." In this analysis, written almost a year after *Death Weekend* was released, Handling attempts to reconcile his conviction that "Fruet is an auteur – an author in the true sense of the word" with the "anger and hostility" he felt after watching the film (Handling 1977, 44).

Ironically, Handling struggles to accept Fruet's strong female character throughout his article, and adopts an attitude much like Harry does in the film. He suggests that "paradoxically, it is [Diane] who is really responsible for the holocaust of violence precisely by [fighting back]. Her aggressive 'masculine' driving is skillful enough to push Lep and his gang off the road at the beginning of the film. It is her ability to think like a man that not only gets her into the whole mess in the first place, but is also responsible for getting her out of it" (1977, 46). Instead, he implies, Diane should not assert herself, but simply submit to Lep's view of women as passive creatures that must be dominated, or Harry's view of women as little more than possessions. Handling's interpretation is at odds with Fruet's presentation of Diane. Although conspicuously lacking a character arc, she stands throughout the film as a strong-willed, modern woman who holds her own against any of the male leads. Fruet does not imply she should be "punished" for failing to accept the submissive roles that Harry and Lep attempt to impose on her. Instead, he indicates that the failure belongs to Harry and Lep. The film's insecure male characters are obsessed with proving their masculinity by gaining power over Diane, which ultimately leads them both to their deaths.

Written just three years before the release of *Death Weekend*, Fothergill's seminal essay "Being Canadian Means Always Having to Say You're Sorry" discusses the male lead characters in early 1970s English-Canadian films. Fothergill looks not only at Fruet's work in *Goin' Down the Road* and *Wedding in White*, but also the male leads in more than a dozen other films, noting that "to the extent that one identifies with the protagonists one is likely to be disheartened. For a man, identification means involving oneself in the experience of impotence" (Fothergill 1973, 25). Fothergill goes on to trace the three different types of male characters common in these films – the Clown, the Coward, and the Bully, noting that these films "dramatize and identify with the demoralizing exposure of a male protagonist as shallow and contemptible ... We are not particularly encouraged to respond sympathetically to the protagonist. He comes across as a selfish and unappealing person, trapped in his own limitations. Much of his talk seems hollow and insincere, as though his real feelings are blocked or stunted, and he is relating to other people inauthentically" (1973, 25).

In discussing Fruet's work, Fothergill identifies *Goin' Down the Road*'s Pete and Joey as Cowards who realize their rural east coast upbringing and values are almost worthless in the prosperous, white-collar city of Toronto. In the film's conclusion, the hapless Maritimers cannot bring themselves to tell Joey's pregnant wife they are leaving Toronto and heading off to Vancouver, leaving her to fend for herself. Fothergill also notes that they occasionally act as Clowns, "drinking and frolicking in a fashion that is likeable enough but rather trying to the women who have to put up with it," and shying away from adult responsibilities (1973, 25).

Fothergill devotes a larger part of his essay to describing the Bully. With this archetypal 1970s Canadian male character, "the threatened and insubstantial male ego is shown attempting to assert its dominance through displays of brutal inconsiderateness and sullen rage. In addition to the hollow nastiness of his general disposition, the Bully specializes in the sexual degradation of his womenfolk. It's the ugliest of the three faces, and the scenarios usually work to punish the characters who display it" (1973, 26).

In *Wedding in White*, Doug McGrath and Paul Bradley make cameo appearances as drunken soldiers in a virtual repeat of their *Goin' Down the Road* performances. Though Billy does intimidate Jeannie so he can rape her, Fothergill notes that it is her father, Jim Dougall, who emerges as the Bully of the film. He is portrayed as a cruel drunk who, in one scene, physically attacks Jeannie when he discovers she is pregnant, lamenting "I've got a whore for a daughter – I'm disgraced!" To save the family's reputation, he forces her to marry his elderly drinking buddy, a move that upsets many in the film's small-town setting.

Fothergill states that in the process of re-establishing their ego, the Clown, the Coward, and the Bully never seem to grow or change. Fothergill notes, "It is very rare indeed to find an English-Canadian film in which a male character of some worth and substance is depicted as growing towards self-realization, achieving or even working towards a worthwhile goal, playing a significant part in any kind of community, or establishing a mature loving relationship with a woman" (1973, 27).

Aside from the initial car chase scene, the first half-hour of *Death Weekend* is notably similar to English-Canadian dramas of the era, with Harry doling out passive-aggressive abuse to a strong-willed female character. Until Lep arrives at the house, Harry closely aligns with Fothergill's role of the Bully. Harry is a deeply insecure character, a womanizer who uses his wealth to prop up his fragile ego. Like Jim Dougall, he is a shallow and selfish man who only cares how others perceive him. In this case, Harry wants to appear as rich, powerful, and sexually potent, not only to Diane, but to the two friendly locals who run the gas station. Accepting Harry's gift of a bottle of liquor, they muse that he has had a different girl up to his summer house every single weekend that summer.

Fothergill notes that the Bully specializes in the sexual degradation of women, and Harry's humiliation of Diane is primarily rooted in his attempts to assert his power over a confident, independent woman. In her 1975 book *Against Our Will*, feminist Susan Brownmiller began to identify that rape was about control rather than sex. She notes that rape "is not a crime of irrational, impulsive, uncontrollable lust, but is a deliberate, hostile, violent act of degradation and possession on the part of the would-be conqueror, designed to intimidate and inspire fear" (Brownmiller 1975, 6). Harry's domineering attitude towards Diane is an obvious example of Brownmiller's thesis. His first act of sexual possession takes place once they arrive at the house when he – without Diane's knowledge – shoots illicit photos of her changing clothes and taking a shower from behind a two-way mirror installed in the guest bedroom (later, Lep discovers a stash of nude photos apparently depicting Harry's previous weekend getaways). Harry's attempts to seduce Diane escalate as the afternoon wears on – he waits until he has Diane out on his boat to casually ask her to pose for nude photographs. She reacts to his question with surprise and a firm refusal. Already feeling wounded after that blow, Harry later tells her that the party invitation was a ruse, explaining "You're a big girl now and you know exactly what's going on."

A similar line occurs in *Wedding in White* when a drunken Billy yells "Don't play dumb" moments before he rapes a protesting Jeannie. Instead of submitting, as Jeannie does, Diane quickly asserts herself and angrily demands to be taken home, saying "I don't pose in the nude, I don't sleep with men I've just met and especially with men I don't like." Humiliated, Harry reacts as a Bully – he angrily refuses to drive her back to the bus station and passive-aggressively tells her to make the long walk alone. Harry's disastrous romantic weekend in *Death Weekend* is reminiscent of Pete's own failure with Nicole, a buxom French-Canadian secretary, in *Goin' Down the Road*. Pete's ill-fated date illustrates the insurmountable regional and cultural gap between the two characters. At a disco club, Nicole dances by herself while Pete, who prefers country music, sits in the corner nursing a beer. When she does not invite him back to her place, Pete saves face by hiding in the shadows until Joey and some other co-workers who have been watching from afar leave, assuming that their friend has scored. For both Pete and Harry, the disappointment of this female rejection is totally emasculating.

However, once Lep and his gang appear, the tone of *Death Weekend* changes from an ugly, downbeat Canadian drama to a tense and horrific thriller. Although Harry and Lep appear quite different on the surface – a nouveau-riche status seeker and a loutish hoodlum – Fruet clearly implies that they have much in common in their attempts to prove their masculinity and subjugate Diane. Like Harry, Lep is threatened by Diane, but for different reasons – she can race and fix cars, traditionally masculine skills that she says she learned from a former boyfriend. At this point, Fruet uses Lep to introduce a more frightening variation on Fothergill's taxonomy – the Brute. Like the Bully, the Brute is a male protagonist motivated by his threatened ego. However, while Fothergill defines the Bully by the "brutal inconsideration and sullen rage" (Fothergill 1973, 26) he uses to reassert himself, the Brute trades in brutal violence and sadistic rage – a much more frightening, outward expression of his inner insecurities that establishes him as a more traditional horror antagonist.

The escalating, aggressive violence that Lep, as a Brute, wages against Diane and Harry is far more forceful and destructive than previously seen in Canadian film. From the unflinching shotgun murder of Harry to the complete destruction of his home and possessions, this level of physical brutality was completely unique at the time. Even when previous Canadian Bully characters are forced to resort to violence, it occurs only in short bursts tied to emotionally charged moments. Specifically, in *Goin' Down the Road*, penniless and hungry Pete and Joey are almost immediately wracked with guilt after they knock a grocery store bagboy unconscious while escaping with stolen groceries. Dougall also responds violently towards his daughter when he discovers she is pregnant – slapping her and even punching her in the stomach. However, this outburst is restricted to just one scene; Dougall's family quickly stops him from retrieving a belt to beat her and he eventually calms down. Later, he tries to save face through arranging an unwanted marriage, a far more passive-aggressive approach.

Fruet's use of violence in *Death Weekend* is quite different. Lep's attack, which is primarily tied to the power struggle that consumes much of the plot, is sustained throughout almost the entire film and turns decidedly deadly by the conclusion. Humiliated by Diane's superior driving skills, Lep is much more outwardly aggressive than either Harry or any of the characters in Fruet's past films, and his unpredictable behaviour gives the film its most frightening sequences. After he crashes his car into the creek, Lep yells out "Goddamn fucking cunt – you'll get yours, baby!" and then proceeds to tell his pals, "I'm gonna ram that supercharger up her ass!" These sexually charged threats, which echo similar language as the obscene phone calls in the earlier Canadian horror film *Black Christmas* (Bob Clark, 1974), foreshadow Lep's later efforts to reassert his masculinity and perceived power over Diane by attempting to rape her – an act that, as Brownmiller identifies, is about Lep's desire for control rather than sex.

Lep's campaign of harassment and intimidation begins as soon as the gang arrives at Harry's home. When Diane finishes packing and leaves her room, Lep is there waiting. Before she can react or call Harry, he grabs her, kisses her against her will, and squeezes her breast. Unaware, Harry is busy preparing to apologize to Diane when he discovers Lep and his gang in his living room. An interesting shift occurs here – with a much stronger and more terrifying Brute now in the house, Harry is forced into the role of the Coward, unable to assert himself against Lep's cruel acts. Instead, it is Diane who stands up to her aggressors. While Harry pleads with her to just do as they say to avoid upsetting them, she proclaims, "This is disgusting – you're disgusting" and "What are you, a bunch of assholes?" Harry proves equally ineffective when Diane's safety becomes an issue. While Lep and his gang are out in the motorboat, Diane begs Harry to do something before they return and turn their attention to her, but Harry does not help her and appears paralysed by the situation.

Once back on shore, Lep escalates his own attempts to sexually humiliate Diane. First they encourage Harry to chase her, promising that, if he catches her, she will "give [Harry] a blowjob." Harry refuses to participate, and the gang violently beats him while Lep chases Diane into a nearby cabin. In the rape attempt that follows, Lep tracks Diane down and forces her into a corner of the structure so he can remove her clothing. At first, Diane does her best to fight off Lep, until he notes that "nothing gets me off quicker than a bitch who fights." Eventually she's overpowered and stops struggling. In a surprising turn quite uncommon in similar rape-revenge films, Lep is unable to go on sexually assaulting Diane. Instead, Lep changes tactics. He stands up and even gives her a tender kiss, but she responds by slapping him.

Finally, *Death Weekend* upholds the tradition of Canadian male characters that refuse to evolve but instead are ultimately punished for their brutal behaviour towards others. Fothergill notes that 1970s Canadian dramas do not "present the humiliation as a wry misadventure or a painful step towards maturity, but more like the pattern of his fate, a nail of his coffin" (Fothergill 1973, 25). In this case, the coffin is literal – all the male characters in the film are killed for their attempts to overpower Diane without ever acknowledging their harmful view of women. Although *Death Weekend* largely focuses on gender, Fruet also touches on related issues of class and urbanism, highlighting the disparity between rich, "sophisticated" city dwellers and the crude rural inhabitants. Fruet explored the tragic side of this theme in *Goin' Down the Road* but again pushes the idea into horror territory by playing up the inherent class conflict in a way that taps into audience fears. In this way, *Death Weekend* aligns with the sensational depictions of anger and violence in *The Texas Chain Saw Massacre* (Tobe Hooper, 1974), *Deliverance* (John Boorman, 1972), *Straw Dogs* (Sam Peckinpah, 1971), and *The Last House on the Left* (Wes Craven, 1972) (with which *Death Weekend* played as a double bill in the United States). In her 1992 book *Men, Women and Chain Saws: Gender in the Modern Horror Film*, author Carol J. Clover notes that "one of the obvious things at stake in the city/country split of horror films, in short, is social class – the confrontation between haves and have-nots, or even more directly, between exploiters and their victims" (Clover 1993, 126).

This social class split is prominently explored in *Goin' Down the Road*. Although Pete dreams of a "job in an office, some chick for a secretary, company car, and my name on the door" in the big city of Toronto, he quickly discovers that his dreams are just as unattainable as they were at the cannery in his rural working-class community of Cape Breton, Nova Scotia. Pete even attempts to fit in with what he sees as the more sophisticated city dwellers. At a record store he browses the classical music section instead of stealing country music albums with his friends and pines after Nicole instead of the working-class waitresses Joey has resigned himself to. In one of the film's most poignant scenes, Pete is shocked when, during a job interview at an advertising agency, he learns that he needs more than just a high-school diploma to get the job. Soon Pete is back to working the same kinds of menial jobs in Toronto he had back east – loading trucks with beer, setting pins in a bowling alley, and working a carwash.

While Pete withdraws in bitter disappointment after realizing he will never be accepted by the city, *Death Weekend* has Lep react to a similar class division with violent anger. When Lep realizes Harry is rich and that he is largely unfazed by their attacks on Diane, he realizes the only way to hurt him is to destroy his possessions. Exhibiting some of the characteristics of the Clown, Lep and his gang drunkenly trash the house in a harrowing display of property destruction, using a sledgehammer and crowbars to smash everything from the grand piano to the windows and walls, and even the toilet. But Lep makes the class issue explicit, taunting Harry by saying, "Everything you got is shit. This whole goddamn place is shit. You think it's class. You think you got style." Lep notices Harry's lack of concern for Diane and further berates him, yelling "You're incredible – you don't give a shit what I do to this charming lady, you don't even give a shit what I do to you, do you? But your car, your boat, this crap house."

Death Weekend's uniquely Canadian approach to the rape-revenge horror film can be further illustrated by comparing the portrayal of Lep's gang to the four rapists in the rape-revenge film *I Spit on Your Grave*. Considered one of the most notorious exploitation films of the 1970s, primarily due to the extended rape, sodomy, and degradation of its female lead, the Connecticut-shot film (originally titled *Day of the Woman*) shares many distinct similarities with *Death Weekend* – an isolated rural setting, a strong professional female character, and a despicable four-man gang of hoods determined to demonstrate their control over a woman who appears to be their social better.

In *I Spit on Your Grave*, Jennifer Hills (Camille Keaton), a pretty New York City writer heads out to a rented cabin in a small rural community to work on her first novel. Locals Johnny (Eron Tabor), Stanley (Anthony Nichols), and Andy (Gunter Kleeman) take notice of her arrival. The men decide to rape Jennifer, ostensibly to help mentally challenged grocery delivery boy Matthew (Richard Pace) lose his virginity. The ensuing attack occurs in several different areas of the woods and concludes back at the cabin. At first reluctant, Matthew eventually attempts to rape Jennifer but cannot reach orgasm. Once they finish, Matthew is given a knife and told to stab her to death, but he cannot bring himself to carry out the deed. When Jennifer recovers from the vicious and brutal ordeal, she carries out her revenge, killing each of the men when they are most vulnerable. As with *Death Weekend*, *I Spit on Your Grave* received harsh critical notices, but for different reasons. In his review, Roger Ebert describes the film as "a vile bag of garbage" and "an expression of the most diseased and perverted darker human natures ... a geek show" (Ebert 1980). Ebert was primarily offended not by the film itself but by the disturbing catcalls and inappropriate laughter exhibited by the audience he saw it with. Though depictions of rape on film can run the risk of making a rape look acceptable or even attractive to viewers, *I Spit on Your Grave*'s uncomfortably long sexual assault – it occurs over almost forty-five minutes of the one-hundred-minute movie – seems obviously intended to illustrate how damaging and repellent rape can be. Noting Ebert's review, critic Marco Starr theorizes that the catcalls of men apparently "enjoying" the film's rape are more likely due to male spectators doing anything they can to "prove that they are *not* upset by all this rape business," which may single them out as "woman-identified men" (Starr 1984, 54).

The rapists in *I Spit on Your Grave* take the same attitude towards women as Lep, even noting at one point that "total submission – that's what I like in a woman!" However, Johnny, Matthew, Stanley, and Andy differ significantly from the Bully characters of Canadian film and even the Brute of *Death Weekend*. These characters use the rape and subjugation of Jennifer as a means to prove their masculinity to each other and are largely unrelatable to the audience. In addition, these characters are ultimately punished for their physical actions that result from their demeaning attitude towards women and not the attitude itself, as Jennifer conforms to the men's chauvinistic views before she kills them.

Lep and Harry's sexual humiliation of Diane in *Death Weekend* is primarily intended to reaffirm their superiority over her. By contrast, the rapists in *I Spit on Your Grave* are far more interested in showing off for their friends. Clover notes that the film's notorious rape scene illustrates how a group dynamic can cause individuals to act in ways they would not on their own and to establish the male characters' pecking order. She states: "The pretense is that the assault on Jennifer is an act of generosity toward one of their members, a gift from the guys to Matthew. The fact is that this is a sporting competition, the point of which is to test and confirm an existing hierarchy" (Clover 1993, 122). When Matthew is, at first, reluctant to rape Jennifer, the others tell him to "Come on, be a man" and "You wanna be a man don't you Matthew?" Although the men do humiliate and degrade Diane – at one point they rip up her manuscript while she watches – their motive seems to stem less from being threatened by a female, and more from needing to assert their own masculinity to one another.

The relationship between the rapists and the audience also greatly differs between the films. *Death Weekend* encourages the viewer to identify with Harry and Lep. Fruet often pulls the camera away from the supposed protagonist, Diane, to tell the story from the male character's perspective. And although Diane is a strong, proactive character, more of the script is devoted to developing and clarifying Lep and Harry's motivations, as flawed as they may be. In this way, Fruet emasculates the audience by directly inviting the viewer to experience the male characters' impotence. Clover notes that "although earlier cinematic rapes allow for a large measure of spectator identification with the rapist ... films from the mid-1970s go to increasing lengths to dissociate us from that position. Even when the rapes are shown, they are shown in ways that align us to the victim" (1993, 152). Accordingly, *I Spit on Your Grave* forces the viewer to associate with the victim through camera angles that are almost shot from Jennifer's point of view – in essence Johnny, Stanley and Andy are raping the viewer, who is feminized in the process. This corresponds with Starr's interpretation of the theatre audience's reaction to the film – placed in the position of the rape victim, men will loudly pretend to enjoy watching the rape. Thus, in *I Spit on Your Grave*, the horror comes from the viewer being feminized and "raped" by the men, while in *Death Weekend* the horror comes from the viewer recognizing their own brutish cowardice, as reflected in the film's male characters.

But perhaps the biggest difference between the two films is the way the female protagonist enacts her final revenge. In the conclusion of *I Spit on Your Grave*, Jennifer recovers from the attack and visits each of the male characters in turn. At first, Jennifer pretends that she actually enjoyed the rape and has returned for more sexual gratification. Jennifer lures Matthew back to the woods and tells him, "I could have given you a summer to remember for the rest of your life." She allows him to have sex with her, but then kills him at the moment of orgasm by slipping a noose around his neck and hoisting him into a nearby tree.

Later, Jennifer finds Johnny and, putting on a seductive air, convinces him to take a car ride with her. At a secluded spot she pulls a gun on him and forces him to strip. Johnny begs for his life and tries to justify the rape:

> This thing with you is the thing any man would have done, you coax a man into doing it to you! Look, a man gets the message fast, whether he's married or not. A man, he's just a man. First thing, you come into the gas station and expose your damn sexy legs to me walking back and forth real slow making sure I see them good. And then Matthew ... sees half your tits peeking out at him. And then you're lying in your canoe, in your bikini, just waiting ... like bait!

Listening to Johnny's attempts to put the blame on his victim, Jennifer appears to have a change of heart and they are soon naked together in the bathtub at Johnny's house. In the film's most infamous scene, Jennifer massages Johnny's shoulders and then appears to fondle him under the bubble-bath-filled water. At first Johnny says, "That feels so good it hurts," before realizing that Jennifer has in fact castrated him with a knife she has kept hidden in the water. She then locks him in the bathroom and plays music to drown out his screams of horror.

Like Diane, Jennifer avenges herself against her sexual humiliation but in a wholly different way. Jennifer must initially conform to her attackers' skewed understanding of gender – that "being a man" means possessing and subjugating women better than your friends can. By acting seductively, Jennifer disarms Matthew and Johnny, but in doing so also briefly validates their beliefs that, in their initial attack, Jennifer was "asking for it" and "wanted it all along." As a result, the rapists of *I Spit on Your Grave* are never challenged over their notion that an ideal woman is one who "totally submits" to a man. Instead, they are simply punished for acting on this view.

Fruet takes a markedly different approach in *Death Weekend*. Diane consistently challenges Lep over his beliefs and never gives in to the male characters – she does not compromise herself. She frequently stands up to Lep's gang when Harry is too scared and never entices the men, even falsely. Even though Lep and Harry never display any self-consciousness over the way they have treated Diane, her confident attitude and actions throughout the film demonstrate to the viewer that their view of women is flawed. In *I Spit on Your Grave*, the characters reach some sort of self-realization. When confronted by Jennifer, they first downplay their own involvement in the rape, but just before they are killed they realize they are paying the price for their vicious physical assault. This is not true of Harry, who is shot while trying to escape, or Lep, who gives Diane a twisted smile as she steps on the gas and runs him over in the final reel. The characters in *Death Weekend* pay for their attitudes, but they die without ever fully realizing the errors of their ways.

While Fruet's choice to make a genre film indicates a deliberate move towards a more commercial style of film production, this does not preclude him from exploring specific Canadian themes. Instead, Fruet takes the well-established ideas of a wounded, insecure male character that attempts to subjugate a female and the inherent class conflict between rural and urban Canadians and simply reframes them in an a way not previously explored in Canadian film. Initially, Lep follows the traditional path of the Bully, the quintessentially Canadian "loser" archetype identified by Fothergill. Made to feel inferior by both Diane's racing skills and Harry's rich lifestyle, he unsuccessfully attempts to assert his power over the other two characters, transforming from a Bully to a more frightening Brute with an escalating campaign of explosive violence. While threats and brief expressions of violence do occasionally transpire in English-Canadian dramatic films of the time, Lep's actions go far beyond any other Bully's attempts to heal his ego. His attempt to sexually humiliate Diane results in the death of every character except Diane and almost the complete demolition of Harry's house by the lake. In comparison, Harry first appears as a more traditional Bully, but is eventually revealed as a Coward; Harry is able to passive-aggressively lash out at women who will not sleep with him but is unable to fight back when faced with the possibility of bodily harm or significant property damage.

However, unlike most American rape-revenge films, as typified by *I Spit on Your Grave*, it is not Fruet's sole intention to make viewers uncomfortable with the depiction of a vicious rape. Instead, he pushes the audience to relate to the film's deeply flawed protagonists, thus forcing them to identify with the male characters' impotence – an often identified "Canadian" approach, as explained by Fothergill. While Harry and Lep are both killed without even realizing the inherent harm of their derogatory view of women as either second-class citizens or as possessions, the viewer has the opportunity to critique and judge their actions.

In the same way that Fruet was able to use the horror genre to make an explicit attack on Harry and Lep's attitude towards gender politics, he was also able to reframe the inherent class conflict of *Goin' Down the Road* in violent terms. Just as Diane's acts of retribution towards her would-be rapists can be read as a revenge of a stronger Jeannie Dougall on her domineering father, Lep's destruction of Harry's home and possessions could be interpreted as Pete and Joey's own intensely violent response to their inability to fit in with rich and urbane city dwellers.

The Brute quickly became a standard figure in Canadian horror and exploitation films. Variations of this sadistically violent and destructive character can be seen in *Vengeance Is Mine* (1976, John Trent) in which a farmer (Enrest Borgnine) captures a trio of bank robbers invading his home, including the wildly unpredictable criminal Leroy (Michael J. Pollard). Like Lep, Leroy's ego is wounded and he responds by getting violently out of control – smashing a police car, attempting to rape the man's daughter, and finally engaging his captor in a shoot-out. In *Blackout* (1978, Eddy Matalon), four prison escapees invade an upscale apartment building during a power failure and humiliate and terrorize the rich residents. They rape a woman and burn Picasso paintings owned by a rich resident (Ray Milland), reminiscent of Lep's own violent class revenge on Harry. In *Siege* (1983, Paul Donovan), striking union cops-turned-vigilantes become Brutes when they threaten and forcibly sexually assault the patrons of an underground gay bar. More important than its influence on the films that succeeded it, *Death Weekend* shows that it is possible to reflect nationalist themes in a genre film context. By drawing on the underlying anger and frustration of characters from his past work and then intensifying these emotions into deadly intimidation and violence, Fruet creates a unique horror film–ready spin on Fothergill's identifiably Canadian characters. While *Death Weekend* may not have received critical approval at the time of its release, its power to provoke and disturb the audience while still exploring quintessentially Canadian themes makes it an important landmark in the early development of Canadian horror cinema.

6 *Rituals*: Creating the Forest Slasher within the Canadian Tax Shelter Era

MARK R. HASAN

The Debut of CanCon

The "tax-shelter" policy discussed in Paul Corupe's chapter had many antecedents, all of which sought to bolster the fledgling Canadian film industry. In fact, the first protectionist policy to affect Canada, which has already been referred to in Andrea Subissati's chapter, emerged from the UK in the form of a quota system – the 1927 Cinematograph Films Act – which mandated all distributors to carry a minimum 7.5 per cent British-made films, and 5 per cent of films shown by exhibitors to be British-made (with a minimum constitution of technicians, lead creative talent, and financing requirements originating from within the British Empire, including Canada of course). Its ultimate goal was to provide funding for native productions that could compete for the public's attention in theatres amid the heavy saturation of American product. The number of British-made films did increase, but Hollywood studios were forced to invest a percentage of their revenues in productions that had significant budgets.

The act did aid in the foundation of British studios, a star system, and high-quality productions that could be exported outside of the United Kingdom, but when Hollywood chose to curtail its investment in Britain during the late 1960s, film production dwindled, causing a crash in the film industry during the 1970s. In Canada, the federal government had a more complex series of issues to tackle. Most independent, Canadian-owned, first-run exhibition chains failed to match the financial resources of their American counterparts, and regional leading chains either folded or were swallowed up by the competition, of which the Allen Theatre Corporation is the most notable, being absorbed in 1923 by the Canadian arm of Famous Players Theaters (Morris 1978, 92).

By the late 1940s, film distribution was virtually controlled by American studios and, to some extent, by the Odeon circuit, owned and operated by Britain's Rank Organization.[1] When the Canadian government's extended period of indolence finally ended, they too examined a British model of minimum screen time for native films and the reinvestment of revenues towards a quota of Canadian film production. The latter aspect was championed by the NFB (Pratley 1987, 82), but when Hollywood voiced its displeasure with the plan, the Canadian government threatened to levy an income freeze (1987, 84) – a genuinely bold concept – but after heavy lobbying and schmoozing by the head of the Motion Picture Producer's Association of America (MPPAA)[2], a more benign solution was proposed: the Canadian Cooperative Agreement (CCA).

In exchange for shelving protectionist measures and failing to support independent Canadian exhibitors,[3] Hollywood would mention aspects of Canada in their films to promote tourism (1987, 84) – hence the often oblique Canadian references in US films, such as visiting cousins from Quebec, the occasional use of Canada as a setting (but not necessarily filming a Canadian locale), and the sudden observance of passing Canada geese by cowboys – enriching the "mindless simplicity" of Canadian stereotypes (Morris 1978, 93) perpetuated by Hollywood ad infinitum in film, TV, and other popular culture streams.

The intellectual construction of this plan would allow the local film industry to focus on what it did best – documentaries, via the National Film Board (NFB) – and nothing else, perhaps because the paternalistic government felt Canadian filmmakers were better suited to focus on short-form documentaries, travelogues, educational shorts, and nothing remotely resembling a fictional, commercial, feature-length film – live action, or animated. The CCA was a cultural and industry sellout, and neither it nor a Capital Cost Allowance Program (CCAP) – beginning in 1954, a taxpayer could deduct up to 60 per cent of private funding in a film – yielded the level of productions wanted by the country's talent pool. The disappointment probably mitigated the decision of actors, writers, and directors to move to the US, once they had earned substantive credits, where they enjoyed productive careers in film and TV during the fifties and sixties.[4]

Between 1954 and 1969, roughly sixty-six feature-length films (fiction and non-fiction) were released theatrically in Canada, of which thirteen were produced separately as distinct productions by the NFB and the CBC, plus one co-production; the remaining fifty-two were independent films, insofar as neither of the aforementioned Crown film or TV corporation were involved in their full production. Of these non-Crown corporation films, two were thrillers, one was a psychological shocker, and two were actual horror efforts: Julian Roffman's 3D classic *The Mask* (1961) and Erick Santamaria's *The Playgirl Killer* (1966). In 1974, the government refined the CCAP by boosting the tax deduction to 100 per cent per income year and instituting a point system: the more Canadian (CanCon) talent involved in the production, the closer the taxpayer could get to that magic 100 per cent mark (Pendakur 1990, 170). The system remained in place until 1984, when the deduction limit was rolled back to 60 per cent (Vatsndal 2004, 166) and then 30 per cent in 1987, causing a crash in CanCon film productions which were (ideally) destined for theatrical screens, assuming a significant percentage of tax shelter films were not funded by wealthy dentists and plastic surgeons, but indeed financed, assembled, and sold to international markets with the direct intent for theatrical and later home video exploitation.

The Canadian Parliament, however, formed the Canadian Film Development Corporation (CFDC) in 1967 to help fund low-budget productions. Starting at $10 million, the slush fund was augmented several times over the years, but the corporation's executive directors also found a significant portion of completed films were not being released or making it to theatre screens. The lack of a rival Canadian distribution network, scant independent productions, poor (if any) marketing plans to promote films in print and other media to filmgoers, and virtually no training ground (besides television) for filmmakers to explore long-form fiction films in commercial genres ensured a long wait before Canada would produce its first formal horror film. The reason *The Mask* succeeded, besides use of private funds, was due to its being aimed squarely at the exploitation market.

With the exception of *The Luck of Ginger Coffey* (1964) – a US adaptation of Brian Moore's Governor General Award–winning novel set in Montreal starring British actor Robert Shaw[5] – *The Mask* remains the best-known fiction film produced in English Canada between 1954 and 1969, largely as a result of its cult status as the country's first 3D film (borrowing the concept of 3D sequences from William Castle's 1960 film *13 Ghosts*) and because of a kitschy, mosaic-clad mask that compels those nearby to "Put … the … mask … ON!"

Regardless of their creative merit or social commentary and/or subtext, the fiction and documentary films produced during that period have been largely forgotten due to rare play on television and their general unavailability on home video and online streaming. Roffman's *The Mask*, however, has endured because of its status as an early Canadian horror film, and because it was the first Canadian feature to be distributed internationally by a major (American) company (Vatnsdal 2004, 40). It was a concerted effort by the director to not only transcend his own hallowed NFB filmmaking roots and enter the commercial film arena by directing a vehicle filled with the genre tropes and gimmicks standard to drive-in venues, but also to exploit the North American youth market already weaned on monster movies from the B-movie divisions of Universal-International, Columbia, and American International Pictures (AIP).[6]

Between 1970 and 1987, subsets of horror films[7] were made which benefited from the new production-friendly climate that permeated the decade, and it wasn't surprising to see former NFB directors move from socially conscious documentaries to dramas, and eventually horror. Among Roffman's NFB alumni were Jean-Claude Lord (who would direct *Visiting Hours* in 1982)[8] and Jean Beaudin (director of 1972's *Le Diable est parmi nous*); and from the CBC came Peter Carter (director of 1977's *Rituals*), whose father had been a documentarian before the Second World War. And yet sprouting from the opportunities presented by the CCAP program were some major talents, including idiosyncratic David Cronenberg; commercial-minded Ivan Reitman;[9] grim specialist William Fruet, already autopsied by Corupe earlier in this book; writer and future director Allan Moyle;[10] and producers John Dunning and André Link.[11]

Foreign directors were also lured to direct films, and the resulting works – perhaps best designated as "mortgage movies" – are often ranked by critics as career lows, regardless of the director's pedigree. For John Huston (*The Man Who Would Be King*, 1975), J. Lee Thompson (*The Guns of Navarone*, 1961), and Michael Anderson (*Around the World in 80 Days*, 1956), Canada provided an opportunity to make movies during major career ebbs, and perhaps cover personal expenses, but they had to settle for underdeveloped screenplays and casting choices influenced by the tax shelter point system while keeping an eye on marquee value.

Huston directed the whodunnit-slasher *Phobia* (1980), written and rewritten by a committee of disparate veterans, hacks, and one psychiatrist;[12]

Thompson directed Canadian ex-pat Glenn Ford and TV star Melissa Sue Anderson in the overlong slasher *Happy Birthday to Me* (1981);[13] and director Michael Anderson attempted to turn a ringing telephone into a doomsday device in *Bells*, aka *Murder by Phone* (1982).[14] Beyond gimmicky plot hooks, neither film offers a fully satisfying horror experience, but for connoisseurs, the films do contain a sufficient quotient of amusing kitsch and dramatic imbecilities. Since these films were not made by locals, there was no invested effort to make a creatively successful film. Unlike government-funded films which had to appease the appointed "civil servant" producer, the tax shelter films offered savvy Canadian filmmakers a unique quirk: because most investors merely needed a completed film to enjoy the 100 per cent write-off, it didn't matter whether the films were any good. They simply had to be a motion picture.[15]

Working the System

Unlike Peter Carter, who had worked within the clichéd parameters of CBC quality drama and whose prior experience with grim subject matter only went as far as the crime series *Wojeck* (1966), fellow directors Fruet and Cronenberg quickly moved towards emotionally grisly subjects early into their careers. After co-writing *Goin' Down the Road* and directing *Wedding in White* and *Death Weekend*, Fruet made a number of other gruesome thrillers, including the *Psycho* riff *Cries in the Night* [*Funeral Home*] (1980), and exploding-bodies shocker *Spasms* [*Death Bite*] (1983). These revealed Fruet as a filmmaker who wanted to explore taboo subjects and deviant behaviour within commercial genres, but his work inadvertently became the antithesis of what critics wanted to see in theatres: small or socially conscious dramas about being Canadian – a challenging state to quantify, even in literature.[16]

On one level, Canada's first horror films stand as individual rejections by their filmmakers of the government's ill-conceived position in the late 1940s which believed that film culture lay only in NFB documentaries; heritage and nature vignettes celebrating the country's verdant wealth for the benefit of Commonwealth tourists; and small character films about eighteenth-century struggles on a prairie farm, cross-country road trips, or friction between the English and French solitudes in gauzily focused period sagas. Canadian horror isn't subversive; it's a visceral, sometimes vulgar reaction against an imposed philosophy about what kind of films a country's artists should make as regulated through controlled funding and stiff guidelines by federal and provincial governments. The following hurdles were – and, to some extent, still remain – significant deterrents to any filmmaker who wants his or her film to reach the average filmgoer: a limited quantity of theatrical screens for limited engagements in deeply entrenched American-controlled theatre circuits; and local censor boards who could restrict the degree of rebellion by refusing an exhibition rating without the necessary removal of overt cuts towards extreme sex, violence, gore, or utter weirdness for commercial exhibition.

Although Malcolm Dean's chronology *Censored! Only in Canada* focuses heavily on sexually provocative films which ran afoul of individual provincial censor boards, a glimpse into the moral grey zone with which censors could affect the distribution of Canadian horror films is evident in this excerpt from guidelines used by the Ontario Censor Board, circa 1981: "Films may become restricted if they contain scenes of heavy violence, torture, or abuse, extremely graphic depiction of accident or horror, full nudity, sexual activity or undue use of offensive language. Films which promote controversial or anti-social lifestyles might also be restricted depending on format and force of presentation." (Dean 1981, 256)[17]

Undoubtedly, filmmakers were frustrated when they had to defend the integrity of key scenes against generalities such as "heavy," "graphic depiction of ... horror" and "anti-social lifestyles." The very nature of any serial killer, certainly in the slasher film, is of a physically imposing (male) brute with anti-social qualities whose graphically vulgar destruction of the human body represents an improper lifestyle choice.

One can arguably assume that Roffman, Fruet, and Cronenberg did not want the national film industry to return to its pre-1969 days when the country's filmic output was limited and the total number of horror films during that era amounted to two features. The production boom during the post-1969 tax shelter years offered previously stifled filmmakers a somewhat absurd filmmaking system: in the case where investors were satisfied with their 100 per cent deduction and did not care whether a CCA film was any good, filmmakers could exploit the vacuum of studio interference and create something personal and commercial.

Perhaps the best case study in which Canadian talent quietly rebelled against the type of ideal CanCon film preferred by critics and government funding agencies is Peter Carter's *Rituals* (released on video as *The Creeper*) (1977), which contained suspense, horror, gore, and a depiction of splendiferous natural beauty akin to NFB documentaries[18] and indigenous family TV series such as *Adventures in Rainbow Country* (1971) and *The Forest Rangers* (1963–6).[19]

From Concept to Early Regenrification

The concept for *Rituals* came from a canoe trip a friend designed to get writer Ian Sutherland back into higher spirits after a skiing accident. While the trip did cure his depression, he realized the isolated mountain locale could prove deadly if any one of the two men had an accident, got lost, or made some grievous error in direction (Bowen 2009, 20). Sutherland admits to making every effort during the writing process to distance his script from *Deliverance* (1972), a film released shortly after he began writing *Rituals*, but it is important to cite the shared elements because *Rituals* "regenrified" the slasher film into the subset described as the *forest slasher* by retaining the mysterious stalking killer and body-count elements found in Bob Clark's *Black Christmas* (1974), but forcing city-bred characters to use their wits after being isolated in dense, dangerous forests. It's a lethal culture clash in which the forest becomes the haunted house and characters experience what Carol J. Clover classifies as urbanoia (Clover 1992, 124).

Clover argues that *Deliverance* is both drama and urbanoid horror, but her regenrification is fixed on young, attractive urban dwellers being tormented by poor, disenfranchised country folks. The forest slasher, however, is more inviting to other societal classes and perhaps retroactive in the sense that the degrees of traditional and recombined slasher tropes are inherently flexible, if not mutative. The selected examples from the early forest slasher corpus to be examined here include the portentously titled *Don't Go into the Woods* [*Don't Go into the Woods … Alone!*] and *Just before Dawn* (both released in 1981), and *The Forest* (1982). Because *The Burning* (1981) straddles the border between campground and forest slasher, some relevant aspects of that film will also be addressed here.[20]

In *Deliverance*, Lewis (Burt Reynolds), a super-macho outdoorsman, leads a four-man vacationing troupe for a canoe trip down the Cahulawassee River in Georgia before a dam under construction floods a once-pristine natural treasure in a matter of weeks. Part vacation and part expedition, the weekend jaunt offers minor risks of bugs, rough country, and rapids. Lewis is joined by best friend and fellow alpha male Ed (Jon Voight) and newcomers Drew (Ronny Cox), an insurance salesman and father of two, and Bobby (Ned Beatty), whom the group nickname "Chubby." Whereas Drew and Ed use the trip to escape from their domesticated lives as fathers and husbands, Bobby's along for some fun and a bit of risk. He attempts to assert his own sense of manliness by making crass statements of his sexual prowess – a behavioural pattern that's soon rewarded with sodomy and rape by one of two inbred cousins who is either offended by his big-city arrogance or by city boys trespassing on private land. Or, perhaps the local boys happen to be two sickos who were just plain bored that afternoon.[21] Before the second tormentor can sodomize Ed, Lewis kills the first with his bow and arrow, sending the other cousin scurrying into the forest.

After burying the body, the men head back to the river and make a hasty canoe journey to reach their cars at the river's end, hoping the inevitable flooding of the valley will smother evidence of their crime, except the surviving cousin tracks them down, kills Drew, and causes the three men to tumble from their canoes into the rapids. With Lewis incapacitated by a broken leg, Ed climbs the cliffs and kills their hunter, and the trio eventually makes its way to town, where the film shifts gears and becomes a more straightforward suspense film. The last act's tension stems from whether the three men can manage to leave town and avoid arrest while surrounded by the dead men's friends and families.

Like *Deliverance*, *Rituals* follows a similar premise: after trekking to an isolated forest, a ritualistic male bonding session is disrupted by an unseen, tormenting figure, who pits killer against hero. The warning both *Deliverance* and *Rituals* present to urbanites and gentrified townsfolk is clear: don't make fun of rustic locals, because in their domain, they have the real power. The secondary message in the scripts is much simpler: just don't go into the woods. These two caveats are central to the forest slasher: had the camping troupe and local hikers stayed away from the mountain in *Don't Go into the Woods* the body count would have been restricted to wandering locals; if Warren (Gregg Henry) hadn't felt the need to exert a sense of ownership by manning a camping expedition to a large plot of mountain land he inherited in *Just before Dawn*, his best friends wouldn't have been slaughtered by inbred twins who roam the land and hack to death trespassers; and if a game of friendly gender competition – wives betting husbands they could not only reach a remote campsite days before their husbands, but survive without their aid for a few days – had simply been laughed off during a banal dinner between friends, one-half of the group would have lived out a natural life of connubial bliss instead of being hunted, gutted, and eaten by an ex-suburban father hiding out in *The Forest*, tormented by the ghosts of the unfaithful wife he bludgeoned to death and the kids who committed suicide because of extreme hunger.

Relationships and Lethal Choices in the Wild, Wild Woods

The relationships within the *Rituals* group are unique: as they fly to an isolated lake and trek through swamps, creeks, and bug-infested forests to an idyllic riverside campsite, their joking and side comments establish the hierarchal social pecking order. Screenwriter Sutherland, however, establishes the dominant alphas in a simple dockside scene where Harry (Hal Holbrook) refuses to leave his low-paying, rewarding post as head neurologist of a marginal clinic and accept a high-paying executive post at a private clinic set up by Mitzi (Lawrence Dane, who also co-produced the film). Their rivalry and political camps are immediately demarcated before their flight to God's country, and the already strained civility between the two will become the leading conflict, right to the inflammatory finale.

The characters in *Rituals* are also a collegiate group of older men, similar in age to the quartet in *Deliverance*, but non-standard for the slasher film set in suburban and campsite locations, such as the iconoclastic *Halloween* (featuring an overabundance of high school kids played by twentysomething actors) and *Friday the 13th* (young adult councillors arriving early to prepare the camp prior to the kids' arrival), respectively. Genuine twentysomethings dominate the camping troupe in *Don't Go into the Woods*, whereas the couples in both *The Forest* and *Just before Dawn* are closer to thirty; the socio-economic status of the latter group, like the men in *Deliverance* and *Rituals*, is similarly middle-class.

Adults can also symbolize the wizened veterans who eventually save the young trespassers from danger in the final act – for example, the elder sheriff in *Don't Go into the Woods*; the trucker who rescues screaming Sally from Leatherface and his whirring chainsaw at the end of *The Texas Chainsaw Massacre* (1974); and the sturdy park ranger in *Just before Dawn* who tried to warn the campers that the mountain was harbouring uncontrollable dangers. Sutherland's group in *Rituals* all went to medical school, but their assorted mid-life crises encompass finding a satisfying career balance between financial and personal rewards (Harry and Mitzi, at polar ends of their life philosophy) and the inability to maintain a long-term relationship (Martin, played by Robin Gammell, whose sexuality as a gay man is generally a non-issue with the group). The remaining colleagues are still important to the group's social DNA: D.J. (Gary Reineke), the group's camping leader, is the prime force that organized the trip, cajoled the men into coming, and eases their fears about any dangers before venturing off for help after the killer begins his teasing games; and shutterbug Abel (Ken James) is a generic family man, yet he adds colour to the group's monochrome campfire drinking and juvenile teasing. He also represents a different breed of urbanite: with the exception of D.J., the men in *Rituals* are completely fish out of water. In comparison, the *Deliverance* boys generally have experience in the wild woods and have come expressly to indulge in manly activities (canoeing, hiking, and hunting). A key aspect to most doomed characters in the forest slasher is the lack of manly skills, which ensures they can't survive on their own: they'll often take the wrong route, and certain weaker individuals will frequently hurt themselves due to an overwhelming unfamiliarity with forest and mountain terrain.

The group's trek to the campsite begins quite clumsily: several fall into a brackish swamp and almost lose their tourist gear. Only D.J. was sufficiently disciplined to bring along a second pair of boots; the rest ignored his itemized list which expressly recommended that every man bring appropriate redundancy gear. When the men's boots are stolen by the killer and a bloody deer's head is found at the end of camp, the men are (quite understandably) spooked. Unable to trek back in sneakers, D.J. makes the decision to seek out civilization before the group's provisions are devoured and their poor wilderness coping abilities bring on paranoia. As Sutherland explained about the design of his drama, "I wanted it to be the most civilized people on Earth who fall into a situation and get stripped of everything and have to survive. What would they do to each other? What would you do to a friend to survive?" (Bowen 2009, 24).

D.J. makes the first proactive move by heading upstream in search of help at an old government-operated dam ("It's a hydro dam, and operations that big don't run themselves. There'll be someone there!"). But the moment he leaves, the group's pecking order shifts, and while Mitzi, the larger, more masculine of the remaining four ought to be the leader, the real decision making is ultimately awarded to Harry because the group respects his intellect and reasoning instead of Mitzi's bravado and aggressive persona. Harry's power to motivate an increasingly exhausted Mitzi remains potent to the end: not only does Mitzi help carry a wounded Martin up the side of an unsafe mountain, he also returns twice to Harry after stomping off on his own in a rage – first when Harry insists on carrying their comatose friend down the mountain, and again after Harry euthanizes a badly wounded D.J. The death of D.J. destroys the last shred of civility between the two remaining men, and by leaving Harry, Mitzi ultimately walks straight into the arms of the killer.

Struggles between friends are also vital to the developing conflicts in *The Forest*, though director Donald M. Jones tends to have his characters bickering over the same issues instead of crafting an elegant arc where power is passed among the characters and bad decisions worsen their circumstances. In *Rituals*, the mounting trauma Harry experiences as his friends are maimed and as the killer leaves peculiar clues – a war medal, an X-ray of an army surgeon's ineptitude (which Harry quantifies as "butchery"), and the killer's official discharge papers – transforms the gentle intellectual into an alternate self that's been subjugated through banal civic duties: a war vet. Harry's instincts quickly lock into gear, and he becomes cold, obsessive, and paranoid, but his unwavering drive to get every wounded or captured man out of danger is what ultimately causes the dwindling group's disintegration.

Though the killer maims the group, it is Harry who shares responsibility in testing the mortality of the men: he takes the group across a river, where Martin's foot is quickly damaged in a bear trap laid by the killer; he insists a wounded Martin be floated on a stretcher upstream, causing them to lose half their gear and Mitzi's seething rage to explode; he voices a homophobic epithet towards Martin, bringing Mitzi another step closer to severing his friendship with Harry. Power struggles are less important in director James Bryan's *Don't Go into the Woods* because the film's structure and Garth Eliassen's script (his sole feature film effort) are so poorly laid out;[22] the main campers wander around and lose a member now and then, but the film doesn't shift into any measured gear until the local police are called to hunt down the killer. At the film's climax, the two survivors take power away from the police by catching, maiming, and meting out raw justice by hacking the wild mountain man's cadaver to shreds – a cathartic act of rage almost identical in tone to the bludgeoning of the killer in Wes Craven's *The Hills Have Eyes* (1977) by a formerly peace-minded suburbanite.

In *Just before Dawn*, however, director Jeff Lieberman opts for an effective, carefully drawn power shift between the group's leader, Warren, and his mousy girlfriend Constance. Early in the film, she wears no makeup, has her hair tied up in the back, and enhances her bland sexuality by wearing pattern shirts and tan slacks. As she becomes more assured of her relationship with Warren, her sexuality begins to blossom: she lets down her shoulder-length hair and wears a pair of short-shorts given to her by the group's tart, Megan. Lieberman's heroine arc goes further when she decides to take responsibility (and revenge) for the remaining twin killer by luring him to Warren's camp while wearing heavy makeup and placing herself in a submissive body position by the campfire. Not only does her baiting work, she kills her tormentor.

Warren was the group's manly leader until the death of the first killer twin, but the experience of previously seeing Constance in peril has traumatized him to a level of shell shock; he virtually quivers as she fights the second twin and kills him by orally fisting him to death – perhaps the most bizarre death of a serial killer in any slasher film.

Unlike the more restrictive and populated physical settings within a slasher film (the multi-storey dorm in *Black Christmas* or the suburban streets in *Halloween*), lethal assaults in the forest slasher exploit the sheer remoteness of winding hills, dark valleys, and environs where the victim's senses are often limited to restricted sight and a fear of unfamiliar "wild" sounds. With less clearly demarcated boundaries, filmmakers can easily establish a vast unknown where someone can be snatched and taken to a hidden lair to be slain according to the killer's "anti-social lifestyle" and mordant peccadilloes.[23] *Deliverance* is neither exclusively a slasher nor a horror film,[24] but as we have seen, it does contain the partial DNA for the forest slasher, including sexual power struggles.

"Chubby" Bobby feigns a grand sexual persona so he isn't wholly overshadowed by buffed Lewis and his two married friends, but Bobby is soon sodomized, not by a powerful alpha hunter, but by an inbred who reduces his victim to a pig – an animal with which the inbred has had a bestial relationship. When the sounds of a wandering hiker spook the camping leader in *Don't Go into the Woods*, his female companions laugh, a key point where the supposed male lead is completely emasculated and so walks a little farther ahead to be out of earshot of the women's hurtful comments.

The battle between the sexes is almost exclusively at the core of *The Forest*'s premise: the wives challenge the husbands to a bet in which they will prove their ability to manage the same camping trip and endure hardships without their aid and support. Sex also plays a role in the killer's genesis: he murdered his wife because of her loose ways, and he can only regain his sexual authority by becoming a hunter in the woods, proving his machismo by killing and eating both men and women like some ultimate alpha male.

Location, Location, Location

It is fair to presume that any influence *Deliverance* had on the visual design of *Rituals* is coincidental due to the inherent beauty of each film's natural settings. As was the case with Peter Weir's *Picnic at Hanging Rock* (1975), where a filmmaker wanted to tell a story under budgetary duress and impress foreign buyers with his filmmaking skills, sometimes the best production value can be had using extant natural resources.[25] In Canada, the wild natural country that lies north of major cities features striking terrain, and filming near Lake Superior gave *Rituals* some remarkable locations that remain unique to that film. Sutherland chose the location because he had canoed in the area, and Carter showed full comfort in capturing the rawness of the remote terrain through expert camera placement.

The director designed some spectacular shots which make it quite clear the actors are walking, swimming, and hiking along dangerous ground. Perhaps taking a nod from Boorman, who similarly placed his actors, instead of stuntmen, in the violent water rapids, Carter made sure his actors went through their characters' discomforts, including being stung by a mass of real honeybees. The first outstanding sequence in *Rituals* occurs near Wawa, Ontario, when Mitzi and Harry carry a wounded Martin (actor Gammell was actually on the stretcher) along the dangerous edge of a mountain, trying their best to avoid losing a step and tumbling en masse down a valley. When they reach a plateau, camp is set up, and Carter has the camera focused on Harry – now decked out in green military-styled clothes and a red bandanna, brewing rice on a camp cooker. As the camera pulls back, the shot reveals the gorge and a distanced Mitzi and, after a winding, elegant tracking shot, the massive distance between the men and the barren valley below.

The actual location had apparently been scoured to its sandy core by a fire, but sections were also affected by the airborne chemical effluent from industrial factories in a nearby valley. One can hypothesize that Sutherland and Carter used the location to add a slight subtext about man's mismanagement of nature (an issue that causes Lewis to choose the Cahulawassee River for his group's trip in *Deliverance*), but like the diverse landscapes exploited by Australian filmmakers, the northern

Ontario locations are exceptionally composed for the benefit of the characters, the story, and the production.

The second major location is the dam where D.J. had believed he could find aid. Carter's camera reveals the dam by juxtaposing the men against its massive bulwarks to impart a sense of both scope and man-made rot – the structure looks abandoned, and its industrial and engineering components have been reduced to rickety shacks, roofless control rooms stripped of metal control panels, and rotting wood and rusting gears atop the dam. In this scene, the wasteland is the man-made structure rather than the natural terrain, and the images of the men carrying Martin on a stretcher across the dam's top enhance the subtextual theme of nature reclaiming the elements man has chosen to mismanage.[26] If there are civilized structures in a forest slasher film, they are in a degenerative state: the dam and the killer's pack-rat cabin in *Rituals*; the cave where the cuckolded killer cooks, eats, and sleeps in *The Forest*; the dim mine entrance where *The Burning*'s Cropsy lives among corroding rails and mining cars; and the disarrayed cabin wherein the mountain man stores bodies as well as souvenirs and trophies from his victims in *Don't Go into the Woods*.[27]

Unlike the slasher film, where familiar locations such as a house, factory, dorm, or apartment building consist of stark geometric shapes, recognizable angles, and navigational routes designed for human conveyance, there is no form and function within the seemingly random patterns, colours, and structural order inside a forest; animals (and humans) must adapt to their surroundings in exposed weather conditions in day or night, because failure would result in death.

Fear the Forest Reaper

The last important element of the forest slasher is the mad mountain man, a character whose presence is inferred through actions or end results, much in the tradition of a masked killer leaving clues, dangerous objects, dead animals, or human cadavers prior to his unmasking. In *Rituals*, the killer begins his tormenting session with minor but peculiar offences (stealing the men's boots) before advancing towards shock tactics (a freshly killed deer's head left as a warning sign), a lethal bear trap, and select clues (the war medal, X-ray, and discharge certificate). He also destabilizes the group's confidence through his more primal displays of rage: the severed head[28] of Abel that Harry finds piked at the edge of their mountain campsite, and the still-living but mentally destroyed D.J., whom Harry finds atop the dam's valley, tied to a chair with thick-gauge cables, and a spike rammed through a thigh.

Like the abandoned dam, D.J. appears dead but is actually in a coma, awaiting a coup de grâce before nature can claim him. When Harry strangles him to death, it is a mercy killing, but by accomplishing the kill, the good doctor has gone to the polar extreme in his role as a life-saving surgeon and fulfilled Sutherland's transformation where two feral-minded men are poised to fight each other to the death. What is unique within *Rituals* is how the men are given choices: they could have avoided becoming terminally victimized by the killer (who lived closer to the dam than the men's original campsite). For example, D.J. could have gone downstream to the lake as the men suggested; Harry and Mitzi could have floated Martin down the river to the lake; and Harry could have left Martin at the dam and turned back with Mitzi instead of taking the killer's bait – discovering and euthanizing a dying D.J. – to track the killer to his cabin.

Though Lieberman's *Just before Dawn* is a near-perfect forest slasher, *Rituals* is much more sophisticated with its balance of horror, gore, character arcs, and subtext, and a convincing, tense narrative. It would have been simpler to have a mountain man who kills until he is hacked to bits – as occurs in *Don't Go into the Woods*. The lone flaw in *Rituals* lies in the killer's modus operandi. In Sutherland's original script, the narrative was open-ended: the tale of the horrible camping ritual gone wrong is told by a survivor, but it's not clear whether he's telling the truth to the police, bending facts, or devising a grand scheme to massacre his friends.

As Sutherland recalled, "We were forced by [the government funding body] to put in a bad guy. In the original script, in the end you don't know who it is. They wanted an explanation and it was no use explaining to them that films aren't always filled with explanations" (Bowen 2009, 24). Sutherland wanted a similar level of ambiguity as was present in Peter Weir's *Picnic at Hanging Rock*, where mood and a measured pacing replace any clear explanation of how and why a teacher and several students disappeared during a school trip to a rocky outcropping. In the *Rituals* DVD commentary track, Dane classifies *Rituals* as a drama, but he adds: "The best horror pictures are scary dramas ... If it's written properly, the horror will come." And *Rituals* was designed to be a horror film: "We wanted to give it a veracity that you don't normally see with horror pictures."

In the shooting script, Harry finds the killer's mountain cabin and, mistaking an old blind man for his target of rage, fatally gores him. He then discovers his victim is the brother of the killer, who will eventually return to the secluded home. When the brother returns in the evening, he torments Harry from outside, eventually goring him in the leg and cutting an artery. From a tree, dangling beside a fresh deer carcass, Mitzi is suspended by rope over a fire – his second decision to return back to Harry being a fatal move. Relaying his demands through Mitzi,[29] the still-unseen killer once again offers his victim a horrible choice that foreshadows the core elements of the *Saw* franchise: to save oneself and let a friend die horribly, or risk one's own life and perhaps save the friend, risking further traps and harm along the way and the possibility that the killer will replay the game with a new and equally insidious scenario.[30]

To avoid bleeding to death, Harry uses gunpowder to cauterize the gashed leg artery, but by the time he recovers from the brutal pain, Mitzi is ablaze and burns to death like a condemned witch during the Middle Ages.[31] With a gun and nowhere to go, Harry waits until the killer enters the cabin and is confronted by a weathered man with severe facial disfigurement that interestingly presages the warped and silent visage of *The Burning*'s Cropsy. As his speechless opponent slowly approaches, he seems to beckon Harry to fire the gun, and the killer exploits his own ugliness by teasing Harry until a fatal shot is fired, ending the game and the killer's own personal torment. For audiences, the killer's modus operandi is grievous moral offence: the killer, maimed during the Second World War, was hastily patched up by "butchers" and discharged as a physically grotesque figure who could no longer exist in any society. Whether he and his blind brother grew up in the forest is never clarified, but the two misfits fended for themselves. For thirty years they maintained private lives until society began to encroach upon their terrain. The opportunity to exercise some justice for the army doctors' "butchery" proved too easy – hence the killer's decision to focus on the vacationing doctors.

According to Dane (who provides a more precise explanation on the DVD commentary track), the killer's reason for snapping is more precise: the two brothers had been aware of campers, hikers, and forest workers for years, but when the disfigured vet overheard the doctors making cheap shots about saving lives fixing up patients for money during the campfire, his offence was channelled into full-out revenge. This explanation is never detailed in the shooting script (muddying the reason for the killer's mental snap), but Sutherland left enough clues to validate the core moral of the film, and of the genre: *just don't go into the woods.*

The desire to see "the bad guy" may have confused the film's plot in the finished version, but it did result in the addition of a peculiar development in the shooting script's completion: the lone survivor has a face-to-face battle with the killer of his companions, the last major element to complete the forest slasher template. Pitting a survivor against the killer is arguably the most necessary ingredient in a slasher film because it is the reward for audiences who have been led down various paths and witnessed assorted mayhem; the slasher film mandates a cathartic finale.[32]

In the forest slasher film's ideal form, the audience witnesses the bloody demise of the killer after a lengthy cat-and-mouse fight in a dangerous, claustrophobic locale: the mining cave in *The Burning* where Cropsy's head is split open with an axe and his cadaver goes up in flames; the couple who intensely hack to bits the wild mountain man killer in *Don't Go into the Woods* in a finale directly lifted from *The Hills Have Eyes*; Constance orally fisting her aggressor into a state of lethal asphyxiation in *Just before Dawn*; and in *The Forest*, the killer's efforts to murder the hero foiled when he hallucinates and freezes, believing the heroine with the knife running towards him is the spirit of his dead wife bearing a big stick – the most dramatically unsatisfying finale among the aforementioned forest slashers.

Conclusion

While the tax shelter system did enable Sutherland, Carter, and Dane to make a personal commercial project, Dane had to sign over rights to a distributor, whose efforts to sell the film were, quite frankly, amateurish. The US trailer is edited to convey a whodunnit montage, and the music is neither horrific nor enticing, but a dreadful recording of children singing "The Teddy Bears' Picnic." Though *Rituals* has remained largely unavailable save for VHS releases and cheap DVD editions, it has developed a cult following as a kind of "lost" horror film.[33]

Unlike their British counterparts,[34] horror entries crafted in part or whole by Canadians during the peak tax shelter years were often denigrated by Canadian critics, who wanted to see highbrow culture on cinema screens. As a result of this bias, tax shelter productions, as a specific cultural genre, were and still are regarded as cultural nadirs, if not works inherently flawed due to the kind of national inferiority complex that Subissati describes in her chapter.[35] As Dane, who has co-starred in and produced numerous films, explains, "People always thought they could differentiate between a Canadian production and an American production. I don't think the average person would know the difference, but … if you label it a Canadian picture, they'll look for flaws" (Bowen 2009, 22). *Rituals* illustrates the inventiveness that existed among film-makers hungry to create good commercial films during the country's tax shelter years. The film may reflect aspects of Canadian drama, col-legiality, humour, and fear of the vast natural world outside of urban centres but remains the first and best example of the forest slasher.

NOTES

1 The Rank Organization was founded in 1937 by British media mogul and flour manufacturer J. Arthur Rank, one of the chief corporate benefactors of the British quota system. The need to fill screens enabled Rank to build his own American-styled vertically integrated filmmaking model, where a single corporation controlled a film's life from script to production to theatrical distribution

2 Renamed the Motion Picture Association of America (MPAA) in 1945, the organization has overseen the rating and classification of films exhibited within the United States since 1968. The MPAA, during the epic regime of Jack Valenti (1966–2004), also managed to thwart subsequent efforts by the Canadian government to readdress the issue of American-dominated film exhibition, most tragically in 1987 (Pendakur 1990, 269).

3 Vancouver-based exhibitor Lew Perry soon discovered the power of American lobbying when Liberal cabinet minister C.D. Howe buckled, withdrew his support for a quota system, and in 1947 supported the Canadian government's traitorous Canadian Cooperative Agreement (CCA) in which aspects of Canadian culture would be sporadically larded into US scripts to promote the country and NFB films were distributed in US cinemas. The arrogance of the CCA and its architects and point men – chiefly Blake Owensmith – were profiled in a February 1975 episode of the CBC series *Prime Time*.

4 Those Canadians who retained their citizenship proved to be a gold mine for tax shelter productions decades later. By the mid-seventies, silver screen and TV icons such as Glenn Ford and Robert Vaughn were past their prime, but their enduring recognition factor made them ideal for

meeting the CanCon point system; hence their involvement in films such as *Happy Birthday to Me* (J. Lee Thompson, 1981) and *Starship Invasions* (Ed Hunt, 1977), respectively.

5 *The Luck of Ginger Coffey* (Irvin Kershner, 1964) marks one of the first appearances of the uniquely Canadian co-production whose creative chemistry is designed to appeal to an international market. Paired US and Canadian firms produced a film version of a Canadian novel written by an Irish-born novelist (Brian Moore) living in Canada, filmed in Montreal, and starring British actor Robert Shaw with additional American and British actors, and several supporting roles filled by Canadians.

6 The best-known drive-in fodder produced by these three studios include Universal-International's *Monster on the Campus* (Jack Arnold, 1958) and *It Came from Outer Space* (Jack Arnold, 1953); *The Werewolf* (Fred F. Sears, 1956) from Columbia's expert exploitation man Sam Katzman; and the multi-genre efforts by prolific AIP producer/director Roger Corman, such as *The Wasp Woman* (1959) and *House of Usher* (1960).

7 Subsets of early Canadian horror include the supernatural slasher *Death Ship* (Alvin Rakoff, 1980); the whodunnit thriller *The Clown Murders* (Martyn Burke, 1975); the occult thriller *Le diable est parmi nous* [*The Devil Is among Us*] (Jean Beaudin, 1972); the serial killer thriller *Deranged* (Jeff Gillen, 1974); and the ghost story *The Changeling* (Peter Medak, 1979).

8 *Visiting Hours* (Jean-Claude Lord, 1982) is one of the very few Canadian films to make the infamous Video Nasty list, compiled by Britain's Director of Public Prosecutions [DPP] and made public in 1983. Included films were either banned outright from exhibition and home video distribution, or required cuts to receive a formal ratings stamp (Kerekes and Slater 2000, 267), as enforced by the British Board of Film Censors (BBFC).

9 Prior to *Ghostbusters* (1984), Ivan Reitman directed *Cannibal Girls* (1973), and produced William Fruet's *Death Weekend* (1976) and two of David Cronenberg's early films: *Shivers* (1975) and *Rabid* (1977).

10 After writing *Montreal Main* (Frank Vitale, 1974), Allan Moyle penned the vampirism-by-virus eroto-thriller *Red Blooded American Girl* (David Blyth, 1990) for the Canadian exploitation firm SC Entertainment, although he is best known for writing and directing the teen angst and rebellion classic *Pump Up the Volume* (1990).

11 John Dunning and André Link formed a memorable production team, beginning with the Québécois softcore tease *Valérie* (Denis Héroux, 1969). Several of their productions were supervised by Ivan Reitman (see note 10). The pair also produced Reitman's first comedy hit *Meatballs* (1979) and the slasher diptych *My Bloody Valentine* (1981) and *Happy Birthday to Me* (1981).

12 The five credited screenwriters on *Phobia* [*Phobia: A Descent Into Terror*] (1980) are emblematic of the rewriting that resulted in John Huston's worst film. The esteemed writers were Americans Gary Sherman (1973's *Raw Meat*), Ronald Shussett (co-writer of 1979's *Alien*), and Peter Bellwood (later to co-write 1991's *Highlander II: The Quickening*); British writer Jimmy Sangster (author of several Hammer classics, including the 1958 version of *Dracula*); and Canadian Lew Lehman (writer and director of the 1981 Canadian shocker *The Pit*).

13 Like Canadian ex-patriot Glenn Ford, American TV actress Melissa Sue Anderson was an ideal choice as co-star of *Happy Birthday to Me* (1981) because after seven years of playing a gentle, morally spirited schoolteacher who loses her sight but succeeds in career and marriage in *Little House on the Prairie*, the instantly identifiable actress was ready for a career change. The natural genre to shatter her family-friendly image was horror, in which she played a dual role of tight-laced morality and unbridled sexuality.

14 *Bells*, aka *Murder by Phone* (1982), is a perfect example of the revolving CanCon talent pool during the tax shelter years, as the film contains two co-stars from *Rituals*: Robin Gammell and Gary Reineke, plus familiar faces Sara Botsford, Alan Scarfe, and TV star Barry Morse, who also appeared in the CanCon shockers *Welcome to Blood City* (1977) and William Fruet's *Cries in the Night*, aka *Funeral Home* (1980).

15 Or to paraphrase director William Fruit, "a piece of junk that got rejected in the United States" (Vatnsdal 2004, 212).

16 Although he devotes more than a quarter of a page to assessing the forgotten drama *Riel* (George Bloomfield, 1979), noted Canadian film historian Gerald Pratley provides a singular perfunctory sentence about *Rituals* in his *A Century of Canadian Film*: "As gory and unpleasant as they come" (2003, 184). This mere log line is emblematic of the conflict between artists who want to express themselves in unbridled stories, and critics who are biased towards risk-free emotional stories and familiar social commentary.

17 Malcolm Dean, *Censored! Only in Canada: The History of Film Censorship – The Scandal Off the Screen* (Toronto: Virgo Press, 1981), 256. By contrast, the "Restricted" category in Ontario 2011 now reserves the following (and highly specified) elements for audiences age eighteen and over: "Visually explicit portrayals of violence which may be characterized by extreme brutality, extreme bloodletting and extreme tissue damage, torture, horror and sexual violence … Frequent detailed gory/grotesque images will have a more prolonged or graphic focus and greater frequency … Scenes and situations may cause adverse psychological impact. May involve

intense and compelling terror, acts of degradation, threats of violence, and continuous acts of violence; situations could be accompanied by coarse, abusive, and degrading dialogue. Explicit substance abuse."

18 The irony is severe: in spite of a yearning to break the mould of the traditional documentary form, the makers of *Rituals* couldn't completely eliminate these aspects from their film technique. As film historian Peter Morris reflects on a defining (albeit "tentative") quality within Canadian-made films, "it lay in relating fiction and reality, in the idea that stories could be filmed not on sets but in natural locations, in applying a documentary approach to drama" (1978, 93), or as Caelum Vatnsdal quipped, "Nothing could be more Canadian – it's like a documentary about suffering in the woods" (2004, 115)

19 Perpetually in syndication, these two CBC co-productions were seen country-wide by several generations of kids and nascent members of the Canadian film industry, and the nihilistic tone of *Rituals* may have been a deliberate repudiation of the NFB's propagandistic, tourist-friendly portrayal of Canada as a natural wonderland, and the CBC's G-rated family-friendly adventures.

20 Tony Maylam's *The Burning* (1981) is a hybrid of three horror subsets: the prank-gone-wrong horror (Cropsy knocks over a shock flaming skull and sets the cabin and himself on fire, instilling a deep hatred of campers and a bloody revenge quest); the vengeance-driven campground slasher (the scarred Cropsy begins his slaughter at a kids' camp); and the forest slasher (once the young adults are trapped on an island, Cropsy assaults them from under the darkness of the forest cover).

21 The suggestion in *Deliverance* (John Boorman, 1972) that remote mountains and forests are home to inbred families with warped sexual practices is an important but inconsistent element within the forest slasher. Inbreeding led to the creation of the grinning murderous twins in *Just before Dawn* (Jeff Lieberman, 1981), whereas the killers in *Don't Go into the Woods* (James Bryan, 1981) and *Rituals* (Peter Carter, 1977) are mountain men whose isolation enhanced their anti-social demeanour. Wes Craven borrowed the concept of murderous inbreds for *The Hills Have Eyes* (1977) – essentially a forest slasher transposed to the desert – whereas inbreds comprise the core aggressors in the *Wrong Turn* franchise begun in 2003 by Rob Schmidt and extended in lesser imitations such as *Timber Falls* (Tony Giglio, 2007). While *The Texas Chainsaw Massacre* franchise, begun in 1974 by Tobe Hooper, similarly exploits a family with inferred inbreeding who snatch wayward and overly curious travellers, the central location of the film's main dramatic scenes are within the family's house.

22 *Don't Go into the Woods* [*Don't Go into the Woods … Alone!*] (James Bryan, 1981) has few merits due to its technical incompetence (cinematographic composition excepted), yet it continues to be regarded as a must-see title because of its appearance in the original 1983 Video Nasty list, enforced by the BBFC. As Kerekes and Slater (2000) noted, the film is "a shining example of how inclusion on the DPP [Director of Public Prosecutions] list has bestowed a piece of complete crap with notoriety and near-legendary status" (137).

23 An alternative to the forest slasher would be the forest abduction subset, of which the Canadian-made *Abducted* (Boon Collins, 1986), and to some extent its late-coming sequel, *Abducted II: The Reunion* (Boon Collins, 1995), mapped out the basics of another wild mountain man with feral priapic desires who snatches a wife for his own. In the first film, as the madman hunts down his escaped bride, he at one point screams "I … smell … WOMAN!" A direct successor to the genre would be Simon Boyes and Adam Mason's gory *Broken* (2006), which managed to successfully focus on the power struggle between a sadistic mountain man and his potential mates in spite of a flagrant torture porn prelude, a preposterous tongue extraction, and a twist finale that may espouse the nihilism and misery of *Rituals* but is completely ludicrous.

24 In separate interviews on the 2007 *Deliverance* DVD, Jon Voight reflected on the script: "When I first read the film I was a little bit concerned about it … I hit that sodomy scene and it pushed me back a little bit; I didn't know what it was all about … It was a little bit more like a horror film. " But as author James Dickey's son Christopher explained, Dickey and director John Boorman "wanted people to walk out of [a] theatre feeling like they had been run through a ringer, and you can't forget *Deliverance* because you can't write it off emotionally or psychologically." Scenes of emotional intensity are hardly unique to dramas or war films, but the rape of Bobby (Ned Beatty), captured in slow, deliberate ugliness, is typical of the traumatic circumstances characters experience in a horror film, much like Harry strangling D.J., or Mitzi burning to death in *Rituals*. These moments are contrived to haunt audiences long after they've left the theatre.

25 The polar opposite of the ornate *Picnic at Hanging Rock* is *Wake in Fright* (1971) by former CBC director Ted Kotcheff. Once reviled and now lauded as Australia's first great independent film, the adaptation of Kenneth Cook's novel focuses on the mindless animal slaughter perpetuated by drunken blue-collar workers in a wretched, dusty eyesore of a town, whereas the horror that affects upper-class debutantes in *Picnic* is discreet, if not wholly off-screen.

26 In *The Long Weekend* (1978), Australian screenwriter Everette De Roche depicts nature itself using its resources to taunt, tease, and smother humans for disrespecting the environment (setting fires, chopping down trees, leaving broken beer bottles in virgin areas, and using animals as cheap targets). Even a bullet-riddled bunyip manages to crawl up a dune towards its aggressors like a very patient and stealthy Jason Voorhees or Michael Myers.

27 Although the house of the killer family in *The Texas Chainsaw Massacre* (Tobe Hooper, 1974) is filled with the bones and skins of animal and human victims, the gathering and accumulation of trophies – a clutter of victims' belongings – is in fact an important characteristic of the mad mountain man in the forest slasher. The mass of sleeping bags, boots, clothes, and other paraphernalia inside the killer's cabin in *Don't Go into the Woods* predates the rusting car and Winnebago cemetery maintained by the inbred killers in *Wrong Turn* (Rob Schmidt, 2003) and the shed filled with the personal belongings of the men, women, and children slaughtered after sadistic torture in the vicious *Wolf Creek* (Greg McLean, 2005), a forest slasher transposed to Australia's rocky cliffs.

28 Both the severed head of Abel and the prosthetics for the facially scarred killer were designed by Oscar-nominated makeup artist Carl Fullerton, who also designed some of the effects for *Spasms* (William Fruet, 1983). Fullerton achieved his earliest fame with the effects for *Friday the 13th Part II* (Steve Miner, 1981) and *Part III* (Steve Miner, 1982).

29 The killer is never heard in the film, but one must presume he is capable of some speech, given that he lives with his blind brother with whom he must communicate to survive. Therefore, the device of having Mitzi reiterate the killer's options to Harry to come out to stop the imminent immolation is plausible.

30 Written by James Wan and Lee Whannell, and directed by James Wan, *Saw* (2004) virtually launched the torture-porn genre, in which narrative and characterization are subordinated to gory set pieces in which one character must choose some level of physical trauma to either save himself or another's life. Each unwinnable challenge functions as a "test" for the characters and is a simple device for the filmmakers to whittle useless characters to a handful of banal archetypes. The series has thus far produced seven films, the last of which (2010) was filmed in 3D.

31 Writer/director Michael Reeves was extremely adept at (and perhaps overly fixated on) depicting the human misery effected by real and perceived witchcraft. The paranoia within a witch-fearing England during the Middle Ages was best illustrated in Reeves's horrific drama *The*

Witchfinder General [*The Conqueror Worm*] (1968). Like the witch killing at the beginning of Reeves's *She-Beast* (1966), the film features much screaming and suffering, and a world view as bleak as that of Sutherland's *Rituals*. In both films the victim smites the monster by becoming the monster through violence, be it an axe blow to the back, as occurs to the eponymous character in Reeves's film, or the shotgun blast inflicted upon the killer in *Rituals*.

32 The gory Italian thrillers, known as Giallo, often have finales, if not plot logic, that are often completely ridiculous. In *Bay of Blood* [*Ecologia del delitto*] (Mario Bava, 1971), the reasoning for hacking, piking, and bisecting humans is to acquire a land deed, but the perpetrators are obliquely done in by their children, who possess superb shotgun marksmanship. *In Five Dolls for an August Moon* [*5 bambole per la luna d'agosto*] (Mario Bava, 1970), the cadavers of beautiful women are packed into a freezer by a killer determined to convince a patent owner to sell his interest.

33 Perhaps a fitting conclusion to *Ritual*'s commercial release history was its delayed premiere on DVD in North America. Dane asserted that the film had been poorly handled by the distributor and the film's negative processing botched by one of its investors, Pathé (hence the film's severe levels in contrast, particularly in the climactic cabin scenes). After a videotape release, the film vanished from circulation but eventually appeared on a European DVD. After a rare screening in May 2007 at Toronto's Bloor Cinema with Dane in attendance, the film was slated for a US DVD release by Code Red in the fall of 2009 but didn't emerge until May 2011. By November 2011, the DVD had gone out of print.

34 Hammer Films continued to produce horror entries during the seventies, but their reliance on classic monsters (werewolves, vampires, mummies) ultimately doomed the company in spite of its regular use of heaving bosoms, bloodletting, and peculiar hybrids such as a band of itinerant, shape-shifting vampires in *Vampire Circus* (Robert Young, 1972).

35 *Rituals* producer Lawrence Dane laments on the DVD commentary track: "During this era ... you had two parallel things happening: one was filmmakers who wanted to make a good movie ... the other was people [who] wanted to take tax advantages of it ... and not promote it well and try to get it out to a large audience. [You had] the poor filmmaker, breaking his own heart, working within the confines of the system, and it really was sad ... A lot of carpetbaggers came into Canada and made a lot of tawdry movies."

PART FOUR

The True North, Strong and Violent: Eco-Horror in Canada

7 The [Hostile] Nature of Things: A Dialogue on Environmental Survival and the Canadian Eco-Horror Film

GINA FREITAG

The clichéd image of Canada is a land of pristine lakes, snow capped mountains and thousands of kilometres of untouched forests – an environmental paradise.

(Karpenchuck 2009)

The more exquisitely enamelled the face of the wilderness is made to appear, the more conscious one becomes of the possibility that violence lurks just below the surface.

(McGregor 1985, 38)

The clichéd image of Canada as an "environmental paradise" is one which we have taken for granted. Environmentalism has an increasing presence in our social consciousness; it is no surprise that such issues are informing the cultivation and projection of our national image. We tend to internalize a certain ideal, a "pristine" image of our surroundings. But as Margaret Atwood points out in *Survival: A Thematic Guide to Canadian Literature*, there is another underlying conceptualization with which our minds are often preoccupied: Death by Nature (Atwood 1972, 55–6).

Canada boasts a number of vocal environmental activists whose presence in our culture is a constant reminder of the tension between environmental awareness and ignorance. David Suzuki, the renowned voice behind CBC's *The Nature of Things* and other works, is a landmark figure devoted to encouraging a profound recognition of the interdependence of humanity and nature. Many prominent environmental activists, including Atwood, celebrate Suzuki above others, stating that "no other living Canadian has done so much – nationally and internationally – to make us aware of the world we live in and of its precarious state" (Atwood 2010, vii). Alas, even the cautionary and empassioned words expressed by icons such as Suzuki are not enough to sway all minds.

There is a trend in Canadian cultural expressions which suggests a sense of impending doom: instead of making peace with nature, people tend to fear it. According to Atwood, our cultural expressions often portray nature as "actively hostile to man" (Atwood 1972, 49). Recent Canadian eco-horror films capture this attitude in particular, suggesting that nature is a force to be reckoned with, violent and vengeful. While not entirely unlike the "Forest Slasher" examined by Mark Hasan in the previous chapter, eco-horror films do not focus on crazed mountain men dead set on killing vacationing urbanites. Rather, in the films I propose to analyse below, it is nature itself that seeks vengeance upon humanity.

Eco-horror films from within the past decade conscientiously recycle ecological anxieties expressed in the previous waves of the 1950s through to the 1980s; Canadian eco-horror films are no different. These reflect distinct fears of the depletion of natural resources, the reaction of nature, and the effects of climate change, among other issues. Since the horror genre is a means of reflecting on that which terrifies us, it makes sense that the foundations of this particular horror film subset consist, in part, of a warning that we must change our ways and take action against environmental destruction.

Where Canadian eco-horror films tend to diverge from the general eco-horror movement (which includes such disaster films as Roland Emmerich's 2004 film, *The Day after Tomorrow*), is in its ideological format. True, our home-grown collection of eco-horror also imbues elements of nature with vengeful sentience: the forest in *Severed: Forest of the Dead* (2005, Carl Bessai) the ravens in *Kaw* (2007, Sheldon Wilson), and the strange infectious bacteria contained by a prehistoric corpse exposed in *The Thaw* (2009, Mark A. Lewis). Other films outside the scope of this chapter also follow suit: the insects in Paul Ziller's *Swarmed* (2005), the melting permafrost in *Ice Quake* (2010, Ziller), and the enormous cephalopod in *Eye of the Beast* (2007, Gary Yates), are only a few. But despite the harmful effects of human encroachment, there is still an overwhelming sense in cinematic portrayals that the wildness of the environment cannot be contained. Evidently, the message of eco-awareness is not so much that "Solutions are in our Nature," as the slogan of the David Suzuki Foundation proclaims, but that *nature is the solution*; violent environmental retribution is deemed to be a necessary punishment.

The cultural dialogue taking place in this comparison contemplates not only an environmental crisis, but a social crisis as well. In his essay entitled "It Came from Planet Earth," Joseph J. Foy outlines the eco-horror genre as one which is defined by ecologically minded films where "nature turns against humankind due to environmental degradation, pollution, encroachment, nuclear disaster" (Foy 2010, 167). While Foy's article reiterates the common sentiment that eco-horror films attempt "to raise mass consciousness about the very real threat that will face humanity if we are not more environmentally cautious" (2010, 167), it also suggests that the genre is "an example of popular culture attempting to transform a marginalized, disempowered voice into a mainstream dialogue" (2010, 167).

In ecocriticism (and by extension, eco-horror), there is also a strong preoccupation with issues of morality. Paula Willoquet-Maricondi's introduction to *Framing the World: Explorations in Ecocriticism and Film* highlights "ecojustice" as a moral responsibility upon human agents who are tasked with the preservation of nature, insofar as "human societies cannot flourish unless natural systems flourish too" (Willoquet-Maricondi 2010, 15). The fate of humankind is thus entwined with that of nature, and any failing on our part to maintain the healthfulness of our ecological counterpart renders us morally reprehensible.

But this interdependence is further complicated by anxieties which are visualized in cultural expressions: how do we illustrate "good" humanity and "bad" humanity? How can we adopt a sense of activism when humanity is pitted against itself? What are the implications of representing only a few identifiable "evil" figures who shirk the responsibility of environmental guardianship? And what punitive measures do we envision for those who transgress? Ultimately, there is one question with which we are most concerned: what happens when nature is pitted against humanity?

David Ingram points to the displacement of moral obligation onto other sources in *Green Screen: Environmentalism and Hollywood Cinema*, writing that "this distinction thus allows for the complicity of its ... audience in environmental degradation to be conveniently denied ... and also obfuscates the complex causality of those problems" (Ingram 2000, 3). Surely, environmental destruction cannot be reduced to a singular troubling source. And yet, some creature is invariably first positioned as the "monster," the root of "evil" to be overcome or anni-hilated. The eco-horror film frequently features a creature which has arisen from human mishap and ignorance – furious fauna disturbed in their natural environments like the disgruntled killer whale in Michael Anderson's anti-whaling drama *Orca* (1977) (which Peter Thompson discusses at more length in his contribution to this anthology), or more recently, the terrifying tentacled creature surfacing from the watery depths to attack the inhabitants of a small island fishing community in *Eye of the Beast*. These are nothing in comparison to the enormous beast unearthed just below earth's crust by scientists in *Behemoth* (2011, David Hogan). Experimentation and toxins have led to giant or mis-shapen creepy crawlers, such as David Cronenberg's *The Fly* (further examined in the final section devoted to the filmmaker), angry swarms of pesticide-ridden hornets, as in *Swarmed*, or the giant mutant insects in *Insecticidal* (2005, Jeffery Scott Lando). Anthropomorphic tree roots aggravated by toxic waste are featured in Joe D'Amato and Fabrizio Laurenti's *Contamination .7* (aka *Creepers*) (1997). And, of course, killer climates have been known to unleash terrible threats upon us: the melt-ing Arctic has released a plague of prehistoric parasites in *The Thaw* or has tried to swallow us whole in the melting permafrost that destroys the northern landscape in *Ice Quake*. While nature assumes some villain-ous form and poses a great threat to mankind, it is generally a symptom of a greater trouble posed by humanity.

Such trouble is not easily resolved, and often no resolution is achieved; we reach the conclusion of the film only to have the hint of doom still lingering in the air (*The Thaw* and *Kaw* certainly do this). As such, the resulting "open-ended" narrative structure might suggest not only that human behaviour may never change but that danger is continuously imminent and inescapable; we may never fully attain peace and equi-librium, assuming that such a state was possible in the first place. This calls to mind Robin Wood's discussion of the "collective nightmare" often reflected by horror films, and how it "brings to focus a spirit of negativity, an undifferentiated lust for destruction that seems to lie not far below the surface of the modern collective consciousness" (Wood 1979, 22), and how a significant aspect of a horror film is "the sense of a civilization condemning itself, through its popular culture, to ultimate disintegration, and ambivalently (with the simultaneous horror/wish-fulfillment of nightmare) celebrating the fact" (1979, 22). This certainly promotes an attitude of despair and futility. However, as Wood adds, "we must not, of course, see that as the last word" (1979, 22). On the other hand, we might also interpret an open-ended narrative to offer some small sense of hope: even in the gravest of times, nothing is fully decided, and change is, in fact, possible.

Of course, eco-horror films are useful in stimulating social discourse on environmentalism though perhaps are too often misrepresented as terrifying public service announcements. As Robin L. Murray and Joseph K. Heumann conclude in *Ecology and Popular Film: Cinema on the Edge*, "an eco-critical analysis of films does not necessarily rest solely on outlining blatant environmental messages. It also involves a more studied look at the forms, discourse, and histories that helped define and obscure the possible ecological leanings shared by the films" (Murray and Heumann 2009, 205).

In the interest of adopting a "more studied look" to eco-horror, particularly within a Canadian framework, this essay will examine both pessimistic and optimistic perspectives in environmental politics: the sympathetic, hopeful, and educational tones in the works of David Suzuki, and the grave, apocalyptic horrors depicted in recent Canadian eco-horror films, namely, *Severed: Forest of the Dead*, *Kaw*, and *The Thaw*. Significantly, such a comparison reveals that these differing attitudes both draw from, and even promote, the same basic principle, what Willoquet-Maricondi describes as a *biocentric* world view. While eco-cinema may not stir audiences into immediate action, it turns out that we are, in fact, enlarging "our conception of global community to include non-human life forms and the physical environment" (Willoquet-Maricondi 2010, 7).

There's Something in These Woods ...

Whatever sinister lurks in nature lurks also in us.

(Frye 1971, 141)

In the depiction of a Canadian "environmental paradise," forests play a central role, with their lush greenery evoking an idyllic yet wild landscape. This imagery serves as an ideal horror film setting: within the seclusion and natural beauty of the dense, shaded woodlands a terrible danger stirs. Bessai illustrates this setting in *Severed: Forest of the Dead*, using the forests of British Columbia. The film follows a group of environmental activists and a team of logging engineers. Tyler, the son of a logging industry CEO, is sent to investigate a stoppage at one of his father's logging production sites. At the heart of the issue is an

7.1. Video capture from *Severed*. Courtesy of Voltage Pictures.

experiment gone terribly awry: the genetically altered tree sap intended to reinvigorate the growth rate of forests is transforming people into ravenous zombies. The film uses the controversy of the logging industry as a backdrop for the conflict between humankind and nature, illustrating the clash of environmental politics and ultimately commenting on both the hostility and indifference of *human* nature, especially when determined attitudes are at odds. While Bessai's film depicts the familiar trope of humanity struggling under the weight of environmental consciousness, it introduces the idea that attempts to correct human error are simply not enough or are essentially misguided: the logging company engineers a solution to deforestation, however they are also enabling it in a more efficient way for their own gain.

Suzuki also addresses the condition of forests and the consequences of deforestation, as described in his blog *Science Matters*. As a point of interest, he notes that the UN General Assembly declared the year 2011 as the International Year of Forests (Suzuki and Moola 2011b). In tribute to this declaration, Suzuki writes of "the importance of forests to biodiversity, as well as to our own health and well-being" and how despite this "we continue to destroy them at an alarming rate" (Suzuki and Moola 2011b). He goes on to describe the wealth of forest land that Canada boasts and how "no better country is placed to deliver on the ambitious goals of the International Year of Forests than Canada," what with its "new protected areas, world-class forestry practices, and promotion of environmentally sustainable Canadian forest products in the marketplace" (Suzuki and Moola 2011b). In Suzuki's findings, there is a determined note of positivity, one which he hopes to perpetuate through his legacy.

In comparison, *Severed: Forest of the Dead* expresses similar concerns regarding the consequences of depleting natural resources. It depicts the economic motivations, the determination of environmental activism, the issue of environmental terrorism, and the attempt by science to discover a solution (the possibility for a forestry practice which would enable production while preventing the depletion of the forest). However, the logging company is first and foremost depicted as a typical, heartless industry whose economic drive is as insatiable as mankind's increasing rate of consumption of natural resources; hence, we are the zombies.[1]

As Suzuki notes in his award-winning work, *The Legacy*, this increasing rate is substantial, revealing that "it takes 1.3 years to replace what humans exploit in a year" (Suzuki 2010, 50). In Bessai's film, the self-cannibalizing tendencies in human nature are actualized – humanity is its own destructive force. It is this sentiment that links cultural forces like that of the iconic Suzuki with that of Canadian eco-horror cinema. However, the film employs a fatalistic tone and an apocalyptic sensibility wrought by nature's violence rather than a desperate plea, thereby distinguishing itself from the emotionally charged eco-awareness of Suzuki's work. In a two-hour episode of *The Nature of Things*, entitled "Voices in the Forest," the Canadian eco-icon, with an authoritative voice and sincere face, stands upon a stretch of clear-cut land, a "wasteland of tangled roots and jagged stumps" (Falk 1992), creating a sympathetic image of nature, brutalized by our actions. As Dan Falk describes in his review of the episode, Suzuki's emotionally charged approach brings "this bleak, heart-wrenching scene into living rooms across the country and across the world" (1992).[2] The image of nature is thus presented as a helpless, disempowered victim, one that we must rescue and protect.

While Suzuki's portrayal of nature emphasizes the consequences of human actions by playing upon our sympathies, eco-horror cinema shows us the terrifying results of nature as a vengeful force. In the opening sequence of *Severed: Forest of the Dead*, the logging engineers take chainsaws to the trees, and gruesome shots capture the dark tree sap oozing like blood from the man-made wounds. These dramatic images intensify when one cutter slips on the sap and loses his grip on the chainsaw, which then slices into his own tree-trunk torso. Suddenly there is panic among the workers, who watch as their fellow logger shudders into a seizure, his skin yellowing, and his eyes filling with red, uncontrollable rage. The forest around this fracas encloses the men, swallowing their cries of terror as the zombie-logger rises against them.

Bessai's film depicts the forest as an omnipotent force, continually towering over the scrambling workers and activists. Numerous aerial shots capture a bird's-eye view of the treetops which conceal malevolence under their dark canopy. This impression differs greatly from that of the wasteland – consumed, pathetic, and vulnerable – that Suzuki spotlights in his work; this forest is strong and empowered, capable of turning science against us, and each of us against one another (not to mention that it also terrorizes the film's audience with consumers that are arguably more grotesque: actual ambling, flesh-eating zombies). The connection between the evil creatures and the human beings who fend them off is also a comment on social lethargy and the inability to act together to resolve a common crisis. An analogy of zombies in this film instils not only the fear of future environmental destruction; it speaks of hopelessness in bringing the ecological crisis to a definitive end.

By configuring a zombie born from meddlesome scientific experimentation on the forest, the film imagines that, regardless of the intentions to either improve the situation or maintain our current course in the forestry industry, human efforts are futile and humanity deserves to be held accountable by nature's malevolent and inevitable force. The zombie mutation which spreads from the altered tree sap is communicable, infecting the environmental protesters and the engineers alike, leaving no one unscathed by either the transformation or the ensuing attack. Later, when the dwindling group of survivors is captured by renegade logging engineers and brought to their fortified camp, the true horror of human behaviour unfolds. The renegades taunt the zombies who claw at the station's fences and partake in a disturbing game of cage fighting, where small zombie clusters are corralled into a makeshift pen, all for sport. Tempers flare and primitive violence ensues among the survivors, escalating in the murder of a disoriented renegade who preaches of their doom and in the near-rape of one activist, Rita. The forest has rounded up these survivors, forcing them to confront one another while the zombies attack. All are held responsible, including the sole survivor,

Rita, who flees the zombie attacks and stumbles out of the forest onto a roadway, presumably to safety. The evil is contained to the forest for the time being, it seems.

The film places each character type under suspicion, criticizing the heartless industry; the outrage of the environmental activists (some of whom are extremists); the naive and ignorant son of industry; the logging engineers; the ethics of the scientists. In the final scenes, Rita's struggle for survival is intercut with Tyler's father (the logging company's CEO) drinking solemnly in his study, contemplating a framed photo of his son before taking a despairing turn about his house. On all counts, the hopelessness is palpable. Beyond the debate that surrounds logging practices like clear-cutting, it is evident that the film is trying to remind us: that which one group incurs will invariably affect the whole.

While one can ponder whether Bessai's representation is more affecting than Suzuki's, perhaps the more interesting afterthoughts can be derived from their depictions of both nature and human nature. These images not only warn us to change our course of action; they stir troubling questions about our general mindset: how many of these depictions of a victimized nature and its imagined vengeance are reflected in our own defeatist attitudes? Can such devasting or imaginative exaggeration of environmental vengeance instil reason into social consciousness? When it comes to environmental activism, are we plagued by pessimism?

The "Aflockalypse":[3] A Bird Omen

"'Hope' is the thing with feathers," wrote Emily Dickinson. Too often, these days, it isn't.
(Atwood 2010)

An "environmental paradise" can be deemed so only with consideration to its inhabitants, the flora and fauna which are also integral parts of the ecological chain. The relationship between humans and nature is a delicate one, and the slightest change in its balance can alter the future of biodiversity. The cultural interactions of birds and humans, for instance, offer a reflection on the influence of one species over another. In *The Nature of Things*, an episode which aired on CBC 12 June 2011 entitled "A Murder of Crows" discusses the similarities shared between both crows and humans: our sense of community and habitat, a strong sense of memory, and sophisticated communicative abilities. As Suzuki points out through voice-over narration, these capabilities are examples of "a potential evolutionary advantage shared only by certain intelligent species" (Suzuki 2011b). Suzuki's discussion of these corvids and their relationship to humans mirrors a concept which John M. Marzluff and Tony Angell describe in their work, *In the Company of Crows and Ravens*. The term they use, "coevolution," occurs "when animals exert an evolutionary influence on each other" (Marzluff and Angell 2005, 24). Just as our attitudes towards crows have varied over time, "the behaviour of theses corvids has been moulded by their interactions with humans" (2005, 11).

In Wilson's eco-horror film, *Kaw*, a similar connection is drawn in relation to another member of the corvus genus: the raven. Like the crow, whose intelligence Suzuki champions, the raven is also understood to be a clever creature, capable of skilled behaviour, particularly when banding together in a determined pursuit of prey. These two species of birds are remarkably alike in appearance, especially given their black plumage and other distinctive physical attributes. In large numbers, these corvids are described by terms that have negative connotations: a "murder" of crows, an "unkindness" of ravens. But beyond these parallels in behaviour and appearance, they bear remarkable similiarities in the way they are each represented through history and literature. These birds share ominous reputations as sinister tricksters and scavengers; they partake in the creation myths in various cultures[4] and in lore relating to death and bad luck. In certain periods of history, crows and ravens have been treated as symbolic indicators or "powerful omens of future events" (2005, 125), and have been linked with "the inevitability of death" (2005, 132).

Interestingly, they are also viewed "as transporters of the dead, carrying souls to the land of the dead" (2005, 136). This fearsome perception is propagated in literary works varying from Edgar Allen Poe's *The Raven* to Lewis Carroll's *Alice in Wonderland*; through film and popular culture in such films as Alfred Hitchcock's *The Birds* (1963); and in worrisome news stories that warn of diseases like West Nile virus or avian flu, or that describe unexplained, mysterious mass deaths of birds.[5] That these creatures are used as a sign of forthcoming disaster or the approaching apocalypse in contemporary culture, and particularly in *Kaw*, is therefore a significant aspect of eco-horror, which derives terrifying narratives from environmental retribution. The differences in the perception of these black-feathered avian varieties are thus worth comparing.

Suzuki's educational episode minimizes the negative perception of such birds by celebrating the skills and abilities of the crows. His portrayal praises their intellect by investigating the nuances of their behaviour and learning systems through tool usage and memory-based demonstrations. He continually emphasizes the coexistence of humans and crows, and the impact of the relationship on the latter's population. Evidently, when humans move into crow territories, the birds flourish by adjusting to the ways of urban life, even adapting their diet to include the waste and refuse from human presence. Suzuki links the intelligence of this species to that of humans and biological human ancestors by portraying crows as "feathered apes," whose brain size is proportional to its body much in the same way as that of apes rather than that of other birds.

In "A Murder of Crows," Suzuki narrates a number of demonstrations, from a facial recognition experiment, where masked subjects are repeatedly "scolded" by crows that are wary of the strange appearances, to a course in which a crow must retrieve a nugget of food by strategically using a small twig to obtain a larger stick which will enable it to reach the nugget. These demonstrations are crafted to display the exceptional memory and mental abilities of the crow, reflecting an appreciation for an intellect which mirrors our own in many ways. By establishing this linkage between humans and crows, Suzuki aims to encourage a stronger understanding of and appreciation for interconnection in the web of life.

In contrast, Wilson's film, *Kaw*, amplifies the iniquitous image of these same birds and cultivates fear of the creatures by exploiting their unique capabilities in menacing ways. In turn, this distances us from such creatures, rather than allowing us to connect with them. Ravens are depicted as horrifying harbingers of doom, where hordes swarm and attack the seemingly innocent townspeople in the film. This terrifying behaviour is made even more so by the incessant, shrieking "kaws" which virtually drown out all other sounds in the town. In the film, ravens in particular are portrayed as insidious winged fiends, haunting a small rural town and a nearby Mennonite community in astounding numbers. They encircle farmers and dogs, mob vehicles on old country roads, assail a school bus and its passengers, and peck apart members of the community while the general townsfolk look on in horror and confusion. The town's sheriff, Wayne Hayborn, takes charge while investigating the bizarre bird behaviour as the flock becomes increasingly vicious.

Later in the film, the scavenging ravens seize control of the town, swarming a gas-bar diner and cornering the people of the town. One by one, the ravens shatter each of the yard lights in the parking lot before smashing against the diner windows. The surviving inhabitants desperately strategize while one Mennonite farmer breaks down, revealing that the furious flock have become enraged after feeding on cattle in his community that were fatally afflicted with mad cow disease. This biological explanation, an infection, is not the only explanation that is uncovered. The film brings into play religious undertones in relation to this death and destruction: an earlier conversation between two Mennonite elders reveals the epidemic as a sign of the conflict between tradition and modernity, a punishment dealt from God for not respecting certain customs and natural laws.

Human complicity in the creation of such a dangerous state of nature is openly expressed; there is much anxiety that human behaviour has wrought this terrible retribution. The hostile ravens spare no victims, attacking men, women, children, and even other animals, including a dog belonging to the surly bus driver, Clyde. The crazed corvids hold the local authorities accountable when they overwhelm an officer as he draws his weapon in the middle of the street. Upon breaking into the sheriff's office, the ravens tear apart and feast on the face of the dispatcher. Despite his heroic leadership, even Sheriff Hayborn is susceptible to danger. After Clyde sacrifices himself in an explosion to save those seeking refuge in the diner, a final scene depicts the sheriff returning home with his wife, only to be overwhelmed by a mass of ravenous ravens patiently awaiting inside the house for their arrival.

The thematic tension in the film resulting from the conflict of tradition and modernity is further expressed as a contrast between peaceful living and destructive ways of life. And, while the surviving townspeople are lulled into a false sense of security, believing the terror to be over, the open-ended narrative suggests otherwise. Small-town living is no longer the idyllic, pastoral paradise it has been imagined to be. For the townsfolk in *Kaw*, it may be too late to stop the terror that awaits the rest of the world; these ravens are an omen, a force which hints of worse things to come.

Arctic Meltdown, Social Breakdown

The crisis is real, and it is upon us.

(Suzuki 2010, 36)

The "crisis" in environmentalism is not simply that humanity must change its actions to protect and conserve this "environmental paradise," but that people must change their way of thinking. Not only are we troubled by climate change, ecological damage, and the impact of human encroachment, but we are divided between an outlook of hope and one of despair. The trouble lies in the tendency we have to imagine ourselves as being above nature, and at times, vice versa. As Ingram's sentiments suggest, there is a "drawback of this need to conceive of nature as pristine … it tends to position human beings as fundamentally opposed to, and excluded from, nature" (Ingram 2000, 25) when really we are as much a part of it as ever. In *Ecology and Popular Film*, Murray and Heumann echo the ideas of Joseph W. Meeker in outlining our problematic thought processes: too often are we under "the assumption that nature exists for the benefit of humanity; the belief that human morality transcends natural limitations" (Murray and Heumann 2009, 94). As a result, humanity is faced with anxiety over environmental issues and our part in shaping these issues. What precisely are the causes? How did we let things progress so far? How do we address such change? Can we prevent further climate change? Will we adapt, and what happens if we cannot? These concerns are often met with denial and indifference, and are directly deliberated in both Suzuki's work and the film *The Thaw*.

In an episode of *The Nature of Things* entitled "Arctic Meltdown: Adapting to Change," Suzuki sheds light on the climate change debate by focusing on the Bylot Island Study. This project is set in the Canadian Arctic and analyses the eco-systems within a protected area of 2,500 hectares, land that is sanctioned for preservation. He also discusses the impact of industrial development in the north. Similarly, Lewis's film *The Thaw* is set in the Canadian north (on Banks Island), where a team of environmental scientists and a group of environmental studies students make a troubling discovery as a result of climate change.

Once again, Suzuki's approach differs from that of an eco-horror film which centres on the same environmental issue. Granted, both reflect on the dramatic changes associated with climate change, such as the melting tundra and the drying out of wetlands; both feature the unsettling imagery of a dry landscape which stands in stark contrast to the wintry regions that the term "Arctic" calls to mind; and both place science in the forefront. But each one illustrates the clash of attitudes by ultimately adopting opposing outlooks.

Suzuki's examination of the impact of climate change on the Arctic is presented as an attempt at understanding a connection with and a dependence on ecosystems. His voice hovers over images of the Arctic as it emphasizes that in nature there are still "mysteries to solve before we fully comprehend" the effects of climate change; we need to consider that which "plants and animals reveal about their changing world," as it offers insight into the world we know. Through excerpts of interviews with various scientists and ecologists participating in the Arctic study project, Suzuki promotes research as a crucial factor in the effort towards eco-awareness. The latter part of the episode is dedicated to exploring the economic factor behind industrial development in the north by describing the Arctic as not only a "storybook land of ice, snow and polar bears," but one that is also "covered with petroleum plants and pipelines carrying fossil fuels." He speaks with a sense of urgency regarding the troubling exploitation of resources found in the northern regions and the need for an impact study to examine the consequences of development, beyond the effort of creating "safe" technology.

The theme of communication is a fundamental aspect of Suzuki's approach to environmental activism. However, despite attempts to communicate with one another, there is less effort being made to understand: the ongoing conflicts between environmentalists, scientists, industry figures, governments, and members of the nearby Aboriginal community, whose heritage is regarded for its role in the guardianship of nature, are evidence of this.

A similar sense of social conflict is conveyed in *The Thaw*. In the opening sequence, a collage of voices express worry, dejection, and urgency: "I don't think people are going to do enough in time"; "What can we do about it?"; "What does it mean to make a real difference?"; "The time is now." These comments and questions reflect the social climate, itself a crisis of indecision and uncertainty. A final comment summarizes the general tone of the film: "It's too late to do anything."

The film operates through an ongoing debate among the main characters, a collection of graduate students selected to join a research team on Banks Island in the Canadian Arctic. Confined together en route by helicopter, they are forced into an open discussion of their own opinions, mirroring the opening sequence. Of these characters, two in particular, Atom and Evy, bear names which recall the biblical image of a natural paradise, and the expulsion from said paradise following disobedient acts, thus hinting at the inevitable outcome that awaits the group. While Atom points out that "we can't ignore the reality of what we're up against" and wonders "what are we really doing to stop it?" Frederico, the voice of both hope and naivety, fawns over the wisdom of

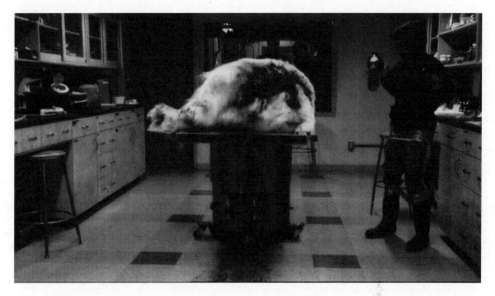

7.2. Video capture from *Thaw*. Courtesy of Voltage Pictures.

his idol and the leader of the research team, Dr David Krupian, whose ambition lies in "changing how people think." Amid the bickering, the students turn to Evy, the daughter of the renowned Dr Krupian, and ask for her opinion. She hesitates before replying, "Honestly, I think that people are incapable of change, and our days are numbered."

Upon reaching the northern station, the team learns that something has gone wrong in the research project – the station has been left abandoned. Meanwhile, Dr Krupian's field team has become afflicted with a strange illness and spirals into dissent and violence. After one member of that team shoots her colleagues in panic, she flees back to the station only to succumb gruesomely to the oozing effects of her mysterious illness. The group of students and their helicopter pilot soon discover that an infected polar bear specimen in the station's lab is similarly afflicted, and in very little time several members of their group are infected as well. It is only in the search for her father that Evy and Atom uncover the source of the illness: her father's research team have encountered a thawing mammoth infected with an ancient parasite, an evil exposed by the effects of climate change.

In a fight for survival, the group struggles to comprehend the disease and its impact and quarrel in their quarantine facility while searching for a solution. They come across Dr Krupian's video diary, appalled to learn that he has committed a "sacrifice" by voluntarily infecting himself as a message of extreme activism and desperation. In the final sequences, Dr Krupian stumbles back to the station, and a confrontation between father and daughter leads to a conflict ending in a helicopter explosion that kills the rescue team and her ailing father, who is determined to get society's attention by inflicting the terrifying parasite on the public through his return. As the sole survivor, Evy contemplates "What is sacrifice? We keep saying we want change but we just keep doing the same shitty things everyday ... I used to believe that people couldn't change ... But now, now I don't want it to end."

Before these words can leave a lasting impression of hope for humankind in the film, the final sequence plays out: a truck is parked out in the woods, a hunter prepares to return with his kill to the city. The truck's radio crackles with the conversation of debate: some voices are sceptical about the global warming "propaganda," while others emphasize humankind's vulnerability and claim that it's "just a matter of time before the big one hits." The final images of the film are of a dead crow – an omen, if you will – lying in the tall grass and crawling with the ancient parasites, while the truck drives ominously off into the sunset. The film concludes with a dialogue on climate change, reiterating the common sentiment that it is too late to change. We have survived thus far, but we will invariably parish from Death by Nature – that is, by *human* nature, and its social crisis.

Conclusion

This comparison of environmental concerns – as expressed by Canadian eco-horror films and by the didactic works of a prominent Canadian environmental activist – illustrates the dialogue Canadians have with one another on a larger social scale, a dialogue that must continue, for as Atwood's sentiment relates, "a country needs to hear its own voices" (Atwood 1972, 24). The theme of survival is central to the social discourse on environmentalism, in which we are constantly reminded that we are interconnected with nature. As Atwood emphasizes, "a preoccupation with one's survival is necessarily also a preoccupation with the obstacles to that survival" (1972, 33).

The Canadian cultural productions examined in this essay also emphasize a theme of connection. David Suzuki's work in *The Nature of Things*, his articles, and his additional projects promote a positive attitude regarding the "web of life." In a blog entry for *Science Matters*, Suzuki points out that "the only way to come to grips with this crisis and find solutions is to understand that we are biological creatures" (Suzuki 2011a) also; he encourages a recognition of the connections human-kind shares with the environment. To this onging dialogue, eco-horror films such as *Severed: Forest of the Dead*, *Kaw*, and *The Thaw* contribute a further connection between human beings and nature through the depiction of disease. In each narrative, nature and human nature both become violent so that hostility itself is a disease, communicable and deadly. Fortunately, ecocriticism enables us to examine such hostility as but one of the "obstacles to our survival" with the hope that we address it before it becomes our apparent doom, what Atwood describes as the "obsession with surviving [which] can become the will *not* to survive" (Atwood 1972, 34).

NOTES

1 This analogy is certainly not a new concept – George A. Romero's *Dawn of the Dead* (1978) drew the connection between consumerism and zombies; similarly, Edgar Wright's *Shaun of the Dead* (2004) suggested that society's lethargy is also likened to those fumbling creatures. Obviously, it is a common trope to interlace a social agenda into a horror narrative.

2 The episode, which aired in February 1991, explicitly favours the preservation of nature's splendour by describing the consequences of clear-cutting in a drastic and pleading tone. In an archived article from June 16, 1992, found online through the Ryerson Review of Journalism's website, Dan Falk describes the negative response to the episode at the time, which argued against Suzuki's distinct, and apparently uniformed, bias. Many outspoken members of the Ministry of Forests were "incensed that Suzuki did not interview known ecologists, academics and professional foresters on the government side who are promoting and practicing new forestry concepts – people who know what is actually happening in the forest as far as replanting and survival are concerned" (Falk 1992).

3 The term "Aflockalypse" is drawn from the title of David Suzuki and Faisal Moola's "Aflockalypse Now: Mass Animal Die-offs and the Ongoing Extinction Crisis," *Science Matters*.

4 Marzluff and Angell tell of religious heritage accounts from the Acoma of central New Mexico, the Tutchone Athabaskan Indians, and Christian creation narratives, of the story of the great flood, "which clever and

industrious Crow survived and created the world anew by piecing together fragments of land. Then, because he wasn't satisfied with the result, Crow summoned a second flood to cleanse the world and start again" (Marzluff and Angell 2005, 117).

5 In their blog entry of 13 January 2011 entitled "Aflockalypse Now: Mass Animal Die-offs and the Ongoing Extinction Crisis," David Suzuki references the sad and strange epidemic of mass bird deaths, including the "5,000 red-winged blackbirds [which] dropped out of the sky in Beebe, Arkansas" (Suzuki and Moola, 2011a).

8 Eco-Horror and Boundary Transgressions in *Orca: The Killer Whale*

PETER THOMPSON

On the surface, the appeal of horror films is pretty straightforward: they provide the audience with an opportunity to experience gory, sensational attacks and situations in the controlled and safe environment of a theatre or home. Aside from offering such seemingly cheap thrills, however, horror films also shed light on broad cultural anxieties, including, for example, our fears of increased weaponization, advances in medical science, religious fervour, immigration, and environmental crises. Although critics almost unanimously panned 1977's *Orca: The Killer Whale* and dismissed it as a poorly directed, poorly acted, and cheap knock-off of *Jaws* (1975, Steven Spielberg), the film actually speaks to complex cultural, economic, and political apprehensions that were coursing through Newfoundland and the rest of Canada in the late 1970s.

At first glance, *Orca* resembles a terrifying vision of the landscape plucked directly from Northrop Frye's garrison thesis (1971, 214–249). As has already been pointed out elsewhere in this anthology, in the 1960s and 1970s, critics such as Frye and Margaret Atwood popularized the idea that a profound fear of the North American wilderness is an essential element of Canadian culture, one that developed centuries before Confederation and can be found to this day. In *Orca*, an unwelcome visitor to Newfoundland tries to tame the natural environment by catching a killer whale, finding instead that he has angered it, causing nature, in the form of the orca, to attack him and the community in which he lives. As the film progresses, the residents of the village hunker down, staying off the ocean and in their homes until the threat of the whale subsides. The characters in *Orca* cower in fear of a natural environment that seems uncaring and hostile, a dynamic which is further explored in Gina Freitag's "The [Hostile] Nature of Things" in this volume. Thus, the film's focus on the terrifying power of nature and the wilderness appears to make *Orca* an effective examination of anxieties that circulated in cultural nationalist rhetoric of the mid- and late twentieth century in Canada.

The film's final battle scene resonates with Canadian cultural nationalist concerns as well: the whale lures Nolan, his crew, Umilak, and Bedford to the extreme north, where they have to contend not just with the whale but also with incredibly harsh northern conditions, including ice floes that threaten the ship and an avalanche that kills Umilak. At the end of the film, the orca actually tries to push an iceberg towards Nolan's boat to capsize it, bringing together two of the most important and supposedly essential fears that Canadians harbour.

I would like to dig a bit deeper, however, and suggest in this paper that *Orca*, like other contemporary eco-horror films, engages in a non-essentialist reading of the landscape and derives its horrific power from a series of boundary transgressions. The film confronts the audience with a set of impurities and crossed borders: the resilience, intelligence, and actions of the orca throw the distinction between human and animal into chaos; Bedford, Umilak, and the fishermen clash over the distinction between scientific, indigenous, and local forms of knowledge; and the setting of the film resides in a liminal space between Canada and the United States. While the whale's attacks are certainly scary, the more profound darkness of the film comes from these shifting and unstable boundaries.

Orca: The Killer Whale

Shot in Petty Harbour, a small, picturesque community in Motion Bay, about 20 kilometres south of St John's, *Orca* is the story of a fisherman named Nolan who comes to Newfoundland from Ireland to poach sharks and killer whales in order to pay off the mortgage on his boat. The film was produced by Dino De Laurentiis, directed by Michael Anderson, and starred Richard Harris (Nolan), Charlotte Rampling (Dr Rachel Bedford), and a young Bo Derek (Annie). In the opening scene, Nolan finds a shark, only to discover that there is a team of scientists already in the water studying it. When it attacks one of the scientists, a killer whale saves him by fighting off the shark – possibly heading off anticipated comparisons to *Jaws* at the pass by demonstrating that the killer whale is a much more terrifying animal than a shark. Nolan then turns his attention to the killer whale. He tries to harpoon it, but his shot goes through the fin of the orca and hits the whale's pregnant mate by mistake. His crew drags the female orca out of the water and hangs it on the ship, where she miscarries.

Calling back to an earlier scene where Bedford, the lead scientist, tells her students that whale fetuses look like human babies in the womb, the crew is horrified by the human-like appearance of the fetus and immediately washes it over the side of the ship. The injured male then rams the ship and attacks the crew, leading them to throw the corpse of the female overboard as well. The opening scenes establish the whale as a sympathetic and even potentially heroic character (Muir 2002, 498): in addition to saving Ken, he protects and ultimately avenges his mate, and seems to have the best interests of his pod in mind. The film humanizes the whale and asks the audience to side with him, at times portraying Nolan as the irrational and even monstrous character. As the film moves along, Nolan starts to relate more and more to the whale. He recounts his own story of grief: when he was younger, a drunk driver struck his pregnant wife, and he lost both his partner and his unborn baby. As he reflects on the intense pain that this experience caused him, he becomes less angry with the whale, and begins to understand his enemy's position, even passing up a clear shot at the whale towards the close of the film.

The rest of the action features an ongoing battle between Nolan and the whale, which stalks him both on shore and in the ocean. Nolan becomes obsessed to the point of insanity with catching the whale, eventually leading Bedford, Umilak, and the remains of his crew into the Strait of Belle Isle and chasing his tormentor even after they realize that they do not have enough fuel to make it home. Bedford is the only member of the crew to survive the ordeal, and the orca swims off under the ice as the credits roll.

Eco-Horror and Boundary Transgressions

Orca is a good example of an eco-horror film, a genre that exploits cultural anxieties surrounding the environmental crisis that has enveloped North American society in at least the last thirty years. The eco-horror genre includes films that represent fears of ecological catastrophes such as *The Day after Tomorrow* (2004, Roland Emmerich) and, in their most basic form, films that play on fears of simply being food for other species (Kerridge 2000, 242; Simpson 2010, 48). Timothy Beal writes that "ecohorror gives popular cultural expression to the ecological nightmare that has pursued us since the dawning of the atomic era ... these monsters stand in for deep anxieties about the effects of modern science and technology on complex ecosystems that we do not fully understand" (Beal 2002, 161). Like standard eco-horror narratives, *Orca* taps into anxieties surrounding the management of resources. In the case of Newfoundland, factory trawlers had ramped up fish harvests to unsustainable levels in the 1960s and 1970s. The action of *Orca* centres on a fisherman who overreaches the informal limits enacted by members of the community and places their livelihood at risk.

In her 2001 article "Discomforting Creatures: Monstrous Natures in Recent Films," Stacey Alaimo notes that although most ecocritics focus their attention on positive representations of nature, monster movies provide insight into cultural anxieties surrounding our relationship with the landscape and with animals, especially fears over environmental and resource-related crises (279). Alaimo argues that the relationship between such films as *Jaws* and *Open Water* (2003, Chris Kentis) and ecological politics is complicated. On the one hand, these films may "vilify nature," giving justification to campaigns to tame and subdue it. This critique resembles the way in which scholars in recent years[1] have suggested that the deep terror of nature of which Frye and Atwood write provides a way of naturalizing the conquest of Canada's land mass, pushing civilization farther into the "empty" recesses of the west.

As Alaimo argues, however, there is another way to read many eco-horror movies. While some position man in a war against nature (a war that in some films he is losing and in others he is winning mercilessly), others employ scary animals to tap into anxieties over systems of knowledge and collapsing cultural boundaries. As theorists such as Donna Haraway (1991) and Val Plumwood (1993) argue, modern medical science and technological advances have a profound impact on our understanding of differences between genders, and even such seemingly straightforward distinctions as the one between animals and humans. In what follows, I would like to suggest that *Orca* capitalizes on these kinds of boundary transgressions.

In "The Nature of Horror," Noel Carroll (1987) suggests that in addition to the threat to physical well-being implicit in being chased by a monster or finding oneself in the midst of a zombie apocalypse, horror films upset us because they threaten our very understanding of the world. He notes that many classic horror films open in peaceful suburban settings or in happy households in order to accentuate the normal lives of characters who are about to be terrorized (1987, 52). This way, when an "abnormal" monster arrives on the scene, our sense of the civil ordering of the society in which we live comes into question: the monster seems even more grotesque, and the feeling of safety we associate with these tranquil settings starts to slip away. Vivian Sobchack argues that many "monster on the loose" films play up this idea of a community or even a way of life under threat by featuring a struggle not simply between a single protagonist and the monster but between the deadly presence and the institutional infrastructure of the society he attacks: even if a hero ultimately vanquishes the monster, the police, the military, the scientific community, and the government always get involved (Sobchack 1987, 49).

For Carroll, the epistemological crisis engendered by cinematic horror comes from a series of boundary transgressions: to use Carroll's term, these films exploit and undermine "thresholds," such as those between natural and unnatural, pure and impure, dead and alive, sacred and profane, and clean and unclean. Horror films attack the complex and intangible distinctions that patrol the "natural order" that our culture works hard to construct and maintain. Carroll contends that in this way, monsters are revolting or disgusting to us because they are "unwholesome," filthy, or decaying. Horror films often feature amalgams between human and monster, medical experiments or treatments that go awry, and wounded or mutilated versions of humans or animals such as zombies. The key to all of these versions of filmic monsters is that they defy easy explanation: it is not clear if a zombie is dead, alive, or something in between. Our fear of the monster stems in large part from a metaphysical crisis that accompanies seeing something that violates our schemes of knowledge: monsters are, as Carroll writes, "interstitial" beings that float between these strict distinctions and cannot be classified in the way to which we are accustomed. Carroll notes that for this reason "monsters are not only physically threatening; they are cognitively threatening" (1987, 56).

At its most basic level, *Orca* gets at the threshold between the sea and the land: the orca often violates this boundary by jumping out of the water to attack humans, reaching them even when they are seemingly safe on shore. In the most extreme example, the whale rams into the stilts holding up the house where Nolan and his crew are staying, eventually breaking a hole in the building big enough to enter and bite Annie's leg off. In the same incident, the whale manages to smash apart the fuel lines linking the community's houses, setting a fire that engulfs the entire dock and eventually spreads to the refinery on top of the hill, which immediately explodes.

However, the most dramatic threshold that *Orca* deals with is the one between human and animal. As Susan Davis notes in *Spectacular Nature: Corporate Culture and the Seaworld Experience* (1997), it is relatively easy to humanize a killer whale. Because they are more round than dolphins (which, according to Davis, makes them resemble sea pandas) and because the white spots near the front of their head give them a human-like appearance, killer whales resemble people and can be readily animated (1997, 192). The ease with which we humanize killer whales is reflected in the popularity of Shamu, the corporate logo and main attraction of Seaworld and Willy, the gentle killer whale from the *Free Willy* franchise. Bedford talks constantly about how humans and whales share an evolutionary background, how their levels of intelligence are remarkably close, and accuses Nolan of being more animal-like than the whale he hunts, insisting that she and her team should be studying him rather than the orca. At several points in the film, the camera focuses in on the whale's eye and then quickly switches to a close-up of Nolan's eye, calling attention to connections between the two possible heroes/villains of the film.

Bedford also tells her students and Nolan that whales project emotion in much the same way as humans; she notes that whales, like humans, are monogamous, and the other whales in the pod follow behind the male orca when he is bringing his mate to shore, almost like a funeral procession. Bedford's comment (mentioned previously) regarding the resemblance of the whale fetus to a human baby also mentions that they even have five fingers and two hands. This sets the stage for what is possibly the film's most jarring image: the whale fetus, which looks uncannily like a human baby, being cut from its mother and lying on the deck of Nolan's ship.

Towards the end of the film, Bedford begins to believe, against her better judgment, that the whale has specifically targeted Nolan. She writes in her notes, "Perhaps I am projecting something on to the whale that is not there. Just because the whale is as intelligent as man doesn't mean that it has our most primitive emotion: vengeance." Like Nolan and the other fishermen, Bedford comes to be perplexed by the whale's behaviour and seems to lose perspective on the distinction between humans and whales as the film moves forward. She mentions several times that whales are in fact more intelligent and have evolved more sophisticated survival techniques than man; here, she finds it difficult to come to grips with the idea that the whale might even share less desirable traits with humans.

Beginning with the film's title sequence, which plays above the sounds of whales in the ocean and the beeping of radar equipment, *Orca* examines the relationship between the sophisticated technology of the fishermen and scientists and the equally complex but seemingly primitive "technology" the whale uses. In addition to mentioning that whales are capable of communicating in a way that is far more complicated than human speech, Bedford mentions that whales use refined radar technology to identify schools of fish and obstacles in the ocean. The killer whale in *Orca* harnesses this skill to track Nolan's boat, figure out which house he lives in, and generally to wreak havoc on him and the rest of the town. The idea that an animal such as a whale could outmatch the technological achievements of human society is another unsettling element of the plot. *Orca* provides an example of animals using technology against humans and suggests that these particular whales might actually be technologically superior to humans.

Alaimo argues that part of what drives our fear of movies such as *Planet of the Apes* (1968, Franklin J. Schnaffner) is the thought that the animals in these films are living in a kind of organized civilization and that they are acting on rational decisions rather than their base instincts (2001, 279). This is a key element of *Orca*. While Bedford and her colleagues are excited at the prospect of whales interacting like humans, Nolan and the rest of the inhabitants of the community seem disgusted at the thought that the orca is watching them, following their patterns, and acting like a human might act. Bedford expresses admiration for the fact that in spite of their superior intelligence, whales demonstrate none of the contaminations that plague contemporary society. In this sense, the idea that whales might live in a "civilization" that is more like the one that we live in than we would like to admit is frightening, as it unsettles the certainty of our claims to superiority over all other species.

In his treatise on whaling culture in Newfoundland, *A Whale for the Killing*, Farley Mowat (2005) also writes about the relationship between humans and whales. *Orca*, like Mowat's book, picks up a key debate taking place in 1970s Newfoundland (and one that persists in some circles) about the corrupting influence of modernity on residents of the province as well as the rest of Canada. In doing so, *Orca* goes beyond the generic concerns of standard horror films to engage with a threshold specific to its Newfoundland setting: the distinction between the pre-modern world of the outport and the highly technologized remainder of North America.

In the middle of the twentieth century, cultural producers and governments of the Atlantic provinces contributed to a movement that branded the region as pre-modern, a bastion of "traditional culture," and untouched by many of the defining elements of North American modernity, including technology, consumerism, and urbanization. The state promoted this version of Newfoundland (and still does) because it makes the province attractive to visitors. One of the most important strands of this campaign to establish Newfoundland as a tourist destination is the idea that residents of the island (particularly those living in "outports" and isolated communities) are authentic representations of "us" – in other words, because distance and geographical obstacles shield them from contact with the rest of the continent, they have been able to maintain a "traditional" way of life, one that, if not for the influence of cities and modern conveniences, would exist in every corner of North America. Thus, visits to Newfoundland by people who live in Toronto and Halifax stem less from the desire to find exotic and unknown people than the hope of discovering primitive and uncorrupted versions of themselves.

In his opening chapter, Mowat identifies a conflict between the "traditional" Newfoundland found in the small outports that dot the southwest coast of the province and the industrialized Newfoundland that Joey Smallwood's modernization schemes looked to cultivate during the second half of the twentieth century. Like many other artists and writers, Mowat viewed Newfoundland as a romantic and inspirational space that offered reprieve from the shallow lifestyle of cities such as New York and Toronto.

In keeping with the cultural nationalist revival of the late 1960s and 1970s, Mowat wrote about the need to protect Canada from the influence of American mass culture and consumerism. In his estimation, the people of Newfoundland were well positioned to fight off these forces because of their spirit of non-conformity, their ability to survive harsh environmental conditions, and their history of ambivalence towards Ottawa and the rest of North America. In his article "Sparking A Cultural Revolution: Joey Smallwood, Farley Mowat, Harold Horwood and Newfoundland's Cultural Renaissance," James Overton (2000) states that in "Newfoundland, Mowat found a place and people who seemed to him almost untouched by the modern world – an ideal base from which he would lead the revolutionary struggle to stem the tide of creeping Americanism" (170). In this way, Mowat and others viewed

Newfoundland as a place where an authentic and traditional culture survived and thrived and could be a staging ground for "restoring" the rest of the continent.

A Whale for the Killing documents an extended trip that Mowat and his wife Claire took to Burgeo, a small outport community east of Port aux Basques. The first pages of the book detail changes taking place in Burgeo: in recent years, a fish processing plant had arrived in the community, offering workers "wage jobs" that took them away from their traditional way of life on the sea. Mowat notes that along with the plant, Burgeo had been infected with the materialistic desires of the rest of North America: people bought televisions, even though they had no access to a broadcast signal and bought cars to drive on paths that lead nowhere and would inevitably wreck them.

For Mowat, centralization and the industrial schemes advocated by Joey Smallwood threatened to destroy the distinctive way of life he saw and loved so much during his first trips to Burgeo. Part of the reason for this is that technology serves to separate people from interacting with the natural environment, an element of the community's culture that Mowat views as absolutely essential:

> Clinging to the landwash, often at the very foot of a towering cliff, these sparse encrustations of human life were separated one from the other by many miles of unquiet waters, yet united by the sea which was the peoples livelihood ...
>
> It was a rock-hard land and an ice-cold sea, and together they winnowed the human seed through generations of adversity until the survivors themselves partook of the primal strength of rock and ocean. (2005, 18)

Shifting his focus to the other object of his obsession during his time in southwestern Newfoundland, the fin whale, Mowat later draws a connection between the intelligence, industriousness, and resilience of Newfoundlanders and the same qualities of the whales he observed:

> When [whales] returned to the sea they brought with them an intelligence of a radically new order – one that had evolved as a direct consequence of the ferocious difficulties which all terrestrial animals must face in order to survive, and which reached its peak in the mammals. This legacy was shared by the ancestral whales and by the nameless creatures who were to become the progenitors of man. (2005, 45)

Mowat focuses on the way in which Newfoundland's harsh environmental conditions have produced a noble, pre-literate, and authentic culture that in many ways resembles the whales who live off the coast. The main thrust of *A Whale for the Killing* is that modern society threatens both of these treasures: just as a taste for disposable goods and regular hours at a plant makes the residents of Burgeo greedy and complacent, advances in whale-hunting technology promise to wipe out their entire population if left unchecked.

Like Mowat, Bedford reveres the intelligence and grace of the whales. She also talks often about the corrupting influence of modernity, comparing the great killer whales she encounters in the wild with the feeble and demoralized specimens found in places such as Seaworld. While Bedford does not make the comparison between humans and whales as explicitly as does Mowat, like him, she rejects the influence of civilization on her subjects and decries the way in which modern society has turned them into tourist spectacles who are weak and dependent on human assistance.

The fishermen who populate the community seem very suspicious of Bedford's motives and her scientific methods. She mentions several times that she is surprised at how ignorant the local fishermen are about the whales that she studies. She says that they are interested in fish and whales only to the extent that they are economically valuable: they want only fish that they can catch, clean, and sell, and have no interest in the science behind their behaviour.

One of Mowat's deep concerns about the future of outport Newfoundland and the whales found off its shores was that both would become resource material for the tourist economy that was creeping into the province during this time. While *Orca* rejects the sentimental reading of Newfoundland found in *A Whale for the Killing* and employs the province as a vaguely interesting and dangerous, rather than preciously authentic, space, the film fits with the province's tourism infrastructure in unexpected ways. The film's hunt for killer whales parallels the province's popular whale-watching industry, and the production itself has become a tourist attraction.[2]

In this sense, *Orca* disorients our understanding of what the authentic Newfoundland might look like. While the idealized and nostalgic reading of the province popularized by writers such as Mowat certainly have traction within Newfoundland's tourism brochures, *Orca*, a film that claims the outport as home to cutting-edge scientific research, the latest whale-hunting technology, and transplants from around the globe, provides an alternative reading of this place.

Insiders vs Outsiders

Catherine Simpson suggests that the eco-horror genre lends itself very well to post-colonial anxieties surrounding the land, including the issue of who belongs and does not belong in settler spaces such as Australia and Canada. She notes that post-colonial articulations of ownership over the land rely heavily on the idea that the colonizing power has supremacy over nature. Simpson argues that in the context of Australia eco-horror films often feature scenes in which tourists, ignorant of local customs and practices around nature, are killed. For Simpson, this element of Australian eco-horror has a kind of nationalist function, in which locals "perform the role of knowing guides [and] claim a greater sense of belonging" (2010, 47). Just as Mowat works out his ambivalent feelings about belonging in Burgeo in his relationship with the land, the characters of *Orca* measure the degree to which they feel comfortable in the space of Newfoundland through harvesting resources from the environment. In addition to threatening the population of whales through his actions, Nolan puts the livelihood of the entire community at risk, as the whale takes it upon himself to drive all of the fish out of the harbour. Films such as *Orca*, where nature not only is hostile to such forces but also overpowers them, unsettle our secure sense of ownership over the land.

In keeping with nature's unsettling power, *Orca*'s characters have ambivalent claims to ownership or belonging in the space of Newfoundland. Frye and Atwood's reading of Canadian culture's relationship with the landscape is informed by environmental determinism, a concept that Cynthia Sugars contends is also very influential in cultural production in Newfoundland. She argues that "the traditional rhetoric of Newfoundland identity has invoked a seemingly constitutive interconnection between people and the land, making people elementally *of* the land, rather than mere inhabitants upon it" (Sugars 2010, 9). The characters of *Orca* have no sense of inheritance to this version of identity and have an ambivalent connection to the province's natural environment.

Nolan and his crew are from Ireland and end up in Newfoundland because its economic prospects would allow him to settle the cost of his boat. Based on her accent, Bedford seems to be from England and works for an American university, and Umilak mentions vaguely that he is from "up north" (presumably Labrador). After Nolan kills the whale's mate, members of the local fisherman's union (the only actual residents of the community featured in the film) tell him that he has violated an unwritten law of the sea they have known for generations. When he finally tries to flee town, they block him from doing so, refusing to give his crew gasoline for any purpose other than going out to sea and facing down the whale.

In keeping with these tensions between insiders and outsiders, *Orca* features a conflict between several different forms of knowledge. Nolan brings to Newfoundland a kind of generic knowledge of the sea and of fishing, but seems to know little about local customs, especially the very important one dictating that people should leave the whales alone for fear of retribution. As a result, he throws the system of the local fishery, something that has been developed over hundreds of years, into chaos. While many horror films feature doctors or scientists who go too far with their experiments or unleash unexpectedly horrific chemicals or diseases into the world, the terrifying events of *Orca* come to pass because Nolan oversteps the established rules of the fishery.

The inhabitants of the town know the patterns of the fish and the whales and reprimand Nolan because of his ignorance. Bedford knows the behaviour of the whales and the science of the fishery intimately but seems alienated from the community at large and in fact identifies most with Nolan, despite seeing him as an enemy. Umilak tells Nolan that Bedford knows that the whale has decided to take revenge on him and that the whales have intimate bonds between them "because of the university," while he knows all of these things "because of his ancestors." He goes on to say that "it is known that [the whales] have great memories" and that he will not rest until the human who has harmed his family has paid for his transgressions.

While the rest of the town curiously mocks Nolan for being too afraid to confront the whale, Umilak takes his fears seriously. He says that he knows that Nolan is not scared of the whale itself but is instead terrified that he has angered a spirit that is acting through the whale. Umilak tells him that if this had happened to his ancestors, they would have had a shaman sew a small skin whale and stuff it with the livers of birds, then throw it into the sea after saying some prayers, and if they did everything properly, they would drive the angry spirit away. When Nolan asks Umilak to do that for him, he tells him that the world has changed and "even our gods dance to a different song," implying that the advent of European modern civilization in Newfoundland has upset some kind of balance and thrown the relationship between even the original inhabitants of the land and the environment into chaos.

Umilak's statement gently points to what Sugars calls the possible haunting of the colonial past (Sugars 2006, 693): it confronts the audience with the idea that invasion, settlement, and the colonial project are both unsavoury elements of history and ongoing processes. For contemporary critics working on post-colonial haunting in Canadian cultural production, the "spectral presence" of North America's indigenous population is jarring to audiences who would prefer to deny the continent's colonial history and throws the bounded and unified notion of the Canadian state into question.[3] Umilak suggests that the absence of an indigenous culture in the community and the spread of European civilization have allowed the actions of the whale to take place. As Marlene Goldman and Joanne Saul argue, Frye and Atwood's "take on Canadian monsters depended on and was a response to seeing the land as empty, silent, seemingly unpeopled, and yet, perhaps paradoxically, threatening" (Goldman and Saul 2006, 647). However, the terror of *Orca* comes partially from the aftermath of colonization, the confused actions of outsiders such as Nolan, the marginalization of Umilak and his culture, and the ambivalent relationship between the white characters of the film and the land, rather than the hostile forces of nature.

The Contradictory Space of Newfoundland

Orca also accesses a complex set of anxieties surrounding the depiction of space in Canadian culture. Newfoundland emerges in *Orca* as a space that outsiders fight over, where people from outside of the community argue about local customs and traditions, and where people accuse each other of being "from away." Newfoundland appears as a kind of floating signifier on which people project their own fears and desires. In engaging these tensions surrounding the space of Newfoundland, *Orca* constructs the province itself as a liminal space.

In her article "Framing the Local: Canadian Film Policy and the Problem of Place," Zoë Druick (2006) suggests that the physical setting of Canada occupies an ambiguous space in North American film production. She notes that even though editorialists and cultural nationalists complain that Canadians consume too many American films and risk losing a sense of their own identity as a result, Canadians do encounter their own country on film much more often than one might expect. While Canadian productions fill the shelves of the foreign film sections of video stores (to the extent they are even there), Canadian settings serve as the backdrop for numerous important Hollywood films, with, for example, Montreal often standing in for New York and Vancouver often standing in for Los Angeles. Druick points out that there is a contradiction inherent in this: Canadian settings are responsible for at once being aesthetically pleasing as well as non-distinct enough that they can easily pose as "more important" locations. In this way, Canadian cities and landscapes are "at once visible and invisible" in mainstream films (2006, 85). She notes that Canadians have a knee-jerk reaction to this situation in which they favour initiatives that depict the uniqueness of Canada's cities and landscapes. However, they claim to reject the influence of North American consumer culture and its penchant for making the country an exploited and homogeneous wasteland, while still going out in droves to see these films. For Druick, accepting and embracing the idea that the experience of place in Canada exists in a kind of liminal space or borderland is more productive than decrying the lack of "distinct" representations of the country on film.

Building on the work of postmodern human geographers such as Doreen Massey, Druick contends that contemporary film reveals a deeper sense of anxiety that Canadians have about their connection to place in general and the relationship between Canada and the United States specifically.[4] The uncanny feeling of seeing Canadian cities and landscapes stand in for American ones challenges the notion that there is a strict distinction between the two countries and suggests that the two cultures and the two land masses are more similar than we might like to admit. Thus, even though it was marketed towards an American audience, *Orca*'s contradictory and elusive portrayal of Newfoundland might be even scarier for viewers in Canada – especially for those who like the safety of clear distinctions between Canada and the United States. In depicting Newfoundland as a kind of liminal space between North America and Europe, constructing characters who traverse the United States and Canada easily and stripping characters of any kind of attachment to place, *Orca* unsettles conventional readings of the Canadian landscape.

Orca reminds us that the straightforward experience of place that theorists such as Frye and Atwood seemed to assume and the premodern connection to the land Mowat went to Newfoundland to find is untenable even in a local setting as supposedly unique and unchanging as Petty Harbour. *Orca* positions Newfoundland as a liminal space that defies viewers' expectations and dislocates their geographical understanding of the country. Newfoundland in many ways occupies a complex space in Canada and North America: its political history gives it a series of ties to the UK that the rest of the country largely has discarded, and by virtue of its ports, Newfoundland has close ties with cities in the US and throughout Europe.

The landscape of *Orca* is at once distinctive and generic: the picturesque fishing village of Petty Harbour provides a unique backdrop for the action, but the film takes place almost completely on the waters of the North Atlantic. Aside from a few establishing shots of the town, the film's setting is ambiguous. On the surface, *Orca* displays no sense of the political or cultural context of Newfoundland, and the province seems to serve as a vaguely exotic, somewhat dangerous, and mildly romantic place that is just far enough away from the United States to be interesting. In keeping with this, references to places are vague in the film, and the final battle takes place in a non-specific northern location. Characters mention Newfoundland only in passing and only a couple of times in the film, most notably when Bedford admits that she is starting to find Nolan somewhat attractive and attributes this to having spent too much time in Newfoundland.

Unlike characters in other standard outsider narratives of Newfoundland, Nolan does not come to the island for restoration or because he is interested in the people who live there (Chafe 2009, 97); he has no romantic attachment to the island and sees it only as a place suitable for harvesting raw materials. Nolan and the other principal character in the film, Bedford, seem completely uninterested in the residents of the island and are obsessed only with the whales. Rather than a distinct place, Newfoundland appears in *Orca* as a liminal and generic space designed to be somewhat exotic and a plausible setting for a deadly battle between a vengeful whale and a group of people with unclear cultural backgrounds and no attachment to the local community. Aside from the establishing shots, the landscape of *Orca* is stripped of all natural scenery, landmarks, or any conventional markers of Canadian or regional identity.

Conclusion

Although *Orca* was an American production, the film brings together a host of Canadian cultural anxieties and seems, on the surface, to correspond particularly well with Northrop Frye's description of the terror of the soul caused by the deep fear of nature that resonates throughout the country's artistic production. However, the film is perhaps unexpectedly ambivalent in its construction of the relationship between human society and the natural environment: like other eco-horror films, *Orca* exploits a series of boundary transgressions, calling into question the distinction between human and animal, modern and primitive, insider and outsider, and, finally, distinctions between representations of Canada and other countries, especially the United States. The characters of *Orca* populate a liminal space stripped of conventional markers of spatial identity where they have no connection to the local community or landscape. Although critics chided the film for its derivative plot, unconvincing action sequences, and poor acting performances, *Orca* does a good job of reminding us that essentialist readings of the terrifying Canadian landscape and nostalgic accounts of the pre-modern setting of Newfoundland fail to tell the whole story.

NOTES

1 See, for example, Mackey (2000).
2 When I visited St John's in 2003, a tour guide took me to see Petty Harbour because it was the setting for *Orca* and other films. There is still a bed and breakfast called the Orca Inn in the village.
3 See, for example, Kertzer (1998), Sugars and Turcotte (2009), and Edwards (2005).
4 See, for example, Massey (1994) and Cresswell (2004).

PART FIVE

Horror by Any Other Name: Animation and the Avant-Garde

9 A Song from the Heart Beats the Devil Every Time: The Fear of Selling Out in Nelvana's *The Devil and Daniel Mouse* and *Rock and Rule*

KIER-LA JANISSE

Expressions of our national fears and anxieties on screen are not limited to Cronenberg, tax-shelter slashers, and *Ginger Snaps*. In other words: "And now for something completely different." Indeed, many filmmakers working in alternative forms, such as animation and experimental films, have also chosen as their preferred topics the nightmarish visions that haunt our polite and orderly collective unconscious. The title of this chapter is taken from Nelvana's *The Devil and Daniel Mouse* (1974, Clive A. Smith), a rock-infused supernatural animation whose preoccupations would later be elaborated upon in Nelvana's first feature film, *Rock and Rule* (1983, Clive A. Smith). *The Devil and Daniel Mouse* and *Rock and Rule* are two strange and fantastical works of resistance against the "American cultural imperialism" that Andrea Subissati scrutinizes in an earlier section of this book. This chapter is devoted to these two films as a means of examining how the three artists who founded Nelvana in 1971 – Michael Hirsch, Clive A. Smith, and Patrick Loubert – emerged from the radicalism of the 1960s with the goal of making intelligent children's animated films informed by their mutual interest in underground filmmaking, alternative pop culture, and anti-establishmentarianism. The three shared a unique aesthetic and artistic sensibility that made Nelvana internationally renowned as a dynamic and progressive complement to the animation being produced by the National Film Board of Canada. But, like many independent artists faced with their first taste of recognition, they had ambiguous feelings concerning their steady immersion into the mainstream. A fear of being hegemonized and artistically neutered by the lure of commercial success made its way into the narratives of *The Devil and Daniel Mouse* and *Rock and Rule* – both of which feature singers whose souls – or more specifically, whose *voices* – are sold or sacrificed to the devil.

Ohmtown Power Plant, sometime in the distant future: A young, barely clad woman chained to a crucifix-like contraption on a gigantic stage is forced by a megalomaniacal rock star to sing an ethereal tune that summons a psychedelic beast from another dimension. As the beast gets larger and closer, transfiguring from one horrifying shape to another, the rock star revels in cosmic chaos while the woman struggles to get free from her sacrificial position. When she is suddenly liberated by intervening parties, including her boyfriend/musical partner, she stands alone and vulnerable before the beast, determined to sing it back to where it came from. But her voice is not enough. The hall echoes with her plaintive lyrics, and the demon's tendrils close in on her, sparking her partner to join her in song. Together, they summon a power stronger than that of the demon and send it, along with the power-hungry rock star, tumbling back into the fiery portal from which it came.

This climactic scene from *Rock and Rule* would stand as the central symbolic image of an independent animation company that struggled with the pressures and demands of an industry that was about to undergo a corporate renaissance after some fallow years – with their help. "One of my goals was to produce animated films of a quality and integrity that was fast disappearing," says Clive Smith, "and at the time Disney seemed no longer to be in the business. Animation at the time was a lost cause and no-one really knew what to do with it."[1] In Canada, the industry in the 1960s and 1970s relied on service deals, meaning that animation projects were farmed out, often by American companies looking for a cheap talent pool. Canadian companies writing, directing, and animating their own original projects were not the norm, outside of the NFB, which produced at most a few short films per year (and did not rely on earned revenue to sustain itself). But Nelvana sought to change that. Says Clive Smith: "Another goal was the belief that we would always be able to write and produce the films we wanted to, original stories or otherwise, with the enthusiastic talent pool we were nurturing and building, without the necessity of having to service the rest of the industry. How could we fail? Clearly it was naive and idealist."[2] This idealism would play out in the narratives of both *Rock and Rule* and its earlier counterpart, *The Devil and Daniel Mouse*.

When *Rock and Rule* first went into pre-production in Toronto in 1979, anticipation was high. This would be Nelvana's first feature film after a string of successful television specials, a veritable dream project, and aside from a talented pool of budding local animators, the project attracted veteran Canadian animators who had previously left to work abroad, such as Chuck Gammage and Robin Budd, the latter a Nelvana alumnus from *The Devil and Daniel Mouse*. "It was the greatest collection of Canadian animators to work in a single studio since Al Guest produced *Rocket Robin Hood*," said Karen Mazurkewich (1999, 109) in her book *Cartoon Capers*. It was hoped that *Rock and Rule* would put original, independent Canadian animation on the map and open the floodgates for the legion of emerging Canadian animators to do some important, lasting work in the field. There was a lot at stake with *Rock and Rule*, financially, culturally, and psychologically.

The film opens with a square-up explaining its post-apocalyptic setting many years in the future, after an unnamed war has wiped out the earth's human population and left behind a hybrid mutant race of anthropomorphized dogs, cats, and rats (known as "Drats"). The Drats seek refuge from the urban crime and starvation of the gloomy metropolis in seedy nightclubs and concert halls where music provides the most ample means of emotional escape. In one of these clubs, Mylar's, run by the obnoxious zoot-suited mouse of the same name, Omar, Angel, Dizzy, and Stretch are about to go on stage. Backstage drama erupts between alternate lead singers Omar and Angel – who are also a loosely defined couple – over whose song will be performed as the evening's final number.

Meanwhile, the reclusive but ubiquitously influential rock star Mok is trawling the dark, dystopian streets of Ohmtown in his elongated future-car, searching for a "very special voice" that will unleash a demonic being from another realm. Mok stumbles upon Mylar's, and as he sits enshrouded in shadows watching Angel sing her signature tune (voiced by Debbie Harry and written/performed by Blondie) his magic ring begins to strobe, signalling that he's finally found what he's looking for. Thus begins a series of dark misadventures that will see Mok – the very personification of the alternately seductive and decrepit nature of American corporate greed – kidnap Angel and whisk her way to the chaotic conurbation of Nuke York, manipulate and drug her friends, and employ any means to isolate and turn them against each other. His plan is to set up a massive concert at Nuke York's Carnegie Hall, where Angel's voice will unleash the beast that will grant him unheard-of destructive powers.

The themes that dominate the film – selling one's soul to cultural hegemons, the ability to recognize one's true allies and to work together to bolster one's chances of defeating corruptive forces – are greatly intertwined with the Nelvana story itself and, by extension, that of the Canadian independent artist in general.

In the late 1960s, Michael Hirsch was already working in a mixture of animation and experimental filmmaking as a student at York University in Toronto. While making a film called *The Assassination Generation* with fellow student Jack Christie, the two met Patrick Loubert, who assisted them with their next project, an art film called *Voulez-vous coucher avec God?* which used split-screen cell animation, pixellation, and claymation. Hirsch and Loubert became campus pranksters, staging multimedia events, performances, and poetry readings, and eventually gained employment at the Toronto offices of Cineplast, a US-based animation company that was doing service work for the then-nascent *Sesame Street*. Disillusioned with subcontract work, Hirsch, Loubert, Christie and fellow filmmaker Peter Dewdney embarked on their own company, christened Laff Arts, which Hirsch described as "an anarchic artist co-op,"[3] friendly with the likes of Toronto's General Idea, a collective which was also known for conceptual media art projects.

They eventually met recent British import Clive Smith when they were looking for a hand with graphic design work. Smith was a young but experienced animator, having worked on *Yellow Submarine* (1968, George Dunning) before being recruited to join the team at Al Guest Animation – then Canada's biggest animation studio – to work on *Rocket Robin Hood*. When Al Guest Animation folded in 1969, Smith found himself increasingly in the orbit of the Laff Arts circle, and after some reconfiguring the seed for Nelvana was planted. "I ended up providing the graphics and worked with them while continuing to service other clients from advertising agencies and networks," says Smith. "They, of course, couldn't pay me, but we continued to develop projects together and at some point realized that we were a good fit, and the three of us founded Nelvana together."[4]

In the immediate period leading up to the founding of Nelvana, Loubert and Hirsch had written and produced a television special for the CBC on Second World War–era Canadian comic books, having recently inherited a substantial collection, along with original art, photo negatives, and printing plates, and took their name from the titular heroine of the Canadian comic *Nelvana of the Northern Lights*. One of the new company's first official collaborations was the mounting of a touring exhibit of the original artwork in conjunction with the National Art Gallery, accompanied by a book called *The Great Canadian Comic Books* (1971), written by Loubert and Hirsch with Smith providing the design and illustrations. But their real interest was filmmaking, and before long, the trio was able to start selling original short films to the CBC as filler between programs.

The Nelvana team did not set out to be an animation studio specifically, but saw a niche and an opportunity in the form of the talent pool emerging from Sheridan College's budding animation department (where Clive Smith was on the advisory board), with which they combined their own knack for animation and keen business sense. "We certainly thought that we could do something slightly different with the animation medium," says Loubert, "perhaps more story, updated music, and fresh designs certainly influenced by 60s graphics. One of the advantages we had was the fact we were too dumb to quit (as one of our early financial advisers put it). We were in a small market (Canada) and therefore had to find themes that would resonate internationally (very Canadian eh?). It was, as you can imagine, an uphill slog."[5]

A Cosmic Christmas (1977) would be the first in a series of holiday-themed half-hour animated television specials, and its success on the international market – the film was sold around the world and syndicated across the US, achieving one of the highest ratings for any syndicated show up to that time (Stoffman 2002, 33) – caught the attention of George Lucas, who hired Nelvana to animate a pivotal sequence in *The Star Wars Holiday Special* (1978), which saw the introduction of the character of Boba Fett. Lucas would be a continuing collaborator in the Nelvana story, and his influence would be a major factor in establishing Nelvana's first partnerships with US networks, something that few Canadian companies had attempted successfully.

While *A Cosmic Christmas* openly spelled out Nelvana's admonitions about the dangers of commercialism, it was *The Devil and Daniel Mouse* that would really put the screws to the establishment with its biting satire of the music industry (both were written by the late Ken Sobol, a mainstay of children's programming at the time). Adapted from a short story by Stephan Benet and based on the classic folk tale *The Devil and Daniel Webster* (and by extension, *Faust*), Nelvana's Halloween-season TV special told the story of Dan and Jan, a folk-singing duo hard up for an audience and on the verge of starvation after being fired from the nightclub where they work. Jan is then offered the opportunity of a lifetime: a deal with the Devil (known here as B.L. Zebub, agent to the stars) that will shoot her to the top of the charts overnight – as a solo act. She leaves Dan in the dust with barely a second thought as she is embraced on the world stage in her new incarnation as Funky Jan, supported by her B.L.-appointed backup band, The Animal Kingdom. But when B.L. comes to claim her soul, Dan comes to Jan's defence in an impromptu mock trial that pits him against the Devil. "This story was conceived during the late 70s," explains Michael Hirsch, "and the news was rife with how music artists had been ripped off as young talent in their teens and spent much of their life trying to get back their assets that they had signed away, just like Jan Mouse."[6]

Like *A Cosmic Christmas* before it, *The Devil and Daniel Mouse* had an indelible stylistic stamp that distinguished it from other animated work of the time. The anthropomorphized animals clearly marked the show as children's programming, but their clothes, their milieu, and, most importantly, their beatnik/hippie lexicon ("like wow, that's heavy") and vocal delivery betrayed an obvious counterculture sensibility. In many ways, these early specials were more family-friendly access points for issues that would predominate in Ralph Bakshi's 1970s-era animated work, such as *Fritz the Cat* (1972), *Coonskin* (1975) and *Heavy Traffic* (1973), as well as his later *American Pop* (1981) – street culture, pop music, cosmic "happenings," self-destructive behaviour – and Nelvana's animation style was somewhere between the grotesque caricatures of Bakshi's universe and the "rockin' sleuths" of Hanna Barbera. Pop culturally, *The Devil and Daniel Mouse* is very much a timepiece: in addition to outmoded expressions and the distinctly '70s pop music of Funky Jan and the Animal Kingdom, the story also shows the shift away from the stripped-down essentials of troubadour-style music – which had gained renewed import in the folk revival of the 1960s – to highly produced, studio-driven commercial music that was canned and exported, with the musicians themselves often distanced from both the fans and the process. Whereas the folk revival prized intimacy, in the 1970s everything became larger than life.

Abandoning her folk background, Jan dons a series of costumes, musical styles, and personas in her rise to the top, all meant to emphasize the shallow, fad-oriented culture that fuelled the star-making music machine. The Animal Kingdom are session players with no personal tie to her; they work for her employer and are quick to abandon her when B.L. gives the command ("Sorry Jan, the union man says you didn't pay your dues"). This conveys a great mistrust of the corporate side of music production, but also brings to light the film's concern with loyalty; Jan left Dan behind to pursue rock stardom at the expense of their friendship and songwriting partnership, and Dan routinely tries to reconnect, only to be told that she's "too busy" to talk to him. But when she is abandoned in turn by her new friends, who have already forgotten her as the clock ticks closer to midnight and her dues to B.L. are about to be collected, it is Dan who encourages her to summon that old folk-music fighting spirit (folk music being intrinsically tied to protest and roots) to defend her soul against the dandy-suited Devil. There is a collaborative spirit here as well – when they sing together (as Angel and Omar would in the later *Rock and Rule*), they win over the B.L.-appointed judge and jury.

In the pre-production stages of *The Devil and Daniel Mouse* (as depicted in the making-of featurette that screened on television at the time and later appeared as an extra on the *Rock and Rule* DVD from Unearthed Films), the Nelvana team conferred about the closing song – the one that will have such undeniable power so as to woo even those vengeful spirits sitting on the rigged jury. Clive Smith asserts that it should be "their own song – the one that got them fired at the beginning." This statement is very telling; first, it places power and value on originality. Second, it reinforces the sentiment that if you stick to your beliefs, people will learn to appreciate that originality. For kids – especially Canadian kids who are brought up to covet and imitate everything American – these were invaluable life lessons. "I think the naivety and the clean moral code in *The Devil and Daniel Mouse* was very Canadian," admits Hirsch. "The characters of Dan and Jan were inspired by Ian and Sylvia, although *The Devil and Daniel Mouse* is not their story. We had worked with Sylvia [Tyson], who did the songs for *A Cosmic Christmas*."[7]

In the world of *The Devil and Daniel Mouse*, originality was necessary to true success, and sometimes being original involved a great risk – losing audiences, losing jobs, losing faith in oneself. At the film's opening, Dan and Jan are at risk of becoming culturally irrelevant. "Nobody wants your kind of music anymore!" barks the tactless club owner, and when Dan goes to pawn his guitar for grocery money, he is confronted with hundreds of other guitars representing the broken dreams of all the musicians who have traversed that same desolate path to the pawnshop before him. Dan and Jan's music may be out of fashion in a world ruled by flash and sarcasm, but believing in oneself can be incredibly powerful and persuasive on its own, an idea that runs through the story and also helped fuel Nelvana in its early, lean years. "It's all about being real and honest," says Smith of the message of *The Devil and Daniel Mouse*. "They totally believed in themselves and pushed ahead with an idea regardless of what others thought or of any negative consequences. The three of us [at Nelvana] were warned on more than one occasion that we were wasting our time building an animation studio, and that there was no future in animation."[8] There is also a great deal to be said about such faith in the lyrics to John Sebastian's opening/closing song for the film, "Look Where the Music Can Take You," and when Daniel Mouse leaps to his feet to exclaim, "I say that music can save your soul – and a song from the heart beats the Devil every time!" B.L. knows he means business.

As a means of emphasizing the sometimes dark motives of mysterious benefactors such as B.L. Zebub, the character design was appropriately horrific when the story called for it. While the roly-poly Devil could take on a cherubic persona when he wanted to win over a naive target such as Jan, his temper was quick to flare if things deviated from plan or schedule, and it was in these moments that many young audiences got their first real taste of terror. It is largely because of this character design – B.L.'s long, spindly fingers and black flaming head turning 360 degrees, *Exorcist*-style – that *The Devil and Daniel Mouse* can fit somewhat comfortably into the horror canon. "We were learning from the Disney model, and using it as our inspiration," says Hirsch of the highly stylized villains that would dominate both *The Devil and Daniel Mouse* and *Rock and Rule*. "Villains in the classic Disney movies, like the Evil Queen in *Snow White* and Cruella DeVille were awesome, and inspired us to go full out with B.L. The first sound mix that we played for our US distributor of *The Devil and Daniel Mouse* went further, and accentuated the horror aspects. We used a lot of tricks picked up from *The Exorcist* – like the sound of bees – and actually had to pull back to make the sound less scary for the audience.[9]

This kind of demonic characterization was essential to creating an arena in which the purity of the Canadian "soul" could emerge triumphant in a battle of wits and wills against corrupt American cultural imperialism. While later CanCon films such as John Fasano's *Rock n Roll Nightmare* (1987) and Bruce McDonald's *Highway 61* (1991) also explore the connections between music, morality, and the selling of souls in ways that interconnect with the Nelvana films' preoccupations (*Highway 61*'s iconic devil Mr Skin in particular, played by Earl Pastko, is a fitting physical successor to *Rock and Rule*'s grotesquely emaciated Mok), the Canadian horror film character that most closely prefigures *Rock and Rule*'s megalomaniacal antagonist is likely Hammer stalwart Christopher Lee as the title character in T.Y. Drake's *The Keeper* (1976).

But in many ways, both *The Devil and Daniel Mouse* and *Rock and Rule* most directly recall Brian DePalma's equally underappreciated *Phantom of the Paradise* (1974), although the latter was purportedly not a direct influence on either of the Nelvana offerings under discussion here. On the surface, *Phantom* is a glittery reinterpretation of both the tale of *Faust* and Oscar Wilde's *The Picture of Dorian Gray* (1891), with diminutive showman Paul Williams playing Swan, the omnipotent, soulless rock impresario who is looking for the perfect voice and music with which to open his new pop palace, The Paradise. Like the character of Swan in *Phantom*, *Rock and Rule*'s Mok has a superficial glamour that only thinly veils the decay underneath; he is an aging rock star who seeks to exist vicariously through others and to live forever through his continued exploitation of their talent (supporting Loubert's belief that "thematically I think that more than 'the times' it was about 'time'").[10]

All three of these films stand as particularly apt chronicles of 1970s excess; but while *Phantom* was wholly ahead of its time, critical of its own context before anyone else clued in that there was something seriously wrong with the decade's fixation on instant gratification (as well as prefiguring today's obsession with reality television), the long production schedule of *Rock and Rule* in particular – nearly four years – ensured that its cultural references would be dated even before its release. Most notably, pulsing avant-rock from Patricia Cullen, Lou Reed, Iggy Pop, and Blondie was posited next to the power pop of Cheap Trick and the disco stylings of Earth, Wind & Fire; with disco having gone out of fashion by the time *Rock and Rule* finally emerged on limited screens in 1983, this unfortunately made Earth, Wind & Fire the most obvious odd men out on the soundtrack. "The music in both shows reflect what we were listening to and liked at the time," offers Patrick Loubert, adding that "we did not all appreciate the same artists."[11]

However, the production of the soundtrack also acted as a parallel for the emphasis on partnership that operated as one of the film's major themes as well as providing insight into what went on behind the scenes in a larger sense. In both *The Devil and Daniel Mouse* and *Rock and Rule*, the monster is brought down by the sound of two people singing together. For *Rock and Rule*'s climactic song, Clive Smith had Blondie, Cheap Trick, and Patricia Cullen each record the song separately, and with an elaborate mix of multiple tracks, they were able to create a version of the song that popped with a collaborative spirit that was convincing in its ability to overcome *Rock and Rule*'s dark forces. "Getting Deborah Harry and Chris Stein – the music and voice of Angel – to perform in a duet with Robin Zander and Cheap Trick performing Omar – when both parties were in different cities and never saw each other once during the entire production – was a feat of old technology and sheer determination," offers Smith. "Add to that the third component, Trish Cullen's score which also had to be integrated into the finale, and it was definitely a challenge."[12] But the results were tangibly affecting: as with *The Devil and Daniel Mouse*, *Rock and Rule* showed that there was an undeniable power in teamwork.

For a company that started out with three visionaries – each with unique skills that made them a formidable whole – this seems like an apt message to impart (consciously or otherwise) through their films. But with *Rock and Rule* being such an epic production, it meant more cooks in the kitchen, and Loubert, Smith, and Hirsch welcomed input from the whole team with sometimes conflicting results that would affect the cohesiveness of the finished film. "We were following the Disney model," explains Hirsch, "to give everyone a chance to comment on the work in progress. This technique did not work for us on *Rock and Rule*, and we dropped it afterwards."[13] Clive Smith elaborates:

> We started pre-production of *Rock and Rule* with no more than an idea and some character profiles, and proceeded with a very organic approach, developing the characters and story ideas in parallel. We had a writing team and a design team feeding off each other with story ideas coming from characters and characters developing with the needs of the story. We had acting classes for the animators to help them understand their characters and we had frequent roundtables where we would tell the story to each other as it developed. Was this crazy or what? Well, yes and no. It was an attempt to have a totally collaborative and democratic studio, and indeed we all benefited from each other's input and consequently explored avenues that one would probably not have done otherwise. But the process was way too idealistic for the realities of production. It was fun and creative but ultimately hurt the production in terms of our budget and delivery commitments.[14]

To add to this, while in production, the success of Gerald Potterton's *Heavy Metal* (1981), which Nelvana was invited to participate in and had to pass on due to their commitments on *Rock and Rule*, as well as the ill-fated advice of some Hollywood producers, created doubts as to whether the under-tens were the best target audience for the film. The result was that juvenile pratfall humour and the silly vocal delivery of Mok's henchmen, the Schlepper brothers, sat uncomfortably alongside existential horror, terrifying creature design, drug use, and shameless close-ups of barely covered female body parts. There was a great deal in *Rock and Rule* that would be deemed wholly unsuitable for children. "*Rock and Rule* missed its target audience," Hirsch laments, "Not tough enough for teen audiences and too tough for the kids."[15]

The film's difficult categorization made it quick to fall through the promotional cracks when United Artists – who was meant to distribute the film in the US – was bought by MGM and its original champions on the UA staff were replaced by executives with little interest in the property. Smith and animator Frank Nissen were left to do grassroots promotion on their own, with discouraging results. "To say I was disappointed with the 'release" of *Rock and Rule* would be an understatement,' says Smith.

> I was devastated. Before its release I spent weeks touring universities and television stations alone or with Frank Nissen promoting the film and discussing the process, to say nothing of the almost four years of production. When the film failed to attract an audience, for whatever reason – and there are a number of them – I retired to Nantucket for a month to lick my wounds and race lobsters across the kitchen floor to the cooking pot. It was as if all our bravado and optimism for the film industry was drastically misguided.[16]

The financial failure of *Rock and Rule* resulted in the sale of 25 per cent of the company's shares and an inevitable dramatic shift in their approach to filmmaking.

While years earlier they had made the decision to build their reputation on original programs, shunning many service-deal opportunities that had come their way, the debts incurred by *Rock and Rule* – a loss of over a million dollars – left them no other choice but to take on service deals as a means of survival. Nelvana went from being anti-establishment to becoming slaves to the establishment almost overnight; that was the gamble they took by risking it all to have their collective voice heard with proprietary projects like *Rock and Rule*. But unlike the characters in their films, they didn't win the bet, and for a short time, they became the session players in that Animal Kingdom known as mainstream television, during a mostly conservative and artistically bankrupt era. "After *Rock and Rule* we had the choice of going bankrupt because we owed millions, or working our way out of debt," asserts Hirsch. "The three of us got together and decided on the latter path."[17] The decision was an emotionally loaded one for Smith.

> What to do ... how to face up to the distinct probability of not recouping our losses? We had a couple of options; close the studio and say goodbye to all the amazing talent we had nurtured, putting dozens of families out

of work, as well as folding up the business the three of us had worked so hard to establish ... or find a way to keep our doors open while we got back on our feet. Then Michael brought in the opportunity of producing *The Care Bears Movie*, purely as a service job, which made me absolutely cringe. But it was a better option than bankruptcy. Little did I realize at the time that this was to be a major turning point for the studio, and in fact, we would never look back to days of thinking of ourselves as an independent studio able to produce original films simply because we believed in them. Yes, a dream was dying and we were waking up to the realities of the "market."[18]

Their service work on projects such as *Twenty Minute Workout* (a sixty-five-episode fitness series), *Inspector Gadget*, the *Strawberry Shortcake* cartoon, and – most successfully – *The Care Bears Movie* (1985, Arna Selznick) saw Nelvana bounce back from veritable bankruptcy to pay off *Rock and Rule*'s substantial debts in under two years. Other than a few hiccups along the way, over time Nelvana steadily climbed the ranks of the animation superpowers to become one of the most successful animation studios in history.

But if anything can be gleaned from the early films of Nelvana, it is that success comes at a price. In *The Devil and Daniel Mouse* the villain is none other than the Devil himself, but Mok in *Rock and Rule* – however demonic in his grotesque character design – was once a regular person, disfigured by success and megalomania, who is spiritually bereft even after achieving the highest level of commercial triumph. Having attained everything, he now seeks only mass destruction. Canadians – specifically those within the arts community – are very suspicious of commercial success. Financial self-sustainability is seen as the result of an Americanized aggressiveness and greed that are not viewed as compatible with artistic integrity. The morality of Nelvana's own early films bolsters these suspicions. As such, these cautionary rock-operatic horror tales for kids reflected a larger Canadian fear of being silenced by US-dominated corporate interests. So what to make of the fact that Nelvana went on to be one of the most successful animation studios of all time, while never leaving its home base of Toronto, Canada? If financial success equals selling out, did Nelvana sell their soul for *Rock and Rule*?

The service deals – what Hirsch refers to as "the dark years" (Stoffman 2002, 50) – do not mark the end of Nelvana's creative cachet. Angel and Jan had their detours as well, and no one thought less of Daniel

Mouse when he sold his guitar to buy groceries because he and Jan were starving. Eventually he got that guitar back, and like Woody Guthrie's guitar decades before, with that immortal sticker declaring "This machine kills fascists," Dan used that guitar to beat the Devil. There is a reason that in both of these films everything returns to the beginning. The song that wins is the song they knew all along, and where the story ends is where it began. At the end of *Rock and Rule*, when Mok stages his giant concert, a power outage at Carnegie Hall forces him to return with Angel to Ohmtown's power plant, the only location with the electric capacity to fuel his elaborate setup. Back where they started, and having learned a few things along the way, Angel and her friends have the resolve and the know-how to kill the beast. The same can be said for the heroes of *The Devil and Daniel Mouse*. "Both Jan and Dan mature considerably during the course of the story," Smith points out. "Jan learns that friendship and loyalty are more important than fame and fortune, and Dan learns not to be such a pussy and to be more considerate of Jan's needs. They are both much stronger at the end, and each of their strengths supports the other. And yes, of course it's magic! Isn't everything?"[19]

As Smith himself has observed, Nelvana would never quite get back to the point of being a fledgling company made up of three dreamers, but after a few years of artistically uninspiring service deals – one hundred hours in 1983 alone – they were again at the point where they could call the shots, being able to find that middle ground between sustainability and fulfilment that proves so elusive to many Canadian artists. "You have to understand what the dream *was*," Hirsch asserts. "By the time of *A Cosmic Christmas*, the dream was the creation of a successful animation studio in Toronto. Even in the early seventies when we operated out of a flat with a 16mm camera over a toilet bowl as our animation stand, we referred to our facility as "the studio." The dream was not about a single movie, but the building of an institution, and the reorganization of our company after *Rock and Rule* left us more focused and disciplined to succeed, and we did succeed, beyond anyone's wildest dreams.[20] So a final question to Clive Smith: *Do you still believe that a song from the heart beats the Devil every time?* "Unfortunately not," admits Smith. "The Devil is a tricky bloke and comes in all sorts of flavours, but if we sing loudly enough, choose our lyrics well and have a sixty-piece orchestra behind us, we can give him a good run for his money."[21]

NOTES

1 Clive Smith, personal correspondence with author, 11 September 2011.
2 Ibid.
3 Michael Hirsch, personal correspondence with author, 9 October 2011.
4 Clive Smith, personal correspondence with author, 11 September 2011.
5 Patrick Loubert, personal correspondence with author, 13 October 2011.
6 Michael Hirsch, personal correspondence with author, 8 October 2011.
7 Ibid.
8 Clive Smith, personal correspondence with author, 11 September 2011.
9 Michael Hirsch, personal correspondence with author, 8 October 2011.
10 Patrick Loubert, personal correspondence with author, 13 October 2011.
11 Ibid.
12 Clive Smith, personal correspondence with author, 11 September 2011.
13 Michael Hirsch, personal correspondence with author, 8 October 2011.
14 Clive Smith, personal correspondence with author, 11 September 2011.
15 Michael Hirsch, personal correspondence with author, 8 October 2011.
16 Clive Smith, personal correspondence with author, 11 September 2011.
17 Michael Hirsch, personal correspondence with author, 8 October 2011.
18 Clive Smith, personal correspondence with author, 11 September 2011.
19 Ibid.
20 Michael Hirsch, personal correspondence with author, 10 October 2011.
21 Clive Smith, personal correspondence with author, 11 September 2011.

10 Where Is Fear? Space, Place, and the Sense of Horror in the Canadian Avant-Garde Film

SCOTT BIRDWISE

Terror has, besides its ordinary forms, the shape of a tadpole; it burgeons, bulges, quivers, disappears. Anger is not merely rant and rhetoric, red faces and clenched fists. It is perhaps a black line wriggling upon a white sheet.

Virginia Woolf, "The Cinema" (1996, 35)

Increasingly angered by the Web's banalization of suffering, I decided to fashion a compilation film, using only material from the Web that would return to the degraded images I found there the full dignity of their horror.

R. Bruce Elder on *Crack, Brutal Grief* [1]

This chapter considers the role of horror in Canadian avant-garde film. As such, it approaches horror, and so "horror (in) film," from a somewhat different perspective than horror in mainstream narrative film. Although one of the films under consideration here, *Crack, Brutal Grief* (R. Bruce Elder, 2000), uses appropriated clips from conventional narrative horror films among its image and sound sources, it does not, as the avant-garde is often purported to do, use them to effect an ironic distance, thus reinstating a kind of class distinction between the discourses of art film, broadly put, or counter-cinema and the pleasures of popular film. If anything, as I will show, *Crack, Brutal Grief* in fact accentuates the truly horrifying aspects of its source material. The two films I will discuss here, Elder's aforementioned *Crack, Brutal Grief* and Jack Chambers's *The Hart of London* (1968–70), are both exemplary Canadian avant-garde films. The seventy-nine-minute *The Hart of London*, for instance, is a crucial, pioneering experiment in cinematic perception, a kind of phenomenological study of London, Ontario, as a site of unending struggle between forces of civilization and nature, where, as Elder writes of the film, "the violence of self, nature and community interlock" and "images of community and nature have the dual characteristic of supporting our sense of identity as well as threatening it" (Elder 1984, 273–4).

It is through an encounter with horror (the indefinite, and the confrontation it provokes with our border consciousness), with horror *as* encounter, that Canadians of varying backgrounds and identities brush up against, and potentially question, the limits of their own "normality" in what Gail McGregor calls "border anxiety," where "space" threatens to engulf or annihilate "place."[2] My reading of Canadian avant-garde films thus intersects, to some extent, with Peter Thompson's interpretation of *Orca* as an experiment in "boundary transgressions, calling into question the distinction between human and animal" (page 186, this volume). In the experience of boundary transgression, the animal's "otherness," and the "otherness" of the wilderness (the wilderness of the landscape as well as the wilderness of other people), returns as sense or sensation in media form – an anxious form that challenges narrative and colonial circumscriptions of place. In this way, Canadian avant-garde film is both connected to and critical of a tradition of Canadian thought associated with such figures as Northrop Frye that returns again and again to the role of the wilderness in the Canadian imagination.[3]

The Hart of London and *Crack, Brutal Grief*, I contend, embody an encounter with horror and the productive anxiety it responds to and provokes not simply as narrative or special effect, but as a kind of *sense* or sensation, as a way to reopen the self (and by extension broader ideas and practices of the community) to the Other. I use "sense" or sensation here in the manner that Davide Panagia (2009, 12) uses it in his *The Political Life of Sensation*, wherein sensation challenges and interrupts narrative's reigning "regime of perception," and in the way Jean-Luc Nancy (1997, 9) figures it as "the element in which signification, interpretations and representation can occur." Sense is that which exceeds and undermines all definition; at the same time, however, it is also the source of definition and its effect: it is sense (as materiality and force) that is a condition of things "making sense." In this way, sense is linked to what I consider here as the Canadian avant-garde film's "sensible" (i.e., aesthetic, material, medial) challenge to normalized, colonized "common sense." It is perhaps useful, then, to think of sense itself as a kind of landscape or stage: a space of potential action and meaning where a self and a place can emerge and be "sensed," as well as challenged, in turn.

In *A Border Within: National Identity, Cultural Plurality, and Wilderness*, Ian Angus (1997) thinks through the relationship between erecting boundaries, creating a sense of place, and imaging the role of the wilderness as the groundless background of representation in the Canadian imaginary. He endorses a "deep questioning of the fundamental polarity" between civilization and wilderness that informs Canadian cultural expression (1997, 129). Canadian avant-garde films participate in such a "deep questioning" through a concern with uncovering our repressed colonial violence linked to the "civilizing" of the landscape and the technological forgetting of the body in the establishment of ideas and practices of place. As the dominated landscape returns as the terror of the wilderness, the repressed materiality and unruliness of the body assert themselves against normative and essentialist definitions of self: both the landscape and the body call into question nationalist ontologies of identity and place as well as epistemologies of narrative and technological mastery. That said, the challenge *The Hart of London* and *Crack, Brutal Grief* pose to the boundaries of normality can be usefully analysed through elements taken from the prism of the horror film.

The Return of the Repressed

The two Canadian avant-garde films considered here share with the horror film an emphasis on sensation and link this sensation to an experience of horror, a sensation of space not occluded by the security, the assumed enclosure, of place.[4] These films also share something else: a concern with mediation and its relation to identity and violence. Various scholars have noted how, due to its generally perceived regressive and sensationalist tendencies, that is, its "B-movie" status, the horror film is not only able to take up subject matter (challenging political, social, and sexual issues, for example) that other films cannot touch or only allude to; it can also challenge established hierarchical distinctions of taste. Moreover, it has been noted that the horror film often responds to and/or reflects anxieties over changes in society. As Ian Conrich (2010) puts it, "The horror film has been seen to peak at times of war, and during periods of economic, political, and moral exigency" (3). And though he rightly cautions that a strictly reflectionist understanding of the horror film can be potentially misleading, presumably due to the complicated relationship between the sheer maintenance and evolution of the conventions of genre and the demands of the market among other factors, he nonetheless maintains that "horror films in particular can act as effective cultural and social barometers" (3). The horror film is thus positioned to stake its claim as either politically and socially "progressive" or "reactionary" in the way it takes up the "return of the repressed" material of society, as Robin Wood (1979) put it in his seminal co-edited work on the horror film, *The American Nightmare*.[5] That is, the horror film can be examined for how it not only reflects but narrativizes and symbolically imagines – generically appropriates in a narrative structure, in other words – the raw, repressed material of popular social anxiety.

Linked to the concept of repression is the figure of "the Other": the Other is not only that which is "external to the culture and the self," but also "what is repressed (but never destroyed) in the self and projected outwards in order to be hated and disowned" (Wood 1979, 9). The challenge the progressive horror film mounts to the dominant ideology is thus posed not only in subject matter but on the level of cinematic form or technique: narrative closure, for example, is resisted by the unredeemable excess of meaning in the progressive horror film. What is often pejoratively perceived to be horror's sensationalism and excessiveness – providing too much space for gore and gratuitous violence, for instance – is part of its potential political and social progressiveness. It is the very progressive power of such "sensationalism" that the Canadian avant-garde films in question tap into.

Where Is Here?

In his book, *Film in Canada*, Jim Leach (2006) employs Northrop Frye's notion of the "obliterated landscape" in his discussion of the representation of the natural environment in Canadian film. According to Leach, the natural environment of Canada was imagined as a metaphysically "obliterated landscape" by the European settlers and colonists, and continues to be conceived of in this way through the Group of Seven and beyond, because its "vastness cannot be comprehended by the human imagination" (41). The Canadian wilderness was/is imagined as an unpopulated (significantly omitting the indigenous Native population, of course), unexplored, and unmastered landscape, a mystifying and unknowable space or non-place concealed from the European (colonial) gaze and hence the epistemological power of the colonist. "At bottom," as Elder, writes, "the experience these settlers had of nature could not be described, let alone conceptualized – another reason why nature was seen as alien and unfathomable, as 'Other'" (Elder 1989, 28). The perceived (and projected) Otherness of the "obliterated landscape" of the Canadian wild generated in the settlers what Frye famously referred to in *The Bush Garden: Essays on the Canadian Imagination* as "a terror of the soul," which confounded them with the question, "Where is here?" (Frye 1971, 227).

The riddle posed by Frye in the form of a question, "Where is here?" persists in the late capitalist wilderness of Canada, as the "normality" of the naturalized Canadian/colonial imagination is "threatened" by the return of the repressed colonial encounter with the (perceived and projected) terror of the landscape (1971, 222). In the twenty-first century, when the majority of Canadians live in hyper-mediated urban environments, transformations in traditional group identities can produce new forms of social atomization. In some respects, these new modalities of isolation strangely echo the fears of isolated settler colonials bereft of the assurances of their former socio-cultural lifeworld; in some measure, technologized social isolation may perpetuate the uncanny experience of the immigrant or the exile, the refugee or the homeless, who drifts within a kind of denaturalized wilderness, where one anxiously and porously borders against the Other. Modern Canadian technological settlers, then, are perpetually exposed to the unknown, or emergent, as threat. In addition, these settlers are never entirely sure when in fact they are exposed: the "wilderness" is potentially everywhere. The threat of the wilderness as exposure leads to what Frye famously calls the "garrison mentality," where solace from the perceived external terror is sought in "communities that provide all that their members have in the way of distinctively human values" (1971, 227). Isolated groups of settlers erect fortress-type dwellings, wherein they huddle together for protection against the unforgiving climate and the alienation of the landscape. One effect of the garrison mentality is that the members of the enclosed community "stress relations with other humans and isolate [themselves] from nature and as a result nature becomes even more alien" (Elder 1989, 31). As the Canadian philosopher of nation and technology George Grant puts it, "There can be nothing immemorial for us except the environment as object. Even our cities have been encampments on the road to economic mastery" (Grant 1969, 17).

In the Canadian avant-garde film, horror as "excessive" sensation – that is, sense not contained by narrative-space; sense "monstrously" transgressing and blurring ontological and epistemological boundaries of civilization and nation – "returns" urban consumer/colonial Canadians to their repressed colonial origins – origins involving an epistemology of terror, a colonial will to mastery at once exercised and thwarted, and metaphysical/psychological isolation in space. In this return, the elements of non-generic horror correspond with the early Canadian settlers' reaction of "terror to the power of untamed nature" and the perceived inadequacy of their previously established (European) forms, genres, and conventions of representation and meaning making (Elder 1989, 25). In the contemporary world, the return of the colonial repressed testifies to what Wood refers to as "the sense of civilization condemning itself ... a negativity ... not recuperable into the dominant ideology" (Wood 1979, 22). The excessive "negativity" of the return of the repressed material challenges the dualistic view of reality in consumerism inherited from the colonial experience (e.g., civilization/nature, conscious/unconscious – what Elder terms "mental stuff" and "physical stuff"), and "progressively" opens it to an expanded, more vital "sense" of the world and one's unsettled, even unhomely, place within it (Elder 1989, 29).

The colonization of space by way of the manufacture and projection of place/civilization upon and within it in the colonial experience, itself a response to a perceived rupture between the European subject and its "natural" home, doubles the ontological rupture between consciousness (or mind) and matter (the material world, including nature). In becoming "unsettled" and exposed to what may be an at once expansive and threatening landscape, the subject can potentially realize the very necessity of an-Other in its own self-constitution; that is, the subject can consciously recognize the necessity of others in an environment, unavailable to mastery and expansion, nurturing and threatening in its (over) abundance of sense. "Where is here?" then is, among other things, a question of space and of place, an inquiry into how we transform space into (a sense of) place. Indeed, if the landscape is not only something that we move through, but something that also moves through us in our imaginations and perceptions, then the "monster" – the return of the repressed colonial experience and its violence as Other – moves through the places of culture, of civilization, and so challenges our sense of place, our dominion over (the threat of) space, by displacing it.

The Hart of London

In an essay discussing the life and work of Jack Chambers, Ross Woodman introduces Chambers's last completed film, *The Hart of London*, as "the nightmare vision of his home town that had haunted and pursued him all his life (Woodman 2002, 45). I will discuss some of the

more "horrible" aspects of Chambers's "nightmare vision" of London,
Ontario, to suggest how this vision of civilization and nature generates
a sense of spatial horror, of place attempting to define itself against
the threat of space. The opening of *The Hart of London* is a barrage of
white light, with white noise suggesting waves or wind layered over
the soundtrack, as representational photographic images of a wintry
landscape start to emerge. Elder contends that this opening passage
connotes "above all that non-existence in which consciousness has its
beginnings, that nothingness that is the ground of our being" (Elder 1984,
264–5). The passage demonstrates how individual perception "endeavours to form a stable image" and "the struggle of consciousness for a
sense of place" (267). These images of primordial consciousness coming
into being eventually lead to the establishment of "being" as "being
there" in a defined place, a city with a history carved out of the wilderness, captured, expressed, and created in a variety of photographic and
filmic images, as well as by the violence of cinematic montage.[6] Indeed,
for Stan Brakhage, the thematic concept – "the city … as walling-out the
heart, the Meat Human, all Animal finally epitomized by 'Hart' … [the]
whatever of Nothing we might know as space" – corresponds with the
aesthetic strategy of the first half of the film, involving the negation of
representational/three-dimensional space when employing found footage, for an emphasis on the flatness of the screen and the "whiting out of
any imagery … [by] a white stuffed full of represented material … which
admits no blanks other than this effect" (Brakhage 2003, 93–4).

As Bart Testa notes in his description of the powerful yet elusive opening segments of the film, where found footage of a deer being killed by the
community leads to archival and present-day (1968–70) images of London,
Chambers "makes the tragic encounter with nature serve as [the] strong
prelude to, almost the condition of, the city's film historiography" (Testa
2002, 148). The deer, one of the "h(e)arts" of London in question, although
really harmless, is effectively perceived as a kind of monster threatening
normality, intruding into the civilized and civic order of London – the
city's name itself a colonial signifier pointing towards the Empire's centre.[7]

The Hart of London depicts the imposition of abstract (meaningful)
form upon space by way of a variety of images, some found and appropriated archival footage (a plough pulled across farmland, a horse-
drawn carriage crossing city streets), some shot by Chambers's own
camera (extreme close-ups on scissors cutting branches and shears trim-
ming hedges). In a film that was black and white up to this point, the
most startling scene involving instruments of cutting is the stunning,

and suddenly in vibrant colour, stationary long-take shot of a lamb being slaughtered upon a stone altar, the anonymous butcher's knife slicing through its neck, the deep red blood flowing onto the floor. This long take is prefaced by a fragmented yet cohesive montage of extreme close-ups of a human child's organs (a crying mouth, clutching hands, wiggling toes), along with shots of butchered and mutilated cows and sheep, and leads up to Chambers's home movie footage of his child's birth. Chambers returns to black and white cinematography after the colour long take, with close-ups of a crying human baby and its genitals.

Following the crying child, Chambers provides newsreel footage of a community bonfire, with the London Fire Department standing close by. Without getting into the many complicated layers of meaning within and between these shots, involving the metaphoric and metonymic, and the intersection of the private or subjective and the public record, it will have to suffice here to note the strong emphasis Chambers places on ritual – that is, ritual as at once the exposure to violence and the mediation and formalization of violence into a tenuously meaningful communal experience. At once excessive and yet absolutely "natural" to our order of things, the conjoined tenderness and butchery of these images testify to the expanding and contracting violence of civilization: the violence which founds the social (and colonial) order that is mediated by the ritualistic killing of animals, of others – a ritual horror that founds and re-founds a sense of place in tragically, brutally consecrating a sacrificial space. Chambers presents this ritual of violence, its "brutal kind of monstrosity" as Testa puts it, as the process of consciousness and perception taking shape, in which birth and death, violence and community, civilization and nature, are not simply dualistically opposed, but intertwined (Testa 2002, 167).

If there is a centre to *The Hart of London*, the heart of the film so to speak, it would be the scene in which the lamb is slaughtered. As stated above, this scene presents the overt spectacle of the controlled violence of civilization taking into itself the excessive "monster" and normalizing it by destroying it. The slaughter of the lamb takes place on an altar as a ritualized action: it is staged in an artificial – that is, closed-in and constructed – space. Framed and staged by Chambers's stationary camera as a kind of theatrical spectacle, the slaughter scene possesses both centripetal and centrifugal force. If the slaughter is indeed the centre of the film, it is charged with a structurally centripetal power that draws meanings from the other parts of the film into itself in a concentrated form and then releases and links them to the other half of the film. The centripetal power of the scene, moreover, is linked to its overt theatricality: the use of the stationary long take in the artificial environment generates a sense of enclosure, akin to the experience of being in a theatre. The theatrical experience suggests the centripetal drawing-together of community – as well as of consciousness – into a unified, collective experience. At the same time, however, the scene has the centrifugal power of the return of the repressed: it exposes the real violence of civilization that parallels the perceived violence of the wilderness. This centrifugal power threatens to displace enclosure by way of the exposure of, and to, abject violence in the non-place of the slaughterhouse.[8] The implication is that the place of civilization, of the self, is also a space of horror.

The framing as well as the vivid colour of the slaughter of the lamb scene, surely the most painterly image in *The Hart of London*, recalls Gilles Deleuze's description of the work of Francis Bacon in *The Logic of Sensation*. Bacon's paintings, which share a number of similarities with Chambers's "nightmare vision" of isolation and exposure, often turn on the depiction of violence in a circumscribed space, framed by and within a suggested shape like a circle or a square – a kind of geometrical grid for configuring the metamorphosis and activity of the body in a place (very often a kind of hybrid man-animal body, the "becoming animal" of man, in Deleuze's terms). These "places," as Deleuze puts it, "render sensible a kind of progression, an exploration of the Figure within the place, or upon itself. It is an operative field. The relation of the Figure to its isolating place defines a 'fact': 'the fact is …,' 'what takes place is …' Thus isolated, the Figure becomes an Image, an Icon" (Deleuze 2003, 5–6). In *The Hart of London*, the lamb's slaughter upon what appears to be a stone table – the table here acting as a kind of altar, as Elder notes, upon and against which the convulsions of the lamb can take place, be seen, and be measured – comes to take on the power of the "fact" in the establishment of place in space. The slaughter, taking its place in a lineage of images of sacrifice going back to the early depictions of Christ's crucifixion, is indeed iconic: it is not only the most "realistic" or "stable" image in the film – an image clearly depicting a "fact" of the world by way of photographic likeness – but, just as it establishes photographic fact, it symbolically brings consciousness up against death and violence into what Testa, quoting Frye, refers to as a "total metaphor" (Testa 2002, 168). The "total metaphor" is, however, in its very "totality" and abstraction, also ever-exposed to the threat of non-meaning in the resistance to symbolization of brute, monstrous materiality: in a word, meat (I will return to this).

The delineated and then annihilated figure in the enclosure of the slaughterhouse exposes what McGregor diagnoses as the "overflowing" presence of "boxed experience" in Canadian art that continually generates "anxiety" about the "integrity and meaning of these enclosures" (McGregor 2003, 8). In a certain sense, the sacrifice is a metaphor for the return of the repressed colonial violence, which still remains and threatens to overflow, in establishing Canada as a place in the wilderness of space. The slaughter – the union of consciousness, photographic fact, and the violent destruction of the sacrificial body – is a metaphor for the "monster" that is the entwined violence of civilization and nature exposed. Even more to the point, the metaphor of violence is achieved through violence (and the symbolic violence of metaphor): the metaphor brings together and achieves meaning, in a totality, by cutting and isolating, by violation. The slaughter as metaphor brings together as it rips apart. Furthermore, placed inside the stationary frame, the fact of the destruction of the animal figure upon the isolation of the altar – recalling what Frye refers to as "civilization conquering the landscape and imposing an alien and abstract pattern on it" (Frye 1971, 248) – is linked to the "monster" metaphor as a kind of sign or warning to the viewer. It is an icon of the violence of turning the world into art – something to be gazed upon at a distance; something brought into proximity and held at bay by way of the frame and the establishment of fact. At the same time, however, it is through the iconic activity of art that civilization comes to know the world, the landscape, and its place in it; the instruments of butchery, then, are also tools of care.

When Deleuze writes of Bacon as a painter who "pities the meat," one again thinks of Chambers (who himself was a famous painter) and the slaughter of the lamb in *The Hart of London*. Deleuze writes: "Meat is the common zone of man and the beast, their zone of indiscernibility; it is a 'fact,' a state where the painter identifies with the objects of his horror and his compassion. The painter is certainly a butcher, but he goes to the butcher shop as if it were a church, with the meat as the crucified victim" (Deleuze 2003, 21–2). The iconic tragedy of the slaughter in *The Hart of London* brings to consciousness – in the reverberation of photographic likeness, fact, and perception – the revelation that the monster, the lamb as both wild nature serving as humanity's meat *and* the icon of the innocent victim, is really as much inside civilization as outside it, and that humanity is as bloody and brutal as nature is perceived to be. The scene of slaughter, Irene Bindi writes, is "the picture of violence that [London/ civilization] needs to grasp its own horror" (Bindi 2008, 3). This horror is both the ground of and the threat to civilization and consciousness.

In laying bare the very real violence of civilization and the generation/management of horror at its centre Chambers also exposes the remains of violence, the leftovers of ritual that make up the meat. After the slaughter, and immediately following the communal bonfire, Chambers cuts to a series of colour images of entrails, apparently sheep intestines, and aborted fetuses, human and animal. Interspersed with these images are shots of children in a family swimming pool learning how to swim and, closing the sequence, men, presumably miners, emerging from a hole in the ground. Obviously, after the "total metaphor" of the slaughtered lamb, we are again confronted with the entwined forces of life and death, creation and destruction. What I am interested in here is how these images of entrails (insides) exposed to the outside, to vision, manifest the sovereign power of civilization to impose itself on life, to cut into and manipulate matter and the natural forms of the body. This imposition is both a material practice and, as we saw with the slaughter of the lamb, a meaning-making activity (making culture, metaphors, ritual, etc.). That said, the very activity of cutting, isolating, and imposing in the activity of meaning making generates not only the more overtly functional objectification of life that is meat, but also the remainder of meaning (and meat) that is tenuously categorized as waste.

The unborn (and thus, in a sense, undead or "never was" and "never will be") but nonetheless brought-out-into-the-world (into obscene being) fetuses, for example, are a very real, that is, material, manifestation of the repulsive horror of civilized violence. These meat-waste things, these leftovers of metaphor (metaphorical leftovers) and remainders of use-value, present, in the words of philosopher Emmanuel Levinas, the "death of death," the "il y a" (the "there is"). The "there is" is the recognition of the sheer weight of being, a kind of ontological-existential experience of horror. Levinas explains this horror as inducing a kind of "nausea" in the subject: "In nausea ... we are ... riveted to ourselves, enclosed in a tight circle that smothers. We are there, and there is nothing to be done ... this is the very experience of pure being ... As such, nausea discovers only the nakedness of being in its plenitude and in its utterly binding presence" (Levinas 2003, 66–7). The establishment of a supposedly meaningful place, London in this instance, in the perceived non-being of the space of wilderness, creates the even more meaningless presence of waste, the sheer material presence of a bloody object, in the "tight circle" of the enclosed place of being. Anything is possible in the enclosed, garrison-like place of civilization, including the systematic annihilation of life, where potential lives (animal as well as human) amount to the plenitude and sickening presence, the "fact," of an obscene mass of guts on the floor. At the same time, in this space filled with nothingness at the heart of closed-in place, nothing is possible; all possibility, as opening, as welcoming to an outside, is extinguished: the ultimate "uselessness of any action" reveals that "there is nothing to be done" in the "there is" (67). Possibility and impossibility, presence and absence, thus coincide in the nausea manifested in the experience of the colonial/colonizing repressed – its brutal and useless activity, its ongoing and futile founding and re-founding violence – exposed in the landscape of leftovers (the leftovers as landscape), the veritable wastes, in *The Hart of London*.

Following the slaughter, Chambers's appropriation of the televisual footage of the Londoners engaged in various communal activities (including barrel boxing and ice swimming) continues the logic of the remainder, of remains, as he estranges the found footage from its typical function as light community entertainment and news, as unproblematic instrument of social cohesion and consensus. In the stark, revelatory (de)construction of place in *The Hart of London*, the found footage repeats the rituals of community with a difference. Among the ways the latent violence and strangeness of the community's activities are exposed in the footage is in the absence of language, of commentary: for instance, the footage is uninhabited by the Voice of God narration so common to the documentary and the nightly news; in its place, the recurrent and meditative sound of water ominously rushing by – a reminder, among other things, of the indifference of time and its passage. In Chambers's reworking of the found footage, the communal activities and the medium(s) of their expression and dissemination are made uncanny, unhomely: following Elder's thesis that *The Hart of London* is about the struggle of consciousness to find, to locate, itself within a sense of place, it is as if the routines and signifiers of "home" and the familiar need to be denaturalized so that a more humane relation with place (and space) can begin to take shape. In other words, consciousness must pass through the anxiety and nausea of the "there is" – including the troubling realization that "there is" violence in the community and its relation to nature – and its deep questioning of civilization's (unspoken) barbarity in order to even hope to break the cycle of violence and the horror it generates and represses.

By way of a conclusion to my analysis, it is important to note the emergence of spoken language at the end of *The Hart of London*. In a kind of repetition (with a difference) of the opening passage of the film where the deer (hart) passes into the threshold of civilization as the intruding Other or monster to be ultimately destroyed by ritualized communal violence, the final passage presents civilization's crossing over into the wilderness, leading to a profoundly ambiguous warning and ethical exhortation. The passage depicts two young boys (Chambers's sons, John and Diego) at the grassy edge of a field in a park near a fence; on the opposite side of the fence two deer stand, framed by trees against the darkness, returning humanity's gaze. As the boys approach the two deer with a curiosity natural to children, what we presume to be their mother's voice (the voice of Olga Chambers) emerges from off-screen space, thus suggesting that the off-screen here is more properly place, the location of safety and civilization.

The first recognizable bit of spoken language in the film, "Be careful with your movements," and the second, again from the mother's off-screen voice, "You have to be very careful," are the closest thing to commentary in the film, the closest language comes to taking upon and into itself, to manifesting, being in relation to the landscape and to nature. Again, the mother's exhortation to her children – the singular "You" addressing the boys plural (and on another level the film viewer) – is an ambiguous warning. On the one hand, it suggests that the children must guard against the possible dangers that the deer present – after all, the deer are wild creatures, the Other to the norms of civilization. In this light, the deer represent all that the ongoing colonial experience must master and repress in the landscape. On the other hand, "You have to be very careful" is a statement of concern for the deer, an acknowledgment of humanity's propensity for its own terrible and incalculable violence. As Elder puts it, "References to the violence of humans and the violence of nature are thus condensed in this ambiguous exhortation" (Elder 1984, 273).

It is crucial to further note, however, that the realization of humanity's and nature's violence takes the ultimate form of a statement, of human language voiced and repeated multiple times before the camera pans up to the sky and the sound of what could be wind or possibly even car engines (traffic) takes over the soundtrack.[9] Indeed, the final sentence, "You have to be very careful," seems to be sampled so as to repeat in the film's soundtrack. What may have been first recorded as a singular statement by the human voice is in the final version of the film sampled and repeated: it is effectively dislocated from its original source by way of the repetitions generated by the manipulation of recording technology. If the voice is dislocated in technological sampling and repetition, it is also relocated through ritual. The voice-statement is effectively technologically ritualized in/as its repetitions: it is repeated because it is a kind of ritual statement; it is ritualized because it is repeated. "You have to be very careful" is not only a statement testifying to humanity's and to nature's (potential) violence; it is also an expression of the ritualized and technologized (automatized) inhabitation/domination of space by way of the maintenance and care of place.

The Hart of London communicates that it is through language and through technology, with an emphasis placed on their potential for violence and for care in ritual and repetition, that the horror of space is necessarily intertwined with a sense of place. That it is a repeating voice technologically manipulated and dislocated, hovering at the threshold of civilization and the wilderness, that helps us to care and to sense this horror, is itself a kind of warning sign and a testament to Chambers's powerful and disturbing insight into our predicament.

Crack, Brutal Grief

In a footnote to an essay on Stan Brakhage's "Faust Series" of films, R. Bruce Elder writes of an exchange he had with the late filmmaker regarding his (Elder's) worries over what he thought to be the excessive "tawdriness" of his film, *Crack, Brutal Grief*. Remarking that "Brakhage took an interest in the tension between (a sort of) visual squalor and formal richness" in his own work, Elder notes how, upon viewing *Crack, Brutal Grief*, Brakhage "allowed that its images were 'grubby,' but likened it to Jack Chambers's *The Hart of London* ... which he described as 'grubby' and yet a masterwork" (Elder 2005, 65–6). Indeed, although a distance of thirty years separates it from *The Hart of London* – and its treatment of the multitudinous and saturated internet images of degrading violence, torture, and sex may appear to deal with different subject matter and formal questions – Elder's *Crack, Brutal Grief* extends Chambers's "grubby" meditation on community and (the nature of) repressed violence, and the latent violence of (human) nature, for a world evermore driven by destructive technological mastery and metaphysical solipsism, a world where humanity has effectively abdicated its responsibility to be "very careful."

Created in response to a close friend's recent (and terribly violent) suicide, the film, in the first instance, serves as Elder's testament to loss.[10] Following this logic, however, Elder's work continues Chambers's meditation on place as it challenges the mediatized and technologized cultural systems of (pseudo-)community and communication that colonize the abstracted and alienated body embedded in such technocratic systems. Like *The Hart of London*, *Crack, Brutal Grief* charges into the relationship between images and community: where Chambers uses archival images of community (a community bound together in its images) to reimagine the city of London's history and identity, Elder uses appropriated images culled only from the internet – and this from a set of internet searches based on a limited number of words (according to avant-garde film scholar Brett Kashmere, the search terms were "suicide" and "power saw" – see Kashmere 2004, 36–9).

Akin to Chambers's "making strange" of archival (tele-)visual footage of the city of London and its communal activities, Elder "denaturalizes" found internet and media images to expose their wild and often formless sense (the film's images are indeed "grubby" – he photographically rubs against the digital images and makes us feel their texture; in this sense, he is concerned with the image's body). Elder's evisceration of the image is also an attack on the narratives – and stereotypes – that the degraded and reified representational images support. In Kashmere's words, "the film is a phantasmagoria of human brutality and debauchery … Hardcore pornography and pictures of physical mutilation and degradation are combined with chaste erotic images and other pieces of sensational early cinema, documentary footage from pre-war Germany, passages from Leni Riefenstahl's films, and various pop culture detritus to fashion an unrelenting vision of a fallen world" (2004, 36).

Crack, Brutal Grief reveals the violent nature and placelessness of the Web's hyper-mediated and fetishized imagescape – he finds, in a word, the Web's spatial horror (physical, metaphysical, psychological, emotional) and uses it to resensitize us to our bodies; for it is in our bodies, or what Elder has called "the flesh," that being and being-with (with others, within the environment, the world) is first and lastly experienced. According to Elder, the flesh is the expression of relation between beings: "Flesh is one; all flesh is the same flesh – it is made one through the reciprocity of sense, that is, through an utterly anonymous and therefore common sensibility inhabiting all humanity" (Elder 2003, 476–7).

Language is important here, of course, but language itself implicates the body just as the body implicates language. Following Elder's writings, one can argue that in this impoverished world with a culture in decline and a so-called natural environment in peril, part of the trouble humanity has found itself in is linked to its active forgetting of the body; not the fetishized and commodified body of the culture industry or dogmatic religion, but the beautiful and terrible mortal body, the living body and its share of horror. This living body is a body bound to other bodies, other beings in a shared experience, in a world, a living environment. I contend that it is part of Elder's concern in *Crack, Brutal Grief* to return us to a sense not only of our bodies, then, but of our bodies (and their meanings, their implications) in relation to other bodies – bodies of flesh and meaning as well as of image, for it is also through and by the image, an experience of the image, that this return can take place.[11] To return to the language of Wood, the return to the body in the flesh can also be figured as the (re)turn to "the Other," to that which was previously imagined as "external to the culture and the self" and "is repressed (but never destroyed) in the self and projected outwards in order to be hated and disowned" (Wood 1979, 9). The flesh thus draws into itself space – the space between inside and outside; the space of the image as projection of self (into space) and the image as Other – to draw beings together into a shared (sense of) place, or, to follow Elder, a shared medium, a "coming-to-be" together (Elder 2003, 478).

Re(ve)lation is, or at least can be, charged with horror, for it is through horror that the body and the being of the Other, in relation, can be sensed. In the limited room that remains, I explore some of the ways in which *Crack, Brutal Grief*, as Elder puts it, "return[s] to the degraded images [he] found [on the internet] the full dignity of their horror."[12] This entails an aggressive attack on the body in the image and the image's body, an uncovering of the intensities of the image, that is, the (e)merging forces of sensation prior to, and beyond, conventions of narrative space and figuration. Tearing the image apart and away from the apparently homely constraints of narrative and/or figurative representation in the Web, and rubbing it against its digital and analogue grain, it is the return of the repressed flesh that returns "dignity" to the image. As Elder has stated in an unpublished piece written to accompany the film, "We must use every extreme means for restoring our connection to our bodies … We must intensify the image" (Kashmere 2004, 36). Elder's call to "intensify the image" is, in a sense, akin to the ethical exhortation in *The Hart of London*: "You have to be very careful." Both statements call for a deep engagement with how we (en)frame the body and experience, and a concern with the violence of this enframing in a given situation, a given space become place. In *Crack, Brutal Grief*, Elder posits internet space as a kind of violent enframing of the body – a body rendered as so many bits standing ready for consumption in the formalized violence of internet space – that the cinematic medium must then deform and "(re)place" with its own counter-violence and intensity. Elder thus eviscerates the image; and in doing so, he gives life back to the experience of it.

In *Crack, Brutal Grief*, previously representational-figurative images (often of fetishized brutal violence ready-made for consumption) become a tactile landscape, a space to genuinely encounter the Other. In this way, Elder draws on a power in/through the image that exceeds cultural, social, and even national boundaries. The flesh, the body he appeals to, is perhaps immanent in the landscape itself: it is the body exposed to the deterritorialization of place/space. This may be its horror relative to the closed techno-rational coordinates of state: a return of the repressed colonial violence turned against itself, against the state. The immanent and violent sharing of the flesh, then, is an affront to the placement of identity and the colonization of being in the techno-apparatuses of capital. Charged by the Other-as-space, the body-image displaced from narrative and figuration thus becomes the "displaced place" of being.

A key touchstone for Elder's caustic attack on the image is the work of the French situationist Guy Debord. Not only is Debord's practice of détournement – a critical artistic intervention whereby popular representational images are reapproriated and turned against themselves as new means for revolutionary ends – a relevant precursor to Elder's own reworking/deformation of reified internet images, but he includes a direct reference to a specific film by Debord in a circling line of text in the centre of the frame that spirals around itself throughout the duration of the film.[13] The line of text reads: "In girum imus nocte et consumimur igni" – a Latin palindrome, which by the film's conclusion is translated (still in spiralling text) as "At night we go down into the gyre and are consumed by fire." The Latin palindrome is also the title of a filmic work of détournement by Debord from 1978. In this film, in a vitriolic voice-over that comments on various images from the twentieth century, Debord registers his disgust with what he deems the contemporary "society of the spectacle," to recall his 1967 book of the same name. Spiralling in upon itself and cryptically transcribing being's nauseously circling journey through the night, burning (expending energy, losing form), the palindrome's structure is itself a kind of unending path to Hell.

Crack, Brutal Grief is, really, Elder's own hellish condemnation of the technologized rituals of the "society of the spectacle." The palindrome's Hell, its night that recalls Levinas's "there is" in the closed-place (or total space) of self-fulfilling/self-nullifying plenitude, presents the horror of repetition by way of repetition. It is a circle, swallowing itself as it repeats itself: a visual metaphor for what Elder sees as the real despair of the internet's closed space of representation. Considered alongside Elder's deformation of the degraded internet images, however, the palindrome suggests the possibility of looking again – a re-seeing of otherwise taken-for-granted images brought about by the (eternal) return of the repressed. In this way, the palindrome of *Crack, Brutal Grief* recalls the disembodied and repeating voice that brings *The Hart of London* to its conclusion, "You have to be very careful," as it returns to the scene of the crime (the encounter with the hart) again and again and again (which in turn brings to mind, in a kind of perverse echo-return, the repetitive audio sample towards the end of *Crack, Brutal Grief* which viciously hisses in a glitchy robotic voice: "We attack without mercy … without mercy … We attack without mercy"). The crime is the division of space into place and the repression of the violence it took to do so. In *Crack, Brutal Grief* the return to the primal scene of the crime is also an intensification of the (appropriated) technological image, an intensification of image-violence intended to return us to our horror: the horror of the return to the place of our bodies in space. The return to the body is also the possibility of the Other: the potential horror linked to the unannounced arrival of someone or something, some unknown and unpredicted sense, in the world. In *Crack, Brutal Grief* it is the intensification of the image and the revelation of its violence – the revelation of its repressed violence by way of a tactile "attack without mercy" on the representational image – that can lead to a more concerned and "careful" being in the world.

Conclusion

In our contemporary technological landscape, mediated by the ubiquitous presence of social media that both screen reality and introduce a host of new forms of uncanny presence, perhaps the avant-garde, in ways different from more necessarily narrative-centred models of social intelligibility, has much to show (and tell) us about Canada and the various fears that populate it. It is precisely the realization/generation of horror as a condition of "opening" to the Other in a shared environment or landscape, however violent and unknowable, thereby involving the Other and the self in a continuously redefined and reopened community of sense, that makes *The Hart of London* and *Crack, Brutal Grief* such powerful cinematic experiences. If, as Jean-Luc Nancy contends, every image is implicated in one form of violence or another, that "perhaps every image borders on cruelty," it comes down to discerning what kind of violence the image participates in and/or testifies to. If every image, as place, "borders" on a "puddle" in space, then perhaps it is a matter of finding and founding the image that does not repress this violence but bears witness to it in its own operations, its own violations and erections of boundaries (Nancy 2005, 25). Perhaps horror is a sign/affect/condition of this opening to the Other: like Virgina Woolf's "black line wriggling upon a white sheet," it is the return of the repressed space that informs and deforms our sense of place, what Angus refers to as "this refusal to be captured [that] may be called 'wilderness'" (Angus 1997, 208). Following Angus, the projected horror of the wilderness "may also be 'our own' to the extent that we participate in a unity that we do not control, but for which we must take responsibility" (208).[14] Again, perhaps Canadians do not control their fear – or rather, what we fear – but in acknowledging our horror, and in perhaps experiencing a certain "unity we do not control" through a sense of it, thus encountering an-Other that exceeds and undoes our own projections in "refusing to be captured," we can begin to assume responsibility for it.[15]

NOTES

My thanks go the editors of this anthology for their valuable feedback. I would also like to thank Lauren Howes, Larissa Fan, and Eva Kolcze of the Canadian Filmmakers Distribution Centre for their generous help in arranging for screenings of work; Michael Zryd for suggesting *Crack, Brutal Grief* as a film suitable for my discussion; and Matthew Croombs who encouraged me in extended conversations on film theory.

1 R. Bruce Elder, artist's description of the film on the Canadian Filmmakers Distribution Centre website, http://www.cfmdc.org/node/1671.
2 For McGregor's discussion of Canadian "border anxiety" and the ways it can close the community in upon itself in the face of Otherness (especially that of the wilderness) while also holding out the possibility of rethinking the boundaries of the closed community, see McGregor (2003).
3 For an excellent introduction to the role of the landscape in Canadian avant-garde film see Testa (1989).

4 As such, the two avant-garde films discussed here have much in common with what Linda Williams calls "body genres," namely the horror film, pornography, and melodrama. See Williams (1991).

5 See Wood (1979). Of course, as is clear from the collection's title, Wood's theory was intended to specifically address the *American* horror film, in the 1970s in particular. When transposing Wood's theory to consider how the return of the repressed takes cinematic form in Canadian film, we should acknowledge a number of important aspects related to the particular national context. One obvious thing to acknowledge is the sheer overwhelming influence of the US culture industry (among other industries) in Canada. Specific to cinema, a key point of difference between the American and Canadian national contexts turns on the role of genre in the Canadian national imaginary.

6 Following the authors discussed, I use "being" and "being there" in terms broadly taken from Martin Heidegger.

7 The consciousness looking for a place to simultaneously emerge and settle with the material world is dislocated from its imperial origins; it is in an-Other zone, a foreign territory. As the film suggests in its elliptical palimpsest of images, the establishment of "place" – emblematized in a camera pan over a sign stating "Welcome to London" – involves the violent imposition and establishment of a "civilizing violence" on "space."

8 Furthermore, in the violence of human culture and industry that establishes place (London) there is also the risk of its spilling over and displacing it; that the sense of civilization can be overcome by a deeper, overflowing sense of space, the element in which representation can take place.

9 It should be noted that there may, in fact, be another statement uttered by Olga Chambers, the boys' mother: "He's going for you." I cannot confirm this at the time of this essay's writing, however, so I will follow the established position that the film's concluding statement is "You have to be very careful." Needless to say, the statement "He's going for you" only adds further intimations of violence and ambiguity to the proceedings.

10 The final credits of the film include the following: "In Memoriam: James D. Smith."

11 A concern with the relationship between image and body in relation to language is taken up in Elder's compelling, and somewhat infamous, essay "The Cinema We Need," in Douglas Fetherling, ed., *Documents in Canadian Film* (Peterborough, ON: Broadview Press, 1988), in which he calls for an experimental, non-narrative Canadian national cinema.

12 R. Bruce Elder, artist's description of the film on the Canadian Filmmakers Distribution Centre website.

13 The spiralling text in the centre of the frame, whose letters appear to shift and replace each other, is sometimes joined by a text that scrolls along the bottom of the frame. The scrolling text is very difficult to follow, but it sometimes appears to describe and/or comment on the obscene images.

14 Future work on the "sense of horror" in Canadian avant-garde film/video could focus on more specific regional practices and articulations, more specifically spatialized and resolutely "placed" senses of horror. Attention could of course be given to such well-known artists as Michael Snow, Joyce Wieland, David Rimmer, and Al Razutis, for example; but it could also be devoted to a range of more recent artists, from Mike Hoolboom, Philip Hoffman, Louise Bourque, and Deirdre Logue to a younger generation including Jason Britski, Solomon Nagler, Christina Battle, Amanda Dawn Christie, Chris Kennedy, and Jubal Brown, for example.

15 The question of assuming responsibility implies rethinking more than just "place" relative to "space"; it also means rethinking temporality. The Canadian thinker Harold Innis's "plea for time" is of relevance here. For a useful introduction to his thought in relation to the broader "Canadian discourse on technology" see Kroker (1984).

PART SIX

Blood, Guts, and Beyond:
An Homage to Cronenberg

11 Traces of Horror: The Later Films of David Cronenberg

WILLIAM BEARD

It might appear strange that this final section of *The Canadian Horror Film*, devoted exclusively to the Canadian "baron of blood," should open with a reflection on Cronenberg's *non-horror* films. But as I will show below, while films such as *Eastern Promises* (2007) and *A Dangerous Method* (2011) seem very far removed from the early gory preoccupations of *Shivers* (1975) and *The Brood* (1978), Cronenberg has been nothing but obsessively consistent in his exploration of the human body and its murky relationship to the human soul. After making *The Fly* in 1986, at the pinnacle of his commercial success, David Cronenberg virtually abandoned the horror film as a form. It is almost literally true to say that before 1987 he made nothing but horror movies,[1] and after 1987 he made no horror movies at all. The director's transition from low genre cinema to high(er) non-genre cinema is a truism of critical commentary on his work.[2] His corpus grew progressively artier, a process that arguably never ceased until his re-entry into the commercial mainstream with *A History of Violence* in 2005 – artier, and less generic, less tainted by the vulgar excesses of horror cinema, even as it was striving still to be transgressive and, on some level, even shocking.

A corollary of this progress was that as Cronenberg's work removed itself from its generic commercial beginnings, it became less and less commercially successful. With the exception of *eXistenZ* (1999), each of his films between *The Fly* and *A History of Violence* – namely, *Dead Ringers* (1988), *Naked Lunch* (1991), *M. Butterfly* (1993), *Crash* (1996), and *Spider* (2002) – found itself opening in art houses rather than mainstream theatres in most places, and most of them lost money. And if Cronenberg had now succeeded in getting recognition as the artist he always wanted to be seen as, it seemed to be at the expense of an "arty" marketplace positioning that made each new production a struggle to finance. His vital and productive bargain with popular genre, so marvellous because the director never had to pay for it with any surrender of artistic originality or creative control, looked in retrospect more appealing, perhaps, than it had at the time, when Cronenberg had had to submit to the moral disgust of respectable commentators who couldn't see anything in his work but blatant "low" sensationalism.[3]

But throughout this whole metamorphosis, another process was going on, one that was by contrast a manifestation of authorial consistency, and entirely coterminous with the filmmaker's desire to be seen to occupy the role of film artist. The genre status and place in the cultural landscape of Cronenberg's work may have changed radically, but the continuance of his thematic concerns and their logically developing, almost dogged, evolution remained entirely true to itself. A critical, constitutive part of that work is the persistence of a set of affective reactions provoked by his films: a profound uneasiness; a particular blending of fascination and disgust; a probing of repressed awarenesses and anxieties about the body and sexuality; and an alarming destabilization of identity and sense of reality that began with the scientific attempt to make human sexuality more overt in *Shivers* (1975), continued through the mad hallucinatory transformations of *Videodrome* (1983), and stretched all the way to the complete undermining of perception, subjectivity, and the world itself in *eXistenZ*. From one perspective – and it is a perspective that Cronenberg himself has encouraged throughout his career – *all* the films have been fundamentally devoted to exploring these questions of subjectivity and reality construction, and however substantial the proportions of bodily mutation or diseased sexuality, the underlying issue was always a philosophical, even an existentialist, one.

Looked at this way, *Videodrome*, *The Fly*, *Naked Lunch*, *M. Butterfly*, *Crash*, and *Spider* are closely related films, repeated attempts to show men trying to recreate and understand themselves in new ways, in spite of the gross divergences between their sense of things and the world's. Obviously, the presence or absence of genre elements has no effect on the persistence of this theme – nor on the persistence of that uneasiness, that bodily and sexual destabilization that is always inseparable from existential transformation in Cronenberg (even if the level of gore and explicit sensation is higher in genre projects). The short summary: there is always, at some level, something stomach-turning about a David Cronenberg movie. And if this profound queasiness may be somehow related to horror, then it might make some kind of partial sense to call Cronenberg a filmmaker who has displaced aspects of horror out of the genre and into other kinds of cinema.

We must turn for a moment, then, to the question of what the horror genre is. There is, of course, extensive literature on this subject.[4] But there is one idea that I find particularly valuable as measuring points to determine what might be "horrific" about Cronenberg's later cinema: the idea that what is disturbing represents the incursion into the world of something that is strange and does not belong. The *locus classicus* for this idea is Sigmund Freud's essay on the uncanny, first published 1919. Near the end of this piece, he says, "the uncanny element we know from experience arises either when repressed childhood complexes are revived by some impression, or when primitive beliefs that have been *surmounted* appear to be once again confirmed" (Freud 2003, 155). He further specifies: "[If] psychoanalytic theory is correct in asserting that every affect arising from an emotional impulse – of whatever kind – is converted into fear by being repressed, it follows that among those things that are felt to be frightening there must be one group in which it can be shown that the frightening element is something that has been repressed and now returns" (146–7).

The idea (extrapolated from Freud) that the horror affect is founded in the *intrusion* into a recognizable world of something that is impossible, or felt to be impossible, is also maintained in Tzvetan Todorov's taxonomy of the fantastic in literature, wherein the fantastic is described in the following way:

> There occurs an event that cannot be explained by this same world [of the fiction] … The person who experiences the event must opt for one of two possible solutions: either he is the victim of an illusion of the senses … or else the event has really taken place … but this reality [where the event has really taken place] is controlled by laws unknown to us … The fantastic occupies the duration of this uncertainty. Once we choose one answer or the other, we leave the fantastic for a neighboring genre, the uncanny, or the marvelous (Todorov 1975, 25).

In support of this fundamental idea, Todorov also quotes Pierre-Georges Castex ("The fantastic … is characterized … by a brutal intrusion of a mystery into the context of real life"), Louis Vax ("The fantastic narrative generally describes men like ourselves, inhabiting the real world, suddenly confronted by the inexplicable"), and Roger Callois

("The fantastic is always a break in the acknowledged order, an irruption of the inadmissible within the changeless everyday legality").[5]

Looking at Cronenberg's work, we can see that these ideas may be applied not just to his actual horror films, but to all of his cinema (Grant 2000, 11–13). Todorov's *intrusion* of alien elements, and Freud's *revelation* of an alarming underlying truth that has been repressed or misrecognized – these are truly consistent elements in Cronenberg. From the sex parasites of *Shivers* to the monster Brundlefly (himself the result of an insectoid intrusion) in *The Fly*, Cronenberg's earlier horror cinema demonstrates its affiliation with the whole genre's standard models of monstrous incursion. But in Cronenberg's case, the monster not only infiltrates the body but also emanates from it. They are also firmly labelled as horror movies by the presence of generic elements of the supernatural or the fantastic – except that in Cronenberg's case these elements are often not paranormal but rather simply the extreme, "intrusive" results or by-products of scientific or medical invention. They are not exactly natural, but they are not supernatural either. Cronenberg said of his horror films on more than one occasion that it was his aim to "show the unshowable" (and Michael Grant [2000, 3–8] has extended this into a project to say the unsayable). What is outside ordinary experience, what doesn't belong or should be left unseen – these are elements as recurrent in Cronenberg's later films as in his earlier. Another aspect arises when we consider the persistent appearance in his films of mad scientists, a staple of horror since Mary Shelley's *Frankenstein*.[6] Over time, it is true, these mad scientists turn into mad artists[7] and their process of monster production becomes so rarefied that it is often difficult to recognize as belonging to the tradition; but in general there is a strong link between monstrosity and derangement in later Cronenberg films like *Dead Ringers*, *Naked Lunch*, *Crash*, and *Spider*. So, I am suggesting, it remains a useful exercise to try to determine how the queasiness of Cronenberg's later cinema relates to the overt horror-ness of his earlier works, and to do so in the terms advanced by the particular ideas in the theorization of horror that I have mentioned. I propose to do this in a film-by-film fashion.

Dead Ringers

Dead Ringers (still Cronenberg's masterpiece) is in some ways the clearest case of the director's particular way of porting horror elements, or something very akin to them, into a different kind of film. It contains no monsters, no slashers, no scares or shocks, nothing of the supernatural (it has one dream sequence) or science fiction. The fact that the protagonists, identical-twin Mantle brothers, can be thought of as biological freaks (hence monsters), that they are gynecological surgeons (hence literally slashers), and that their medical methods are original and radical (hence mad-scientist) shows that the film has links to the horror genre. But by omitting all the necessities of the genre in a literal way, *Dead Ringers* must also be classified as outside the category. Indeed, the story has its basis in a real-life incident (and subsequent book) in which twin New York gynecologists committed suicide in their apartment.[8] The film is a long way from any actual events, but that basis does signal Cronenberg's desire to turn to aspects of real experience that create a profound sense of uneasiness. He has described the reaction of Hollywood people to whom he was pitching the project: It was "too icky." Why did he have to choose gynecology as the twins' specialization? Why not some other medical area?[9] The film's insistence on pursuing exactly that path, of concentrating exactly on the most uncomfortable-making and not-to-be-thought-of intimacies of not only medical science but also female anatomy, is emphatic, and its transgression is further emphasized by the "radical" nature of the twins' practice and their special interest in abnormal female bodies. The latter obsession results in (or is the result of) their own neurotic sexuality, but it is also connected to their freakish twin subjectivity and their implied search for their own origins in the mother.[10]

Freud's essay on the uncanny provides a surprisingly functional tool for interpreting the film as well as mapping its relation to "horror." After expounding the strange etymological connection in German between *das Heimliche* (the home-like or familiar) and *das Unheimliche* (the un-homelike or uncanny), he remarks that "this uncanny element is actually nothing new or strange, but something that was long familiar to the psyche and was estranged from it only through being repressed," and quotes Friedrich Schelling's definition of the uncanny as "something that should have remained hidden and has come into the open" (Freud 2003, 148). He continues:

> It often happens that neurotic men state that to them there is something uncanny about the female genitals. But what they find uncanny ["unhomely"] is actually the entrance to man's old "home," the place where everyone once lived. A jocular saying has it that "love is a longing for home," and if someone dreams of a certain place or a certain landscape

and, while dreaming, thinks to himself, "I know this place, I've been here before," this place can be interpreted as representing his mother's genitals or her womb. Here too, then, the uncanny ["the unhomely"] is what was once familiar ["homely," "homey"] (150–1).

One of these neurotic men is Beverly Mantle, who, maddened by the potential dissolution of his own subjectivity through love for a woman and threatened separation from his brother, begins to rage at his patients ("the woman's body was *all wrong!*") and finally to produce a set of "gynecological instruments for operating on mutant women." Here we see the uneasiness, the uncanniness, of "what should have remained hidden," the fascination of a return to the mother's womb, and the horror of potential neurotic violence. Female bodies are, to this male view, mutant and uncanny, as Aristotle was already suggesting 2,300-odd years ago.[11] The presence of sexual violence and even misogyny in the horror genre is somehow linked to this perception, though Cronenberg is by far the most articulate and self-aware male practitioner in this field.

Added to all this is the fact that the Mantle twins invite reading not only as a single split subjectivity but as mutual doppelgängers – the latter famous inhabitants of Gothic and expressionist horror. The dismaying return of something that ought to be gone, or not there at all, the reflection or shadow of the self as a double, is also among Freud's primary symptoms of the uncanny.[12] Every shot of the two brothers together, every crosscut between the two of them, is uncanny in this sense, all the way to the end of the film. And their freakish and dread-inducing doubleness becomes inseparable from their very strange, forbidden, clearly perverse and sick lives and psyches – which are at the same time somehow familiar, for the film is an allegory of male split subjectivity.

Naked Lunch

Naked Lunch has a completely different profile. It has creatures and horrors galore, but since they are simple transcriptions of the hallucinations of the drug-addicted protagonist-writer, and since the film itself is a (somewhat mutated) species of artist biopic like *Tom and Viv* or *The Hours* and hence distinctively high-culture, it too won't fit into the genre. Once more, it is based on real events – in this instance, events in the life of William S. Burroughs, especially his accidental shooting of his wife and his subsequent writing of the book *Naked Lunch*. Like *Dead Ringers*, it continues what has been throughout Cronenberg's cinema, I have argued, a crucial part of his master narrative: the representation of creativity (scientific, then artistic) as a producer, and also an example, of monstrosity. *Naked Lunch* represents the most literal and explicit of all Cronenberg's films in setting forth this scenario of the modernist transgressive artist-hero whose task it is to delve into his unconscious and recover there what is fundamental and repressed. This is, of course, rather close to Freud's description of the uncanniness of just such repressed and returning psychic material.

In the case of this extended homage by Cronenberg to Burroughs, his revered master of heroic transgressive art, the notion is boiled down by Burroughs (and quoted by Cronenberg both in the film and offscreen) into the story of "the man who taught his asshole to talk."[13] In Burroughs's tale, once the man has gotten his asshole to talk, he can't get it to shut up, and eventually it seals over his mouth and does all the talking: a horror story if ever there was one. What comes out of the asshole is foul and disgusting and also infectious; and those adjectives are fair enough as descriptions of the many obscene, regurgitative, and loathing-filled passages in Burroughs's writing. For Cronenberg it is simply the process of artistic creation for transgressive artists: "It's the part of you that you don't want to listen to, that's saying things that are unspeakable, that are too basic, too true, too primordial, and too uncivilized and too tasteless, to be listened to, but are there nonetheless" (Beard 2002, 151).

All of this is Schelling's "what should have remained hidden." What returns here takes the form of giant insects and creatures hallucinated by the drug-addicted protagonist Bill Lee (and the drugs themselves are also insect by-products): monstrous beetles and bug-typewriters that talk through dorsal assholes, seven-foot boney, lizard-like "mugwumps," all of whom are projections of his own unconscious that Lee talks to and creates his art from. These creatures, unearthly monsters produced by special effects, are representationally close to the stock in trade of the horror movie. But they are clearly labelled as hallucinations, and moreover they are not really very horrifying. Rather, they are presented as bizarre manifestations of the peculiar protagonist's peculiar mind. As such they have no connection to any more general archetype that might exist in the viewer's own experience, and so very little resonance, very little of the uncanny.

The real horror in *Naked Lunch* lies not in this realm, but in the ordinary human one of Bill Lee's shooting of his wife Joan. Indeed, all of Lee's bugs and mugwumps are the expression of his unconscious desire to kill her, and then his horror at having killed her – a return of these repressed facts. In the first instance Lee is told by a talking giant crab-beetle that "your wife is an elite-corps centipede," and his imaginary adventures in "Interzone" end with an attempt at rescuing his newly imagined wife from the clutches of the monstrously evil Dr Benway, also fantasized. In the world of the (repressed and then unrepressed) homosexuality of Lee/Burroughs, women are an entirely different species from men – a line Cronenberg has been known to quote as well – and that species embodies something alien and frightening.[14] The movement of the film, though, is to advance by relentless pressure *through* these hallucinations and towards something closer to the awful guilt and sadness which the hallucinated action is attempting to displace and repress.

M. Butterfly

M. Butterfly is probably the least horror-like of all of Cronenberg's films, including his most recent ones. No creatures, no hallucinations, no violence, no special effects of any kind, not even any scientists or doctors, any gynecology, any drugs. And no sensationalism – or rather, the sensationalism is conceptual only.[15] Instead, it is a rather beautiful period picture set in 1960s China, with lovely costumes and settings, exquisite photography, and restrained performances by Jeremy Irons and a distinguished cast. Its narrative basis again lies in events in the real world. It was the case of a French diplomat, Pierre Boursicault, who lived for many years with a male transvestite performer at the Peking Opera while thinking all the while he was a woman. And yet the film is utterly true to the arc of Cronenberg's thematic evolution, in particular his growing insistence that we all invent our own realities and his continuing emphasis on transgressive sexuality as the catalyst for both the existential transformation of his heroes and their eventual monstrosification and destruction. And in the most discreet and non-demonstrative way, there is also a continuation of that *echt*-Cronenbergian queasiness, here arising from profound self-deception and the instability of reality in the sexual realm.

René Gallimard's infatuation with opera singer Song Liling is enabled by the profound secrecy and intimacy of the sexual body, the uncanny ultimate unknowableness of sexuality and sexual difference. This final frontier of bafflement is what allows the protagonist's comical, but at the same time profound and radically creative, errors about the sex of his partner. His new, liberated subjectivity ends in disaster, as all of Cronenberg's do, when the crushing blow dealt by his clear sight of Song Liling's real male body forces Gallimard into a tragic enactment of his own monstrosity, cutting his throat while grotesquely costumed as the Madame Butterfly he had idealized his lover as. The unavoidable recognition of his lover's maleness is the recovery of an unwanted and repressed truth, the revelation of "something that should have remained hidden" – and thus demonstrates an impeccable, "uncanny" lineage, despite how plainly the film as a whole fails to conform to the category of horror.

Crash

Sensationalism certainly returns in *Crash*, which in fact largely consists of kinky sex and car crashes. Its premise, that Western post-industrial society is emotionally frozen, deracinated by technology, and desperately trying without success to connect with basic animal satisfactions through ever more frantic exercises in decadent sexual perversion, is strikingly similar to that of Cronenberg's first, and arguably purest, horror movie, *Shivers*. In that film, a mad scientist tries to cure this condition by implanting writhing, self-propagating sex parasites into the bodies of his fellow apartment dwellers; in consequence the apartment building itself (a sub-Antonionian piece of off-the-rack soulless modernism) is splattered with blood and squishy creatures, and its inhabitants turned from good little bourgeois into raving wild-eyed sex maniacs. In every way, *Crash* has risen up the cultural ladder from *Shivers*'s bracing trash-genre vulgarity.[16]

Unlike the characters in *Shivers*, the transformees in *Crash* seek the liberation that is instantly created by the sudden and shocking bodily pain and destruction of being in a serious auto accident. The protagonist is jerked out of his habitual profound anomie, with its coldly unsatisfying sexual adventures, by the huge jolt of pain and the terrifying collision with mortality. And he is led to join a band of lumpenproletarian liberationist zealots headed by a charismatic preacher of existential change through car crashes, where he is joined by the widow of the man killed in "his" car crash; then he attempts to initiate his wife, too, into his homicidal/suicidal cult. Once again the literal depiction of something that could be overtly horrifying is muted. The beautiful, hyper-controlled visual style has a deep high-modernist chill; the rather shocking sexual scenes are embedded in an aura of frozen detachment. The sensationalism – of which, again, there is a lot – is desensationalized. The car-crash violence is sudden and very plain, though the one depiction of an aftermath crash scene is operatically lurid. But the real centre of queasy desire is in the damaged bodies: the gorgeous purple bruises, the forcefully punctuating black stitches, the garishly healed scars. (As Barbara Creed [2000] has remarked, in *Crash* the mutated body is present in the form of the wound.) Ballard's attempt to couple sexually with the vagina-shaped wound on the back of a female crash survivor could hardly be a clearer idea. Altogether, *Crash* insists relentlessly and with uncomfortable clarity on a bizarre but explicit connection between sex and death (and does so in a far more arcane manner than the death-of-copulating-babysitters syndrome familiar from slasher movies like *Halloween*). In yoking these two drives together, the film's depiction of transformed, psychically mutated people points a clear path to the Freudian unconscious.

Yet *Crash*'s mixture retains a stubborn detachment, a failure to excite deep psychic stimulation or resonance. It is a cure not for deep-seated repression of basic drives and desires, but for a condition of emotional numbness through technological overstimulation, and even then only for the characters, and only to a limited degree. *Crash* has violence and craziness and moral shock, but very little that is truly uncanny or unnerving, or even existentially challenging. The bourgeois characters are fundamentally unwarmed by their slumming activities. For a film whose principal action involves its central characters trying to break out of alienation and emotional coldness, *Crash* in the end decisively signals the failure of its own project. There is no true breakthrough into the realm of the deeply nauseated, no entry into the revealed underlying world that returns from somewhere primal and induces dread.

eXistenZ

eXistenZ is more strikingly futuristic than *Crash*, its Philip K. Dick–meets–Martin Heidegger scenario has a clearly fantasy or sci-fi content, and its special effects include any number of wiggling little creatures as well as plenty of blood and gore. But "horror movie" just doesn't seem like a good description of this unique film. In one sense *eXistenZ* is even more conceptual than *M. Butterfly*, because it is (among other things) an almost explicitly philosophical tract on the uncertainty and meaninglessness of life that draws heavily on existentialist ideas.[17] Using a futuristic scenario centring on immersive virtual-reality game play as a metaphor for all human life, it repeatedly demonstrates the arbitrariness and unintelligibility of human events and experience. *Everything* in the film is eventually revealed as having no verifiable objective basis whatever. But for most of the film we are given a "real" world that is strangely off-kilter and full of odd events, and then the world of the game "eXistenZ" that is increasingly much *more* off-kilter and odd.

There are tropes from Cronenberg's early horror cinema everywhere, and indeed the film can be read as a kind of self-parody. A vicious, sarcastic, even nihilistic sense of humour keeps asserting itself. The game itself is technically very advanced, but the direction of this advance is, in a fashion highly characteristic of the director, away from hardness-and-shininess and towards viscerality and organic sexuality. The game is played through a direct organic connection between a "gamepod" that looks like a mutated body part surmounted by a nipple-shaped controller and a "bioport" in the player's spine, the connection carried by an "umbycord" that looks exactly like a human umbilical cord. This is all queasy in an authentically Cronenbergian "body horror" way.

The game world evolves from a place that is low-class and grungy to one that is overtly horrifying: the Country Gas Station, where a bioport is installed with a shop-floor jackhammer, the Chinese Restaurant, where really disgusting food is served, and finally the Trout Farm, where "mutated amphibians" are gutted in a spectacularly gross slaughterhouse atmosphere and various operations are conducted on gamepods that look like unspeakable low-tech medical experiments taking place in a concentration camp. At one point the gamepod becomes horribly diseased, shrivels into an ugly grey lump, and explodes into a hideous rain of black spores. This is all imagery entirely proper to horror cinema. It is accompanied, as well, by scenes of explicit violence, where personages in the game world are messily shot or have their torsos explode. We are also reminded that science fiction is always a potential neighbour of horror because it opens the way for "impossible" things to happen. It could be said that *eXistenZ* provides us with a picture of the Heideggerian world into which we are "thrown" – that is, the existential human condition – that is at best drab and disorienting, and at worst truly as loathsome and frightening as a horror movie.

The film makes things complicated for viewers by combining this representation of the human condition, and this immersion in a physically disgusting environment, with a parallel activity of providing a commentary and satire on the world of media, computer games, and finally cinema. The game world has sex and violence, especially violence. But if in human life sex might be ultimately connected to procreation and violence to survival, in the game "eXistenZ" these sensational qualities have drifted free of any possible connection or signification and have become shallow sensation-represented-as-sensation, just as the characters themselves are entirely depthless. Questions do arise about ethical responsibilities in designing and participating in virtual realities, but again these are all conceptual rather than deeply felt. Meanwhile the existential meaninglessness of actual life has become the subordination of everything in the game world(s) to unknowable and effectively arbitrary principles of programming emanating from a place somewhere outside the world. The "body horror" of the gamepods and umbycords is certainly rooted in a fundamental queasiness about sexuality and maternal reproduction, and the gross-out excesses of, for example, the Trout Farm trigger feelings of disgust at mutated bodies and body insides that should be hidden. Tropes of disease and infection run right through the film. But the Cronenbergian horrors from which these are descended are always traceable to deep anxieties, whereas in *eXistenZ* there is nothing deep anywhere, nothing even recognizable about any of the worlds, and this free-floating horror takes on a peculiarly weightless postmodern signification. At its most lurid, the film resembles a nightmare – but it is not the viewer's nightmare at any point. In short, there is nothing much *heimlich* in this *Unheimlichkeit*.

Spider

Spider, based on a novel by Patrick McGrath, tells the story of a released mental patient and his inner attempts to come to terms with the events that made him ill and caused him, as a boy, to kill his mother under the impression she was another woman, a prostitute who had murdered his actual mother. McGrath's novel is told in the first person by its eponymous protagonist and is an ongoing immersion in hallucinatory psychic anguish, as Spider records his environment transforming from the everyday proletarian awfulness of London East End squalor into an expressionist landscape full of terror. The baked potato on his plate begins to ooze with blood; his body is inhabited by a giant worm curled in one of his lungs; his lower intestine is wrapped around his spine and is working its way through the top of his skull; he urinates black spiders into the toilet bowl; and a brazen slut from the pub has collaborated with his father to murder his dear mother and bury her body in the allotments. None but the last of these internal horror images of Spider's are present in the film, which prefers to stage his sad, awful case with restraint, and to unfold his story in a literal and objective way through a set of memories that are simply staged for the camera with his adult self-inhabiting them. Of course these "literal" and "objective" scenes are Spider's (distorted) memories and have no literal or objective status at all: but they are presented in that register. It takes viewers a good deal of time to work out what is going on in the film and in the end to piece together what has gone on in Spider's life (some never manage it).

But, in contrast to *eXistenZ*, *Spider* has at its centre a real human subject of some depth and complexity, and his experience of madness and hallu-cination can be received sympathetically. Moreover his particular insan-ity has a strongly familiar Oedipal cast, and the turmoil of childhood sexuality that is at the basis of everything may still provide a resounding chord for almost anyone. It is indeed uncanny to find the protagonist's mother, played by Miranda Richardson, suddenly replaced by a vulgar, gap-toothed invader, also played by Miranda Richardson; and uncanny to find his father full of love and concern one moment and smashing his wife over the head with a shovel the next. The fact that all of these things have been instigated by the recognition that his mother wants to please his father sexually, and then triggered by the sight of a barroom hooker baring her breast at the boy (and this woman then metamorphosing into the Miranda Richardson substitute mother), introduces a wave of queasiness whose foundation in the primitive psyche Freud would have recognized in a moment. Freud's quasi-ribald citation, quoted above, of the "jocular" phrase "love is longing for a home" (and that home is the mother's womb, or the woman's vagina) is almost literally true in *Spider*, where, from the haunting opening folk song onwards, there is a powerful current of erotic childish nostalgia directed at the mother, and the arrival of sexuality in the boy is simultaneous with a wish to possess his mother. Spider's whole mental landscape is the result of a massive repression of unacceptable truths: of his mother's sexuality, of his own hatred of her for that reason, and of the crime that he has committed. And he is himself a monster – mad and dangerous. Yet the tone of the film is predominantly one of pathos, as the boy's vulnerability and ter-rible mistaken perceptions are presented with a sorrowing detachment that is deeply moving and that finally leaves everything horrifying and uncanny behind in an atmosphere of sadness at this innocent yet mur-derous child, this spectacle of an erring human being atrociously suffer-ing, and at the same time terribly dangerous.

A History of Violence

A History of Violence is a further step – a much bigger one – from the Cronenberg template. So much so that if it and its successor, *Eastern Promises*, had been signed "Alan Smithee," it might take a very long time before anyone came up with Cronenberg's name as the director. Not since *The Dead Zone*, perhaps not even since *Fast Company*, had Cronenberg made a film so completely at home in the Hollywood mainstream. And *A History of Violence* has clear genre affiliations far stronger than any in Cronenberg's cinema since *The Fly*. Except that the genre this film is completely at home in is not the horror movie, but the crime thriller. Indeed, *A History of Violence* dextrously deploys two different familiar narrative/genre strands within that broad classification. First comes the "ordinary good man as action hero" strand, which is enacted when small-town lunch-counter owner Tom Stall saves a roomful of people from two murderous psychopaths, leaving them both dead. This event predictably makes the news with all the enthusiasm that meets any real-life event resembling a mainstream movie, and Tom becomes a local hero. The second narrative arises from the unlikelihood of the first (an unlikelihood that is almost never examined in more naive forms of the popular hero storyline): where did this unassuming straight-arrow citizen get the skills to kill people in such virtuoso fashion? Now the story type switches to a more intricate and sinister narrative family, one that may be frankly labelled "film noir."[18]

Exactly as in the classic noir film of that title, *out of the past* comes into the quotidian life of the apparently blameless hero a vengeful figure, the gangster Carl Fogarty, left over from an earlier life – which it turns out was one of dreadful criminality and violence. Now Tom Stall (or, as he was, Joey Cusack) is compelled to defend himself and his family against threats to their lives, and to journey back into his previous life to take care of this business. At this point the film reverts somewhat to its earlier "popular action hero" archetype, but in a way that is (a) still reminiscent of exactly the same noir narrative, and (b) considerably darkened and complexified from the naive good-vs-evil nature it had earlier presented. The film ends in a couple of bloodbaths and a grimly uncertain last scene of the Stall family sitting around the dinner table, the wife and son having no idea who this man sitting next to them is: he used to be their ideally decent and benevolent husband and father; now he is a ruthless killer with a blood-soaked history.

What one might call the noise of strong pre-existing genre elements in *A History of Violence* almost completely conceals whatever there might be in the film either of a quasi-horror movie or of a David Cronenberg movie. And yet a close examination reveals at least traces of those elements. We may recall that both cinematic horror and film noir have their historical roots in German expressionism, and that the revelation of unstable and ominous realities and subjectivities can produce in noir exactly the queasy, uncanny feeling of a waking bad dream. The *heimlich* world suddenly becomes its opposite without really surrendering its *Heimlichkeit*. The final scene at the family dinner table shows this with great clarity (and in fact Joey's earlier life has thrown up its own uncanny family as well, in the person of his gangster brother Richie). Not only does this uncovering of an unknown, pre-existent underlying world produce a frisson of horror at the spectacle of exactly how comprehensively apparent reality can *lie*, but the scenario also repeats Cronenberg's familiar themes of radical transformation, existential self-reinvention, and the degree to which reality itself has no dependable ontological truth. The imitative transformation of Tom's high-school-student son from a nerdish victim of school bullies into somebody who fights back at them with too much violence and then into a shotgun-wielding killer, redoubles the message in troubling ways. *A History of Violence* plays the Cronenberg protagonist's transformation scenario in a different way, though, since the self-reinvention has already taken place, in the past; and its success is testified to by almost twenty years of "straight life." What then occurs is a transmutation into something disturbing that is not a novel self-invention, but instead a reversion to an earlier, underlying one. At the end of the film, with his whole new clean life in grave peril, Tom might almost echo Brundle's despairing statement from *The Fly*: "I am a fly who dreamed he was a man." Joey Cusack is clearly "something that should have remained hidden."

The most overtly horror-like, and also most Cronenbergian, stroke in the film is the appearance of the gangster Fogarty, who takes off his dark glasses to reveal a hideously wrecked eye and scarred face – damage inflicted by Joey many years earlier. This face transforms Fogarty into something not so far away from a horror movie monster. It is also the objective correlative of Tom's past as Joey: Joey is completely invisible in Tom's decent, exemplary new life, but he is shockingly inscribed into Fogarty's face; Fogarty's damaged face is the objective correlative of Tom's damaged subjectivity. And this use of wounds and scars to signify something much more than themselves is truly Cronenberg.

Finally, though, these are undercurrents rather than grossly defining traits in this mainstream film that is unusually taut, spare, and cold. Where *A History of Violence* ultimately belongs is in the wonderful category of Hollywood genre films that are truly superior in their stretching and mutation of genre conventions to produce something complex, emotionally demanding, and usefully neurotic: the category that houses much of noir, and directors like Nicholas Ray, Douglas Sirk, Anthony Mann, Arthur Penn, Francis Ford Coppola, Robert Altman, and many other honourable examples.

Eastern Promises

Eastern Promises perhaps seems a little less mainstream than *A History of Violence*, if only because of its British setting and its set of personages that includes not a single American character. But it too is essentially a crime movie and, even more than its predecessor, also a certain kind of detective narrative. A gradual penetration into the underlife of the Russian mafia in London that begins with a young woman's desire to care for an abandoned infant leads to unpleasant discovery after unpleasant discovery. Ultimately, *Eastern Promises* replicates the rather typical conventional narratives of an excavation of underlying problems and a putting of them to right through the actions of the good characters; and also the manufacture of new, made-up solutions to actual problems through the will-to-optimism of standard story types. But simultaneously it is replicating the Cronenbergian themes of revelation, destabilization, and transformation. And yet these latter themes are not very marked or visible, and tend to merge into the detective-like genre background.

What does visibly mark the film with Cronenbergian queasiness and uncanniness is the presence of bodily mutation and scarring, the presence of the body as a form of speech that articulates an alarming inner condition. This is the arena of the tattoo rituals of the Russian prison world. Convicts receive tattoos for certain kinds of acts performed or pains suffered, and other tattoos at the hands of the criminal hierarchy in recognition of higher status achieved. These tattooing rituals (one of which we see in the film, performed upon Nikolai), are very similar to the rituals that award military or civil honours. But where the honours awarded by the "daylight" world feature harmless symbolic items such as medals, ribbons, or the dubbing with a sword, the "night-time" criminal world inscribes painful and permanent markings upon the body itself. *Crash* already showed Cronenberg's interest in tattoos as a form of bodily expression, and its articulation of the tattoo as a kind of wound, and the wound as a kind of tattoo, seems a completely logical and recognizable addition to the director's world.

There is an authentic creepiness to the world of tattoos in *Eastern Promises*, one that operates in harmony with similar strands of horror and the uncanny. The inner truth speaks itself in a form of bodily mutation and wounding, which at the same time embodies the similarly mutated and scarred will and desire of the tattooed one. Meanwhile, the film's most remarked-on scene, the attack on Nikolai in the steamroom by two knife-wielding assassins, clearly achieved that status through the extraordinary, horrifying sense of vulnerability that the murderous assault on a naked person in an enclosed space that is itself denuded instantly creates in viewers (as *Psycho* was the first to demonstrate). The body threatened while separated from coverings, from defences of any kind, while existing simply *as itself*, dredges up a deep-seated alarm to which every spectator is subject. Not to mention the fact that this is in its own way simply the most recent of Cronenberg's many surgical assaults with a knife upon defenceless patients. And yet *Eastern Promises*, despite these things and its extensive manipulation of tropes of reinvention and concealed disturbing truths, has departed pretty thoroughly from the Cronenberg line. While it is quite legitimate to say of the film that it represents a world in which the kindly father is a monster, and the family is based on a series of hideous crimes that must be violently erased so that the family may be refabricated from the ground up, still the ending is absolutely the happiest in any Cronenberg film, and by a huge margin.[19] The heroine has her new baby, and her family is safe and protected, while the hero is off to the wars again in the fight against evil (Nikolai's position at the end of the film almost suggests that *Eastern Promises* has been the pilot for a television series in which this intrepid agent grapples anew with the underworld every week).

Postscript: *A Dangerous Method* (2011)

Since *A Dangerous Method* was released only after the first completed draft of this chapter, I cannot comment on it in any but a cursory way (never mind *Cosmopolis* [2012], which had just barely opened in theatres at the time for final revisions, and *Maps to the Stars* [2014], which was just a twinkle in the director's eye). Suffice it to say that a film dealing directly with the historical foundations of psychoanalysis, and containing Freud as an important character, will hardly yield fully to such a brief treatment within the critical context I have chosen. The film is first and foremost a dialogue movie, drawn from Christopher Hampton's 2002 stage play *The Talking Cure*, and displays a very conservative repertory of locations and actions: as such it bears even less of a resemblance to anything horror-generic than *M. Butterfly* does. Nevertheless, the narrative does present a kind of monstrous intrusion, and indeed this intrusion is more or less the point of the story. I am speaking of the shocking discovery by its protagonist Carl Jung that he is deeply aroused by the overt sexual masochism of his patient and pupil Sabina Spielrein, and that in giving way to this desire he is thus compelled to abandon his psychoanalytic detachment as well as large pieces of his moral and ethical bedrock. At the end of the film he suffers a serious nervous breakdown. This outline presents a striking resemblance to a pattern in Cronenberg's cinema stretching back at least as far as *Videodrome*.

In various ways and to various degrees one sees there the spectacle of a male explorer (entrepreneur, scientist, artist) drawn across the boundaries of restraint by the sexual invitation to sadistic behaviour issued by a masochistic female: it is visible in *Videodrome*, *Dead Ringers*, *M. Butterfly*, *Crash*, and *eXistenZ*. When the male moves across this boundary he is reborn, revitalized, newly empowered; but this transformation carries also the seeds of a catastrophe. Because *A Dangerous Method* presents historical characters, and is trying to do so in an at least somewhat faithful manner, it is not allowed the destructive conclusion of *Videodrome*, *Dead Ringers*, and *M. Butterfly*. Jung must recover from his complete nervous collapse and live happily ever after as a pillar of twentieth-century psychoanalysis – a fact duly recorded by the film in an end-title. It scarcely needs mentioning that *A Dangerous Method* is profoundly *not* a horror movie. But the emergence of Jung's unsuspected and "dangerous" sadistic desire does certainly re-enact the revelation of "something that should have remained hidden," and this discovery has enough of that familiar, disturbing proto-nausea to find a kinship with the director's other work. The relationship of Cronenberg's post-*Fly* cinema to horror can almost be expressed as a syllogism: (1) there is something profoundly uneasy and upsetting in Cronenberg's outlook that is entirely congenial to the horror genre, amply demonstrated by his overtly "horror" work up to *The Fly*; (2) there is a demonstrable thematic and affective continuity between this work and the work after *The Fly*, which manifests similarly uneasy and upsetting qualities;

therefore, (3) there is some link between Cronenberg's post-1986 cinema and the horror film. The litmus tests of Freud's uncanny return and Todorov's fantastic incursion reveal how elements crucial to the definition of horror as a genre often produce positive results when applied to Cronenberg's later films.

Let me reiterate that I think none of these films, not even *Naked Lunch* or *eXistenZ*, is well described as a horror movie. But the recurrence of themes, and several overt depictions, of the mutated or perverted body that are much less sensational than what appears in *Shivers* or *The Fly* shows a persistent allegiance to one principle of horror. And the revelation of the unstable, fragile, even mendacious status of the comfortable ordinary world, together with the uncovering of a far more alarming one lying beneath, fits easily into the analyses of Freud, Todorov, et al. Cronenberg's films throughout the last twenty-five years have maintained a quality of artiness, at times almost of gentility. His way has become even more insinuating, a kind of ghostly stiletto-strike at viewers rather than an assault with blunt instruments. One sees this clearly when when we compare his later work not only to his own earlier movies but to para-horror serial-killer films such as *Se7en* or the Thomas Harris adaptations (*Manhunter*, *Silence of the Lambs*, etc.). These latter films and many like them have strongly upped the ante in the thriller/crime movie arena with their sensationally explicit depictions of gruesome violence and its disgusting aftermath (a trend that is now strongly entrenched in cable television as well), and the base-horror affect of revulsion is far more visible here than in Cronenberg's work. But this more overtly shocking kind of depiction is rarely accompanied by anything of the uncanny, and if there is a queasiness it is simply of a kind that needs a sick bag at an autopsy. As so often occurs in the biodiverse jungle of genres, the hopelessness of trying to tabulate genre characteristics and attach generic labels to every kind of hybrid again presents itself. What can be said is that the *unnervingness* of Cronenberg's cinema has been maintained through thick and thin.

NOTES

1 An exception is the non-canonical drag-racing one-off, *Fast Company* (1979), a commissioned project with a ready-made screenplay. Also, his pre-commercial quasi-experimental/avant-garde period, his twin hour-long films *Stereo* (1969) and *Crimes of the Future* (1970) already manifested

science-fiction and body-strangeness elements in profusion, but little that could be classified as "horror."

2 See especially Ernest Mathijs's monograph on the director, which is actually subtitled *From Baron of Blood to Cultural Hero* (Mathijs 2008), and my essay "32 Paragraphs about David Cronenberg" (Beard 2002).

3 The reverse was also true: Cronenberg's later, more openly serious films were slagged by some of the director's early cult followers, who deplored the abandonment of the cheap-and-nasty verve and smart provocation of his earlier work.

4 One only needs to peruse the lengthy Bibliography at the end of this anthology.

5 See Pierre-Georges Castex, *Le conte fantastique en France* (1951); Louis Vax, *L'art et la littérature fantastique* (1960); Roger Caillois, *Au coeur du fantastique* (1965), cited in Todorov (1975, 26–7). Other writing on the genre might be mentioned in this marginal place. James Twitchell in *Dreadful Pleasures: An Anatomy of Modern Horror* (1985) preserves something like Todorov's bifurcation by utilizing the distinction between "horror" and "terror" to distinguish between narratives that preserve the mysterious and inexplicable, and narratives in which there is nothing supernatural or absolutely outside the possibilities of the existing world (monstrous events, then, but not actual monsters). In short, according to Twitchell, terror is explicable, horror is not. The horror/terror dichotomy then is translated into something like a dichotomy of telling vs showing – with contemporary horror's intense devotion to showing the horrific in the most explicit detail possible, the final manifestation of a drift from suggestion to shock. In addition to formalist and psychological perspectives there are other important strains of writing about the genre. Some pursue its potential for political encoding, or both. Robin Wood's (1979) brilliant theorization of the "new" horror film of the 1970s, based on Freud and Gad Horowitz, features most prominently the notion that the genre, and in particular the personage of the monster, acts as a channel for the return of legitimate desires (often related to sexuality and the family) illegitimately repressed by society and hence may embody a progressive politics. Subsequent writing has found in horror a rebellion against the tyranny of elites and the entire Fordist project to rationalize society (e.g., Jancovich 1992), or, in its demolition of existing structures of subjectivity, the potential to evade Foucauldian mechanisms of control (e.g., Shaviro 1993). The arrival of gender as an important lens for critical analysis has yielded especially productive results in the field of the horror film, and especially the Cronenbergian sub-genre of body horror, and has returned

to post-Freudian psychoanalytic methodologies. Bodily sexual difference is revealed in this critical writing as a primary site of desire and disgust (Julia Kristeva's [1982] Freudian analysis of abjection, and Barbara Creed's [1993] Lacanian application of it to the horror genre, are key texts here). Other writers (Carol Clover [1993], Tania Modleski [1988]) map gender/power stereotypes to the extreme positions of perpetrator and victim in horror films and their reception, and observe these stereotypes migrating and transforming in, for example, the narrative's ability to "feminize" characters through mechanisms of suffering and bodily abjection. I have tried to map out the many examples of this mechanism in Cronenberg's films up to *Spider* in my book *The Artist as Monster* (Beard 2001).

6 In his essay "A Body Apart: Cronenberg and Genre," Jonathan Crane (2000) also makes this assertion, and goes on to map all of Cronenberg's outright horror films according to their variations on the specifically Frankensteinian "mad scientist" template.

7 Again I have argued this point at considerable length in *The Artist as Monster*.

8 The narrative of *Dead Ringers* was inspired by the real-life existence of a pair of identical twin gynecologists, Stephen and Cyril Marcus, who frequently impersonated each other and who committed suicide in their Manhattan apartment in 1975. These events in turn inspired a 1977 novel by Bari Wood and Jack Geasland, entitled *Twins*. The film's relationship to the novel is minimal.

9 Cronenberg relates this to Chris Rodley (1997, 137–8) in *Cronenberg on Cronenberg*.

10 Barbara Creed's (1990) essay "Phallic Panic: Male Hysteria and *Dead Ringers*" argues this case in compelling detail.

11 He says, in *The Generation of Animals* (II, iii, 175), that "the female is as it were a deformed male." Cited in *Monstrous Imagination* (Huet 1993, 3).

12 Freud (2003, 141–2). "[Among] those motifs that produce an uncanny effect … [one of the most important variants is] the idea of the 'double' (the *Doppelgänger*), in all its nuances and manifestations – that is to say, the appearance of persons who have to be regarded as identical because they look alike. This relationship is intensified by the spontaneous transmission of mental processes from one of these persons to the other – what we would call telepathy – so that one becomes co-owner of the other's knowledge, emotions and experience. Moreover, a person may identify himself with another and so become unsure of his true self; or he may substitute the other's self for his own. The self may thus be duplicated, divided and interchanged. Finally there is the constant recurrence of the

same thing, the repetition of the same facial features, the same characters, the same destinies, the same misdeeds, even the same names, through successive generations."

13 The original passage is in Burroughs's (2009, 110–11) *Naked Lunch*; Cronenberg's comment is in Rodley (1997, 137–8).

14 Barry Miles in Chris Rodley's documentary *The Making of Naked Lunch* (1992): " I think after [Joan's] death, [Burroughs] unconsciously tried to distance himself from women, maybe partly to cover up the guilt of killing her, or whatever, and towards the beginning of the 60s, particularly 1961, he had developed a very complicated idea in which women were agents for a trust of giant insects on another galaxy, and as such were an entirely separate species, and not even of this planet."

15 The one exception to the "no violence" and "no sensationalism" rule occurs in the final scene, when the protagonist commits suicide in a rather elided and arty fashion.

16 This fact is summoned in evidence against it throughout Iain Sinclair's BFI Film Classics monograph on the film (1999).

17 Heavily and explicitly: in the director's commentary to the video issue, Cronenberg cites, and expounds, Martin Heidegger and calls the film "existentialist propaganda."

18 Bart Beaty (2008) has read the film as noir in some detail in his monograph on the film. He has also taken up Cronenberg's suggestion that there are overtones of the Western in *A History of Violence* in the way the incursion of evil necessitates the hero to act violently.

19 Always excepting *Fast Company*. The runner-up among proper Cronenberg films is *Scanners*, but, as I have argued elsewhere (*The Artist as Monster*), that ending seems not fully considered.

12 The Physician as Mad Scientist: A Fear of Deviant Medical Practices in the Films of David Cronenberg

JAMES BURRELL

Canadians rarely question the health care provided to them by public medical practitioners, placing implicit trust in their doctors' abilities, integrity, and intentions. Though lengthy patient wait times for some diagnostic tests and procedures, delisting of services, and a perceived shortage of family physicians have been well-publicized topics of contention, the majority of Canadians still regard their country's universal health care system to be one that works well.[1] However, misguided ethics, ill-considered decisions, and abuses of power by various medical and governmental bodies have resulted in numerous instances since the 1920s whereby Canadians have been subject to inappropriate procedures, harmful drugs, and various forms of systematic, unauthorized medical experimentation, forming a sad, shocking chapter in the not-always-illustrious history of Canada's health care system.

In 1928, the Legislative Assembly of Alberta enacted the eugenics-based Sexual Sterilization Act, which, over the span of forty-four years forced the sterilization of nearly 3,000 Albertans deemed "mentally defective" (Harris-Zsovan 2010, 5). During the 1940s and 50s, thousands of children living in Quebec Catholic orphanages were incorrectly diagnosed as intellectually disabled with many being held in psychiatric hospitals. Later referring to themselves as the "Duplessis Orphans" after then-reigning Quebec premier Maurice Duplessis, many claimed to have been given electroconvulsive therapy and forced to undergo such psychosurgical procedures as lobotomies.[2]

In 1957, a series of mind-control studies initiated by the CIA began to be undertaken at the psychiatry department of Montreal's McGill University. Experiments involved giving subjects drugs and electroshock therapy in the belief they could be reprogrammed and existing mental illness could be cured by having their memories erased (Collins 1998, 2, 131, 155). Four years later in 1961, thalidomide, a popular sedative used to treat morning sickness in pregnant women, was licensed for use in Canada; however, even after it was discovered to cause severe deformities in thousands of children worldwide, the drug was allowed to be sold in this country (Peritz 2010).

Between 1980 and 1985, an estimated 2,000 Canadians contracted the human immunodeficiency virus (HIV) after receiving infected blood and blood products to treat their hemophilia or in transfusions during surgery (Picard n.d.). From 1980 to 1992, an additional 30,000 recipients would go on to become infected with the hepatitis C virus (HCV) through contaminated blood and blood products.[3] More recently, the fear of nosocomial (hospital-acquired) infections from microorganisms like Clostridium difficile (C. difficile) has been a concern, with the bacterium being responsible for numerous deaths in several provinces across Canada (Eggerston 2006; Silversides 2009). In addition, there are the tens of thousands of cases of "adverse events" – medical errors – that occur each year in Canadian hospitals which lead to further patient illness and death including administration of incorrect medications and/or dosages of drugs and instances of foreign objects being left inside the body after surgery (CIHI 2007; Talaga and Cribb 2007). And most recently, a lack of oversight into the preparation of certain cancer drugs has been a problem in some provinces, with the revelation in April 2013 that well over a thousand patients in Ontario and New Brunswick hospitals had been given diluted doses of chemotherapy treatments ("Ontario NDP" 2013).

Given such an environment of erroneous diagnoses, improper treatments, lack of transparency, negligence, and unauthorized and harmful medical experimentation, the theme of irresponsible or aberrant medical behaviour – with the modern physician/surgeon/psychiatrist supplanting the traditional "mad scientist" or "mad doctor" figure of American classic horror films and European gothic tales – is one that resonates equally well within the milieu of Canadian horror as it does in popular Hollywood productions. And perhaps no filmmaker has been more adept at identifying and commenting on audiences' anxieties over a flawed health care system than David Cronenberg. An auteur whose work has seemingly often questioned the actions and ethics of the medical establishment in Canada, Cronenberg has managed to explore viewers' deep-rooted fears of falling victim to a medical mishap in numerous "body horror" films, often by introducing a mad scientist character, frequently in the form of an experimenting doctor who engages in some form of deviant medical behaviour.

Under a guise of "scientific progress," this medical figure attempts to modify and transform the human body via the introduction of mutation and disease and, in doing so, alters human existence and evolution and creates a new life form or being. This continual fascination with the transgressive application of medical science – particularly on unwitting participants – and the eventual impact it has on both them and society has been a part of much of Cronenberg's work, from his first feature-length experiment, *Stereo* (1969), up to his masterpiece, *Dead Ringers,* and perhaps even as recently as 2011 with *A Dangerous Method.* However, it appears most prevalently – and effectively – in the director's first four commercial efforts: *Shivers* (aka *They Came from Within*), *Rabid*, *The Brood*, and *Scanners.* In these examples, ethical lines are crossed and patients are used like guinea pigs through the application of radical surgery, experimental psychology, or the administering of untested pharmaceutical products.

The Return of the Mad Scientist

A long-time staple of the horror genre, the experimenting mad doctor/scientist views the populace as fair game to be exploited like lab mice. This figure has appeared in a multitude of films, from early classics like *Island of Lost Souls* (1932) in which a vivisectionist attempts to mate a young couple with the animal-human hybrids he has created, to such recent releases as *The Human Centipede* trilogy (2009–2015), the first of which sees a surgeon stitch together three unwilling participants, mouth to anus. In his book *Mad, Bad and Dangerous? The Scientist and the Cinema*, Christopher Frayling notes that mad scientists and their work have been presented as threats in a significant number of horror movies produced from the 1930s to 1980s.

"A detailed survey of more than a thousand *horror films* distributed in Britain between 1931 and 1984 ... reveals that mad scientists or their creations have been the villains/monsters of 31 per cent of them (41 per cent if we count mutations as well); that scientific or psychiatric research has produced 39 per cent of all threats in all horror films (as compared with only 11 per cent 'natural' threats); and – by contrast – that scientists have been the 'pursuers' or heroes of a mere 11 per cent of horror movies, most of them pre-1960s" (Frayling 2005, 41).

Because Canada's involvement in horror filmmaking did not take place until the early 1960s, there were initially very few Canadian efforts featuring such characters as the mad scientist. Examples were limited to the country's first feature-length horror production, *The Mask* (1961), in which a psychiatrist is driven to psychosis after donning an ancient tribal ceremonial mask; *The Vulture* (1967), which sees a professor transformed by a scientific procedure into a half-man/half-bird creature; and the horror-satire *Dr Frankenstein on Campus* (1970), where a descendent of the infamous proto-mad scientist engages in nefarious mind control experiments while studying at the University of Toronto. It wasn't until the emergence of Cronenberg on the commercial film scene in the mid-1970s and onward that the figure of the experimenting mad doctor/scientist would really gain prominence in Canadian horror cinema. Taking the mad scientist out of his cobwebbed, medieval castle and isolated island compound, Cronenberg transplanted him into a clinical, ultramodern environment. Gone were the traditional gothic trappings of laboratories filled with beakers and test tubes of bubbling, brightly coloured liquids and grandiose Kenneth Strickfaden–inspired electrical equipment; instead, they were replaced with stainless steel operating rooms and coldly sterile hospital wards. Under Cronenberg, the mad scientist was no longer a hysterical, lab-coat-sporting, wide-eyed caricature; he now resembled any middle-aged physician, plastic surgeon, or psychologist in both appearance and demeanour (although some remnants of the former version's God complex remained). By removing many of the clichéd characteristics long associated with the character, Cronenberg was able to effectively reinvent the mad doctor figure, making it relevant for modern horror audiences. What certainly remained unchanged, however, was that the deviant actions of these medical personnel would produce dreadful outcomes, not only for their patients but for numerous others as well.

In *Shivers*, a genetically engineered parasite designed to assist in organ replacement is altered by its creator, Dr Emil Hobbes, to induce violent sexual behaviour in its hosts. *Rabid* sees a young motorcycle crash victim, Rose, develop a bloodsucking proboscis after receiving a highly experimental skin graft procedure from plastic surgeon Dr Dan Keloid. She becomes both a virtual vampire as well as a carrier of a virulent rabies-like disease that turns those she feeds on into rampaging, zombie-like beings. *The Brood* showcases a new form of psychotherapy created by psychologist Dr Hal Raglan. This innovative approach proves to be responsible for a woman's birthing of numerous homicidal mutant children. And in *Scanners*, a drug once developed for pregnant mothers by psychopharmacist Dr Paul Ruth is revealed to be the cause of a race of advanced telepaths, some of whom are bent on destroying

12.1. US lobby card for *They Came from Within* (aka *Shivers*). Courtesy of Cinépix.

humankind. Seemingly reflective of past medical abuses in Canada, all four films tap into a fear of unauthorized medical experimentation by both commenting on, and denouncing, new and untested bio-scientific procedures that aid in the creation and proliferation of a catastrophic medical and societal threat. Offering an underlying message of mistrust of medical professionals, these films seem to constitute a criticism of the Canadian health care system itself.

Just What the Doctor Ordered: The Cinema of Cronenberg

Prior to *Shivers*, Cronenberg had completed two 16mm shorts, *Transfer* (1966) and *From the Drain* (1967), as well as two avant-garde 35mm feature-length art films, the aforementioned *Stereo* and *Crimes of the Future*. After shooting several television "fillers" (short documentary programs) for the Canadian Broadcasting Corporation (CBC), he began writing the script for *Shivers* – at the time called *Orgy of the Blood Parasites* (later retitled *The Parasite Murders*, and finally, *Shivers* and *They Came from Within* for Canadian and US release, respectively). Attempting to shop his screenplay around for potential production, Cronenberg found little feature filmmaking taking place in Canada circa 1972 and few options to pitch a concept such as his. One exception turned out to be Cinépix, a small production-distribution company based in Montreal. "There was no filmmaking of the imagination. When I looked around for it, the closest I could come up with was Cinépix," says Cronenberg (Rodley 1997, 36).

Founded by producers John Dunning and André Link, Cinépix had experienced great success with a series of sexy, soft-core films, popularly dubbed "maple syrup porn," such as Denis Héroux's *Valérie* (1969) and *L'initiation* (1969). Responding favourably to his horror script, Cinépix presented Cronenberg's treatment to the CFDC for government arts funding. It would take the agency three years to approve the film for funding, and *Shivers* finally went into production in September 1974.

The film takes place in Starliner Towers, an isolated luxury high-rise outside of Montreal, where a young woman is attacked and killed by an older man who then takes his own life. When police arrive, they are informed by the building's on-site doctor, Roger St Luc (Paul Hampton) that the dead man is Dr Emil Hobbes and the deceased woman a nineteen-year-old named Annabelle Brown. Hobbes's associate, Dr Rollo Linsky (Joe Silver), reveals to St Luc that the doctor had created a parasite to act as a combination of venereal disease and aphrodisiac and used his young mistress Annabelle as a test subject by implanting the organism in her. The pair conclude that Hobbes, sensing danger with the experiment, killed the girl to prevent the parasite from reproducing. Unfortunately, Annabelle had engaged in sexual relations with multiple men in the building, and St Luc and his nurse/girlfriend, Miss Forsythe (Lynn Lowry), had seen male residents visiting the on-site clinic afflicted with unusual stomach growths. It isn't long before this sexually transmitted "disease" spreads through the apartment complex, resulting in numerous cases of rape, sexual violence, and murder. With the entire building's population infected, a procession of cars drives away from the high-rise with the intent on infecting the populace of Montreal while the radio news reports on the rash of violent sexual assaults taking place across the city.

Though the film was slated for release in October 1975, the CFDC found itself under fire shortly beforehand, following the harsh criticism of influential film reviewer Robert Fulford in the September 1975 issue of *Saturday Night* magazine. In an article entitled "You Should Know How Bad This Film Is. After All, You Paid For It," Fulford (under the pseudonym "Marshall Delaney") attacked the film, writing that it was "a disgrace to everyone connected with it – including the taxpayers," and opined that "if using public money to produce films like *The Parasite Murders* is the only way that English Canada can have a film industry, then perhaps English Canada should not have a film industry" (Delaney 1975). Fulford's comments, which sparked a discussion in the House of Commons over the merits of the CFDC's program, prompted Cinépix to respond by publishing a pamphlet for distribution to members of Parliament, entitled "Is There a Place for Horror Films in Canada's Film Industry?" explaining the benefits to fostering such works as Cronenberg's in Canada.[4]

Although Fulford felt that *Shivers* was not representative of what a Canadian film should be, the film earned more than $5 million worldwide, making it the most financially successful film the CFDC had invested in up to that point (Rodley 1997, 52). Despite this, Cinépix still encountered considerable difficulty in securing funding from the agency for Cronenberg's next project, *Rabid* (initially titled *Mosquito*), which continued the previous film's motif of a plague-like virus spreading through the population.

In *Rabid*, a young couple sets off on their motorcycle for a trek along a rural Quebec road. Unbeknown to them, the road ahead is blocked and their bike crashes into a field. The rider, Hart Read (Frank Moore), is relatively unhurt, but his girlfriend Rose (Marilyn Chambers), is severely injured. Rushed to the nearby Keloid Clinic, a cosmetic surgery facility, Rose is deemed to be near death. The clinic's head plastic surgeon Dr Dan Keloid (Howard Ryshpan) suggests an experimental form of skin graft to save her life. As Rose awakens from her coma one month later, the procedure appears to be a success. However, she is left with an unforeseen side-effect: an orifice under her left armpit which houses a penile-like appendage with a needle tip. Unable to digest conventional food, Rose is forced to take nourishment from human blood by using the proboscis to puncture people and extract their blood like a syringe. Compounding the problem is that the puncture or "bite" transmits a virus which produces madness and eventual death. After feeding from other patients and from Dr Keloid himself, Rose leaves the clinic and heads for Montreal, where she satiates her hunger by attacking several people. As her victims become homicidal and begin attacking others, the infection spreads quickly (in one sequence, a television news clip with a representative from the Quebec Bureau of Health discounts the plague as being a strain of "swine flu," a reference to then-current fears in North America over a possible influenza pandemic). City officials declare a state of martial law. Informed that she is both the source and a carrier of the plague that is ravaging Montreal, Rose seals her fate by locking herself in an apartment unit with a man from whom she has just fed.

Released in April 1977, *Rabid*, which will receive more attention in Sean Moreland's chapter, earned more than $7 million and, despite the presence of former Ivory Snow soap box model-turned-porn-star Marilyn Chambers, received a much less vitriolic critical response. After taking a break from horror with the 1979 racing car film, *Fast Company*, Cronenberg returned to the genre with his most personal film, *The Brood*, released the same year.

As *The Brood* begins, Frank Carveth (Art Hindle) travels to the Somafree Institute outside of Toronto to pick up his five-year-old daughter Candice (Cindy Hinds) after a visit with his estranged wife, Nola (Samantha Eggar), a patient at the facility. Nola, who harbours deep resentment towards her parents, is undergoing a radical new form of psychotherapy developed by Dr Hal Raglan (Oliver Reed) called "psychoplasmics," which permits individuals to relive and deal with painful memories by channelling their emotions into physical manifestations (e.g., welts and tumours) on their bodies. One evening, when Candice is taken to visit her grandmother Juliana (Nuala Fitzgerald), the child witnesses the aftermath of Juliana's murder at the hands of a diminutive, child-like figure. Later, Nola's father, Barton Kelly (Henry Beckman), is killed by the dwarf-like being and Frank himself is nearly attacked by the same creature. After two mutants enter Candice's kindergarten class – killing her teacher, Ruth Mayer (Susan Hogan) and taking the girl back to Somafree – Frank heads to the facility to find an armed Raglan, who informs him that the creatures are actually Nola's children; born from her rage, they are a physical manifestation of her emotions. As such, they share a psychic link with her, and whenever she is angry or upset – either consciously or unconsciously – the "brood" will act upon those emotions. Raglan proposes that if Frank can keep his wife calm long enough, he can rescue Candice from the sleeping mutants. However, after giving birth to another creature via an external womb, Nola becomes upset, awakening the brood, who kill Raglan and begin attacking Candice. In order to save their daughter, Frank strangles Nola, which in turn kills the mutants.

Cronenberg wrote the script for *The Brood* during a divorce from his first wife and their subsequent child custody battle over their daughter Cassandra (Sammon 1981, 30), and would go on to refer to the film as his own version of *Kramer vs Kramer* (Rodley 1997, 76). Cronenberg's first horror project to be made without the involvement of Cinépix, *The Brood* was produced by Claude Héroux and executive producers Victor Solnicki and Pierre David; the director would work with the three again for his next film, *Scanners* (originally called *The Sensitives*), a project he had originally planned to make before working on *The Brood*.

Scanners opens in a Montreal shopping mall food court, where a vagrant, Cameron Vale (Stephen Lack), inadvertently causes a woman nearby to convulse violently. This alerts two armed men, who chase and shoot Vale with a tranquillizer gun. Later awakening to find himself in a derelict building, Vale is informed by his abductor, psychopharmacist Dr Paul Ruth (Patrick McGoohan), that he is a "scanner" – an indi-. vidual with telepathic and telekinetic abilities who can hear, or "scan," the thoughts of others and manipulate their actions. A member of Con-Sec, an international security and weapons corporation, Ruth obtains the assistance of Vale to help locate Darryl Revok (Michael Ironside), a psychopathic scanner who has murdered several of the corporation's security agents. Vale's search leads him to a scanner resistance group, headed by Kim Obrist (Jennifer O'Neill), and together they track down Revok to a drug manufacturing plant called Biocarbon Amalgamate, where a drug that induces artificial telepathy, Ephemerol, is being manufactured for distribution to pregnant mothers for the purpose of creating new scanners. Revok, who has ambitions of creating a "scanner army" to rebel against society, informs Vale that they are brothers and that Ruth is their father, and asks for his participation. After Revok's attempts to bring Vale into his plans fail, the two apply their formidable powers against each other in a telepathic battle in which both men wind up merging to become one.

Mad Doctors, Bad Medicine

Although it could be argued that each film's medical procedures start out with the best of intentions on the part of their originators, Bill Beard points out evidence to the contrary in his book *The Artist as Monster:*

The Cinema of David Cronenberg. He writes that "the scientific projects actually depicted in Cronenberg's films are almost never purely rational or altruistic; they are almost always tainted and disavowing. The scientists in *Stereo* and *Crimes of the Future* are irresponsible and proto-sadistic, [*Shivers's*] Hobbes is a comically stylized dirty old man, and the imperious scientists of *The Brood* and *Scanners* are power hungry" (Beard 2001, 32). For instance, Hobbes's apparent reason for creating the parasite in the first place is a noble one: once transplanted into the human body, it would dissolve a diseased organ and then successfully resume the function of that particular organ, becoming, essentially, a form of organ replacement. It is never made clear at what stage, however, Hobbes decides to alter the organism's purpose, or whether his originally stated intentions were just a ruse to obtain more funding for his true project: a parasite that acts as a behaviour-altering aphrodisiac in its hosts and reproducing through sexual contact, much like a sexually transmitted infection (STI). What is clear from his notes (found by Linsky and read by him to St Luc) is that Hobbes believed "that man is an animal that thinks too much. An over-rational animal that's lost touch with its body and its instincts." He created the organism in a bid to "help man get more in touch with his primal self" and to "turn the world into one big, beautiful orgy."

The medical, scientific, and societal benefits that Cronenberg's fictional doctors pursue recall the "altruistic" intentions of individuals associated with real-life Canadian medical abuses. One such notable figure was Scottish-born American psychiatrist Dr Donald Ewen Cameron. The director of the Allan Memorial Institute at McGill University in Montreal, Cameron carried out numerous mind-control experiments on dozens of unwitting patients on behalf of the Central Intelligence Agency's behaviour-modification and "brainwashing" program, Project MKULTRA. Employing such methods as "psychic driving" and "depatterning," Cameron believed that individuals could be reprogrammed and that mental illnesses such as schizophrenia could be banished by erasing memories and rebuilding the mind. Cameron presented test subjects with various psychotropic drugs, including LSD; subjected them to long periods of listening to recorded audio messages which repeated continuously; administered electroconvulsive treatments; and even put some individuals into chemically induced comas for weeks or months.[5] A number of subjects never fully recovered; some developed severe depression, suicidal thoughts, anxiety disorders, and permanent memory loss (Collins 1998, 16, 154, 217).

Many of Cronenberg's fictional medical procedures are performed on vulnerable members of society: the young, the sick or injured, pregnant women, and those with emotional or psychiatric disorders. These groups, along with other minorities (e.g., sexual and cultural minorities), have historically been oppressed and more prone to abuse. The adolescent Annabelle Brown, who has reached physical but not emotional or psychological maturity, is therefore, susceptible to Hobbes's manipulations: he engages in a pedophilic sexual relationship with her and uses her as a test subject to conduct highly sexualized medical experiments.

In addition to Cameron's mind-control experiments, several vulnerable members of society have been exploited by members of the medical establishment. Between 1928 and 1972, 2,822 Albertans were subjected – either unknowingly or against their will – to eugenically inspired sterilization procedures consisting of tubal ligations, hysterectomies, castrations, and vasectomies to prohibit the propagation of "feeblemindedness," which was believed to be passed onto the offspring and lead to a future overburdening of provincial social services, hospitals, and jails (Harris-Zsovan 2010, 5). Some individuals were used as drug trial patients; a number of those deemed to be "mentally defective" were actually not intellectually disabled (2010, 6). In the case of the "Duplessis Orphans," over 3,000 children in Quebec Catholic orphanages were falsely declared to be developmentally disabled; a number of them were put into straightjackets, exposed to electroshock therapy and neurosurgical procedures, and even sexually abused by staff members. What makes the situation particularly tragic is that the children – many of whom were abandoned because they were born of out wedlock – may have been classified as "mentally debilitated" and the orphanages they were housed in converted into psychiatric institutions in order to receive additional government subsidies. At the time, the provincial government provided orphanages with only 75 cents a day for the upbringing of a child, while federal payments for psychiatric patient care was significantly more, at $2.75 per person.[6]

Cronenberg's characters are often unable to avoid becoming targets of these objectionable experiments: In *Rabid*, Rose, who is critically injured and unconscious, is unable to protest any type of surgery by Keloid; and Nola and fellow Somafree patient Mike (Gary McKeehan) are generally in no condition emotionally or mentally to defend themselves against Raglan's psychotherapy techniques. In fact, some, like Mike (whose turmoil stems from a lack of any affection from his father), may become dependent on or "addicted" to the techniques. Others, like former patient Jan Hartog (Robert Silverman), who has developed lymphosarcoma (marked by a cancerous growth on his neck) due to psychoplasmics treatments, attempts to fight back by mounting a court case against Raglan, but this occurs only after his "therapy" has caused his body "to revolt against itself" – prompting his inner turmoil to manifest into a life-threatening physical affliction. It is ultimately too late for lawsuits, as no amount of money (or the prospect of seeing Raglan incarcerated) will restore Hartog or other psychoplasmics patients to normal. The same might also be said for the real-life former patients of practitioners like Dr Cameron. In 1988, after an eight-year legal battle with the CIA, eight of Cameron's patients received an out-of-court settlement with the agency (a ninth died before the settlement was reached) for $100,000 each; seventy-six other patients also received $100,000 each from the Canadian government (Turbide 1997, 61). All of them still had to live with the unfortunate after-effects of their treatments.

Although the audience never meets her, it can be assumed that Dr Ruth's (unnamed) wife and mother of his children, did as any trusting wife would have done in the 1940s or 50s: she took Ephemerol, the drug her physician-husband presented her with – not once, but twice –never thinking it would lead to mutation in her children. Here, Cronenberg was seemingly inspired by a particularly tragic real-life scenario: the administering of the teratogenic drug thalidomide to expectant mothers in the late 1950s and early 60s. First available in 1959 in a sample form, thalidomide was later licensed for prescription use in Canada on 1 April 1961. With clear evidence that the drug prompted severe birth defects in children, thalidomide was still permitted to be made available in Canada until March 1962, approximately three months after countries like Great Britain, Germany, and Australia had banned it.[7] Because of the Canadian government's slow response and doctors' and pharmacists' ignorance about the dangers of the drug, an estimated 120 children were born with conditions such as phocomelia, a malformation of the limbs which produces unusually short appendages and can cause hands or feet to grow from the shoulder or hip, giving them an almost "flipper-like" appearance. While Cronenberg's fictional drug causes neurological, rather than physical malformations, the allusion to thalidomide is undeniable.

The evolution of the doctor/scientist figure in relation to the destruction they cause is interesting to note in the films of Cronenberg. In early works like *Shivers* and *Rabid*, while the devastation caused by the doctor/scientist character is on a grand scale, the figure himself plays a relatively minor role in the film: Hobbes is featured only in the opening minutes of *Shivers*, while in *Rabid*, Keloid appears in a handful of scenes, amounting to only a few minutes of screen time. In these examples, it is the devastating results of the doctors' actions on society, rather than the men themselves that are of significance, as they are not present in the film long enough to fully witness the catastrophic results their experiments will unleash. In follow-up efforts like *The Brood* and *Scanners*, the scientist plays a more significant role in the proceedings, and the characters of Hal Raglan and Paul Ruth are fleshed out accordingly. Bill Beard notes that "the character of Raglan also marks an enlargement of the figure of the controlling male scientist who invents and initiates the experimental medical project. This figure had been a constant in Cronenberg's work right back to *Stereo*. All of the characters occupying this place are in some sense detached from the narratives whose events they have so strongly determined by their experiments" (Beard 2001, 87–8).

Conversely, as the role of the doctor/scientist is enlarged, the destructive results of his experimentation shift from the nameless, faceless crowds (i.e., Starliner Towers) or the large-scale collapse of society (i.e., Montreal) to a more personal level: the destruction of the family unit represented by Frank Carveth's family in *The Brood*; and the two families in *Scanners* – the underground faction of "good scanners," and brothers Cameron Vale, Daryl Revok, and their father, Paul Ruth. In Frank's case, that destruction is evident not only in the violent murders of his parents-in-law by the mutant children and his snuffing out of Nola's life with his own hands, but also by the interloping (and possibly even amorous) actions of Raglan, who has assumed the role of surrogate husband to his wife. Though he and Nola are estranged, any vestige of Frank's patriarchal role has been usurped by the older, more confident, and more physically and intellectually powerful Raglan, who, in addition to being better able to serve Nola's emotional and psychological needs, is also "father" to her rage-spawned brood, giving her numerous children – in a figurative form of insemination – via psychoplasmics. Ultimately, Frank is deemed not only unnecessary for Nola's happiness, but also largely ineffectual in saving what is left of his family – his daughter Candice – from harm, as the revelation of welts on the girl's arm at the end of the film indicates that the intense emotional, psychological, and physical trauma she has endured will manifest itself either physiologically (i.e., her mother's unique birthing capabilities) or psychologically (i.e., a mental disorder).

The father-creator role of the mad scientist is more literal in *Scanners*, as Dr Ruth is not only the biological father to Vale and Revok, but also the one responsible for their telepathic condition as he both created Ephemerol and administered it to his wife during her pregnancies. Despite this familial connection, Ruth displays few paternal instincts – he has permitted both men to live decades of isolation and misery before going on to exploit one son for the purpose of locating and destroying the other. During that time, he has used them like lab rats: after engaging in his act of self-mutilation by drilling into his forehead, Revok is videotaped (presumably by Ruth) and prodded into revealing why he committed the deed; Vale is drugged and detained by his father and subjected to a cruel monitoring experiment in which a large group of people are brought into the same room as him, forcing his telepathy to go into torturous overdrive and sending him into agonizing convulsions. As with Raglan, Ruth has an apparent final realization of the consequences of his experiments and makes an attempt to rectify or minimize their negative effects, but it comes at the cost of both his life and the dissolution of his family.

Of Cronenberg's doctor figures, perhaps the one who has the most benevolent intentions is Keloid, even though he has been dismissive of others' opinions and has been unable to foresee the possible dangers of his work. His erroneous decision to proceed with Rose's skin graft, even after his surgeon-wife warns him that the tissue may become cancerous, makes the procedure and his actions somewhat less altruistic. Interestingly, this graft is a procedure that predates stem cell research and treatments; in the film, strips of tissue removed from Rose's thighs are treated to become neutral and thus able to bind with the burned tissue. In a scene Cronenberg cut from the film, Keloid explains to Rose that he expected the specially treated skin implant to help her grow new intestines destroyed in the accident, but the tissue did not react as anticipated (Rodley 1997, 57).

Medical Rape

Among the troubling aspects of these deviant medical operations on unwitting subjects is that many of them are victims of what can be classified as medical rape. Not only is there a sexual nature to much of the experimentation or medical procedures performed in Cronenberg's cinema, evident even in his most recent "mad scientist" film *A Dan-*

gerous Method (2011), but in many cases the violation can also be seen as an exertion of power by dominant figures over others. Although it takes place off-screen before the film begins, the procedure performed by Emil Hobbes on Annabelle Brown in *Shivers* would most likely have been done against her will, and as such constitutes rape. Hobbes's genetically engineered parasites – which look like a cross between a piece of fecal matter and a penis – would need to be inserted into her either orally or vaginally, or both.

Although we see only the after-effects of her impregnation by the penis-like organism, the sexual violation she experienced during this "medical procedure" is repeated over and over on various other residents of Starliner Towers throughout the course of the film. Once the organism (which incubates in the stomach and secretes an acid-like substance) begins to multiply and spread past the circle of Annabelle's sexual partners, the ongoing effects of Hobbes's quickly replicating medical experiment turns into a series of sexual assaults for everyone in the high-rise (including resident Betts [Barbara Steele], who becomes infected when a parasite crawls up through the drain of her bathtub and enters her while she is taking a bath) and spreading beyond the building into the city and, potentially, the rest of society.

The theme of sexual violation as a result of medicine also plays a role in *Rabid*. Unlike Hobbes, Keloid does not come across as a sexual deviant; the actual operation does not have a sexual element to it, nor is the character of Rose sexualized in any way during this particular scene, even though she is played by adult-film star Marilyn Chambers. However, as in *Shivers*, the medical operation in *Rabid* is once again the catalyst for the events that will unfold, for it transforms Rose – against her will – into the being she will become: a perpetrator of vampiric, sexualized assaults on others. Hidden inside the puckered, anus-like opening under her left armpit, Rose's penis-shaped organ extends outward to penetrate her victims while she embraces them, oftentimes in a sexualized manner – taking away their life source, and giving them an STI-like disease and madness in return. Rose's victims, all of whom except one are male, become subjects of this forced penetration, with Rose taking on a role reversal of the traditionally male rapist/sexual predator who does not typically hunt or attack other men. This shifting of male and female sexual characteristics is noted by Mary B. Campbell in her essay, "Biological Alchemy and the Films of David Cronenberg": "In both *Shivers* and *Rabid*, transformations involve transference and confusion of sexual characteristics, resulting in ominous parodies of the Androgyne, men giving birth to monstrous lumps of flesh in the former, a woman with a phallic organ that sucks in fluids rather than expelling them in the later" (Campbell 2004, 339). In fact, the escalating attacks in *Shivers* and *Rabid*, the ability of Nola to both rapidly conceive and bear mutant children on her own, and the imminent birth of untold numbers of scanner babies could certainly be seen as a form of scientifically engineered cancer, rapidly spreading out of control:

> Cronenberg's oeuvre ... presents the images of sexual life as a kind of cancer unleashed by precisely those scientific practitioners whose function should be to control and regulate it. There is a doctor at fault in each of these films, a doctor searching for a magic trick that will render nature more vital and generative than it already is ... The errors of these zealous medical experimenters seems to be compounded of an unbridled enthusiasm for the generative and regenerative powers of technology and the belief that more is better. (Campbell 2004, 342)

Ultimately, all the doctors involved get their comeuppance in one way or another: Hobbes kills himself in remorse; after being punctured by Rose, Keloid literally turns into a slavering, foaming-at-the-mouth "mad doctor" to be locked up, presumably until he expires; Raglan is literally torn apart by Nola's (and his) brood of mutant children; and Ruth is murdered by ConSec's traitorous security chief Keller (Lawrence Dane), who is working alongside Revok and ensuring the distribution of Ephemerol is uninterrupted. Even though his films ostensibly portray the medical and scientific communities as corrupt entities, Cronenberg himself has stated that he does not personally share that viewpoint:

> People of incredible power and charisma and intellect appeal to me as main characters in a film, just as they do in life. When I'm delineating their downfall, I'm really referring to a much larger canvas. I mean we are all trying to deal with life. We all are trying to make sense out of the world, trying to cope with it and, hopefully, make something creative out of it. I feel a lot of empathy for doctors and scientists. In fact, I often feel that they are my persona in the film. In another way, everybody's a mad scientist, and life is their lab. We're all trying to experiment to find a way to live, to solve problems, to fend off madness and chaos. (Sammon 1981, 26)

Conclusion

Although the mad doctor/scientist had been a firmly established arche-type of American and European horror cinema, the figure nevertheless became a largely ineffectual caricature by the mid-1970s. Camp-filled efforts such as *The Incredible 2-Headed Transplant* (1971) presented uncon-vincing scientists like Dr Roger Girard (Bruce Dern) engaged in fatu-ous head transplantation experiments on animals and people. Revered titles like *Young Frankenstein* (1974) and *The Rocky Horror Picture Show* (1975) were affectionate send-ups of classic Universal and Hammer horror films that gave audiences the endearing Dr Frederic Franken-stein (Gene Wilder) and Dr Frank-N-Furter (Tim Curry) – mad doctors who were more to be laughed at than feared. Cronenberg's deviant, irresponsible mad doctor figures on the other hand, were responsible for unleashing dangers considerably worse than singing and dancing man-made beings or a maniacal, double-headed person running amok.

Cronenberg's multidimensional doctor/scientist figure remains the most effective representation of the modern cinematic mad scientist, especially as the destructive consequences of the mad doctor's actions appear more grounded in reality and are thus all the more tragic and reprehensible. And despite Cronenberg's assertion that he sympathizes with doctors and scientists, his work – in particular these earlier projects – generally tends to portray them in a negative light. What also stands out, as Sean Moreland will detail in the next chapter, is this blending of such trademark "Cronenbergian" themes as bodily transformation, dis-ease, and mutation, as well as the addition of twisted sexuality, blood, and violence, all of which are significant in the work of recent filmmak-ers who maintain the "body horror" aspect in Canadian horror cinema.

NOTES

1 Harris/Decima Poll press release, "Most Say Health Care System Working, No Appetite for Further Privatization," 5 July 2009, http://www.harrisdecima.ca/sites/default/files/releases/071009E.pdf.
2 "A Dark History Revealed," broadcast date, 14 August 1992, CBC Digital Archives: *The Duplessis Orphans*, http://archives.cbc.ca/society/youth/topics/1633/; "Duplessis Orphans Get $26M from Quebec," CBC News (online), 21 December 2006, http://www.cbc.ca/archives/categories/society/youth/the-duplessis-orphans/a-dark-history-revealed.html.

3 Sonya Norris, "Canada's Blood Supply Ten Years after the Krever
   Commission," Parliament of Canada (online), 10 July 2008, http://www.
   parl.gc.ca/Content/LOP/researchpublications/prb0814-e.htm; *Canada's
   Tainted Blood Scandal: A Timeline*, CBC In-Depth, http://www.cbc.ca/news/
   background/taintedblood/bloodscandal_timeline.html (Oct. 1, 2007).
4 Paul Corupe, "Shivers," *On Screen!* Pippin Productions, Soapbox
   Productions, original broadcast date: 10 February 2010.
5 *The Memory Thief*, BBC documentary, http://www.youtube.com/
   watchv=7aPPdKewAHc; Collins (1998), 2, 130, 131, 155.
6 "Life in an Orphanage," *Man Alive*, broadcast date: 8 February 1993, CBC
   Digital Archives, *The Duplessis Orphans*, http://www.cbc.ca/archives/
   categories/society/youth/the-duplessis-orphans/topic-the-duplessis-
   orphans.html.
7 *The Canadian Tragedy*, Thalidomide Victims Association of Canada, http://
   www.thalidomide.ca/the-canadian-tragedy/.

13 Contagious Characters: Cronenberg's *Rabid*, Demarbre's *Smash Cut*, and the Reframing of Porn-Fame

SEAN MORELAND

In his idiosyncratic but penetrating history of Canadian horror film, Caelum Vatnsdal points out that "horror is, along with pornography, among the most misbegotten of genres, and this is perhaps triply true in Canada" (Vatnsdal 2004, 16).[1] Due to the greater role played by government arts support in Canada, as compared to the US, the ethical and aesthetic biases of funding bodies are a major factor in determining which films get made, and what kind of financing they receive. Horror and pornography are both typically deemed to be exploitative and sensationalistic genres, and films perceived as such are thus unlikely to receive support. This ignominious association[2] in part accounts for why a handful of Canadian films have been both motivated and uniquely enabled to effectively reframe the perceived links between horror and pornography. This essay is concerned with the way that two such films, David Cronenberg's *Rabid* and Lee Gordon Demarbre's *Smash Cut* (2009) deploy and interrogate the horror/porn generic intertexts in quite different and yet complementary ways. I argue that both these films provoke their audiences into engaging with received associations between horror and pornography using a combination of cinematic allusion, self-conscious generic parody, and a deft exploitation of what I will term *character-contagion*.

Character-contagion is a familiar cinematic phenomenon that involves a semantic slippage between *character*, understood as a role portrayed by an actor, and *character*, a quality possessed or embodied by the actor.[3] This is a factor that filmmakers frequently exploit and which changes the perception that audiences, including critics, have of films, even before they actually view them. Casting is often tied to audience expectations and can contribute to the implicit "viewing contract"[4] that

.DUNNING/LINK/REITMAN present **MARILYN CHAMBERS** IN **RABID** starring JOE SILVER · HOWARD RYSHPAN and FRANK MOORE as READ written & directed by DAVID CRONENBERG

13.1. Publicity still for *Rabid*. Courtesy of Cinépix.

the film is expected to fulfil. This is especially true of horror films, many of which play with the generic competence of audiences intensively, referencing one another in various ways, including through the actors they employ,[5] which has led to the typecasting of many a performer and the creation of numerous cult horror "stars." Both Cronenberg's and Demarbre's films emphasize their intertexts with the pornographic film roles of the actresses (Marilyn Chambers and Sasha Grey, respectively) who portray their protagonists, but they do so in very different ways, and ultimately, to disparate ends.

Rabid was Cronenberg's second commercial feature film, and like his first, *Shivers*, it is at base a contagion-apocalypse narrative very much in the same vein as Romero's *Night of the Living Dead* (1968) or *The Crazies*

(1973). What chiefly distinguishes both of Cronenberg's films from Romero's contagiously influential classics, however, is their abandonment of the American director's largely asexual eschatology. Instead, sexuality is explicitly situated at the epicentre of Cronenberg's epidemics. The manifold continuities between *Shivers* and *Rabid* have led a number of writers, including the chronically astute Kim Newman,[6] to portray *Rabid* as a sequel to, or continuation of, *Shivers*. In his voice-over commentary for *Rabid*, however, Cronenberg describes that film as not so much a sequel as "a companion piece" to *Shivers*, and I would like to stress that most of the major differences between these films, despite their similar subject matter, derive from *Rabid*'s identificatory and perspectival structures, and it is these that chiefly inform my argument.

Generically speaking, *Rabid* is, as already mentioned, probably best understood as a contagion-horror narrative having many commonalities with zombie-apocalypse fictions. However, unlike *Shivers*, it also displays elements of the slasher genre, which was in the early stages of what Carol Clover has identified as its second cycle at the time of the film's production.[7] Admittedly, *Rabid* does not involve many of the most obvious characteristics of the slasher film; there are no "first-person stalker camera" shots, nor is there even, in the ordinary sense, a single killer – the film's various murders are committed by an assortment of pseudo-rabid, infected individuals. Nevertheless, it shares with slasher films certain thematic and structural continuities that I would like to foreground here:[8] most importantly, its use of a female protagonist as the chief object of identification for the audience. This character, Rose (Chambers), shares many characteristics with what Clover influentially called "the final girl" (Clover 1993, 35) of the slasher film formula. More specifically, Rose's role can be recognized as a fusion of the function of the monster/killer and the final girl. In its synthesis of these character-functions, *Rabid* presents a logical extension of the affinity between the monster and the final girl that both Clover and Linda Williams have observed in many horror films.

Clover boils down the trajectory followed by every final girl as follows: "The Final Girl (1) undergoes agonizing trials, and (2) virtually or actually destroys the antagonist and saves herself" (1993, 59). The first point and the first half of the second clearly describe *Rabid*'s Rose, who finally rises above the impotence and incompetence of the film's many failed figures of masculine authority when she finds a radical, and self-sacrificing, solution to the crisis she has unwittingly precipitated. In effect, she commits suicide, using one of those she has infected as her

instrument. The failure of various institutions and male authority figures to resolve the crisis throughout the film (the source of much of its
black comedy) is typical of the anti-authoritarian sensibility that Wood
praised in many American horror films of the 1970s,[9] but this representation of the failure of masculine authority is also quintessentially Canadian. As Bill Beard has pointed out, "Passivity, ineffectiveness, weakness: these are all qualities recognizable in the male protagonists of a
broad strain of Canadian literary and cinematic fiction" (Beard 2001,
65), and are all qualities that characterize many of Cronenberg's other
films, from *The Brood* through to *Spider.*

I would like to further emphasize that this identificatory structure,
whereby the audience is primarily invited to share the point of view of
a female character, parallels not only that of most slasher films, through
the figure of the final girl, but also Chambers's most important pornographic film roles up to that point, including *Behind the Green Door* (1972)
and *The Resurrection of Eve* (1973), films which *Rabid* visually alludes to.
As Linda Williams observes in her classic study of the generic characteristics of porn, *Hardcore*, these films are among the first to treat the female
"heroine" as the continuous locus of identification for the audience, as
they provide "an abundance of interchangeable men – and their penises –
in relation to a single woman" (Williams 1989, 159). This brings me to
another, closely related, difference between *Shivers* and *Rabid*, and that
is their casting. While *Shivers*'s cast was largely composed of relatively
unknown actors (in part, no doubt, a function of its minimal funding),
Cronenberg and his collaborators were determined to secure a more
high-profile figure to portray Rose. While Cronenberg initially wanted
Sissy Spacek, fresh from de Palma's adaptation of Stephen King's *Carrie* (1976), to play the part, his co-producers, Ivan Reitman, André Link,
and John Dunning, had other ideas. In Vatnsdal's words, their "exploitation muscles were twitching with the possibility of hiring porno star-
let Marilyn Chambers, of the crossover hit *Behind the Green Door*, [mak-
ing *Rabid*] her first 'legitimate' picture" (Vatnsdal 2004, 112).

In his commentary on the film, Cronenberg explains that a "lot of the
story of the movie *Rabid* is the story of Marilyn Chambers," describing Chambers by saying she "was a notorious porno star ... who was
really making her debut as a straight film actress in this movie ... this
was actually Ivan Reitman's idea ... because we couldn't afford a real
star he came up with the idea of getting Marilyn Chambers, who had
become quite famous in the general public because she had been the
Ivory Snow woman."[10] Williams explains: "Originally known as the

100-percent pure Ivory Snow Girl who scandalized the advertising industry by associating herself with 'dirty movies' in the 1972 *Behind the Green Door* (Mitchell Bros.), Chambers was Linda Lovelace's main competitor" (Williams 1989, 156) for pornographic-film fame or, following Cronenberg's characterization, *notoriety*.

According to his commentary on the film, while Cronenberg was aware of Chambers's porn background, he had not actually seen any of her work in that genre prior to casting her, a decision that he insists was motivated primarily by her impressive performances. Yet the popular and critical furore elicited by Chambers's casting effectively underscores the stigma associated with pornographic film work, which serves to make *Rabid*'s interrogation of sexual anxieties, particularly those linked to female desire, more powerful. In short, as Cronenberg readily acknowledges in his commentary, *Rabid* relies on the character-contagion associated with Chambers's earlier career for some of its effects.

Cronenberg's description of Chambers as "a notorious porno star" and his admission that he and his producers were particularly interested in casting her because they couldn't "afford to hire a real star"[11] suggests the degree to which character-contagion is a phenomenon intrinsic to the concept of stardom itself. Robert C. Allen writes that, at "its most basic, the concept of stardom would seem to involve a duality between actor and character" (Allen 1999, 547), a duality predicated on its own labile capacity for collapse. Similarly, in a seminal essay on key differences between theatrical and cinematic acting, Leo Braudy notes that the "line between film actor and part is much more difficult to draw than that between stage actor and role, and the social dimension of 'role' contrasts appropriately with the personal dimension of 'part'" (Braudy 1999, 420). Braudy's phrasing suggests the degree to which the characters portrayed by film actors become perceived as "part" of their own character, or conversely the degree to which the film actor becomes merely a "part" of the character she embodies, feeding into the cult of personality that has surrounded popular film stars since the beginning of the twentieth century. Braudy goes on to write that "the other life of a film character is the continuity in other films of the career of the actor who plays him" (421), acknowledging that both audiences and filmmakers retroactively consider characters previously played by an actor in light of more recent parts they've embodied. Braudy emphasizes that "the film actor does not so much perform a role as he creates a kind of life, playing between his characterization in a particular film and his potential escape from that character" (421). This description of the actor as a "creator" of "a kind of life," redolent as it is of a B-movie figuration of Dr Frankenstein, is particularly apt where *Rabid* is concerned, since Rose, who becomes a form of life other than what we normally think of as human, assimilates, and is in turn assimilated by, Chambers's prior and subsequent parts, including *Behind the Green Door*'s Gloria, *The Resurrection of Eve*'s eponymous heroine, and the *Insatiable* Sandra. By this logic, it can be better understood that, together, Cronenberg and Chambers have woven her previous, highly publicized (private?) parts into the part she plays in *Rabid*, making Rose an assemblage of sexualized parts, reflecting her physical hybridity as a quintessentially Cronenbergian bricolage of fractious flesh.

Rabid is programmatic in its emphasis on Chambers's character's confusion with Rose's character right from its opening scene. The first actor's credit to appear is, of course, Chambers's, and it is accompanied by a langorously dollying shot, beginning from behind, of Rose standing, in full biking leather, beside a Norton motorcycle. The camera circles around nearly 180 degrees until it faces Rose, her gaze distantly off to the side. This opening shot doubly frames Rose as both an object of the audience's gaze (coyly alluding to Chambers's previous pornographic roles by showing, as Cronenberg chucklingly observes in his commentary, "Marilyn Chambers in *leather*")[12] and a locus of their identification throughout the remainder of the film. This 180-degree camera movement is highly conspicuous, breaking from the traditional limitations of a particular shot's range of vision to about 30 degrees, a convention which, as Daniel Dayan and others have argued, suggests the illusion of an extradiegetic character's viewpoint through which the viewer is sutured into the film's narrative.[13]

Thus, this opening sequence of shots represents a deliberate rupture from what Kaja Silverman has described as "the imperative that the camera deny its own existence as much as possible, fostering the illusion that what is shown has an autonomous existence, independent of any technological interference, or any coercive gaze" (Silverman 1999, 138). Cronenberg's commentary stresses the importance of this effect, underlining for the audience the importance that this is *Marilyn Chambers*™, not merely some actress playing the part of a character named Rose, thus emphasizing the importance of this character-contagion.

This device is easily, and often, overused, especially by films aligned with both the porn and horror genres, but *Rabid* employs it to fascinating effect. The film goes on to foreground its intertextual relationship with various other films, including Chambers's pornographic roles, through a series of visual allusions. As Ernest Mathijs writes:

> There are filmic references and winks that testify to Cronenberg's familiarity with popular culture: before Rose approaches Judy in the hospital's hot tub, we see Judy toting a biography of Sigmund Freud; a poster for *Easy Rider* adorns Hart's workshop; and when Rose prowls the streets of Montreal's bustling entertainment district, she enters a porn theatre named Eve (the title of one of Marilyn Chambers' porn films was *The Resurrection of Eve* [Jon Fontana/Artie Mitchell, 1973], where a Cinepix film is playing. After she has consumed the sleazebag who seduces her there, she wanders the streets again, and passes a poster of *Carrie* (Brian de Palma, 1976) – a film that contains, like her, a female lead in a modern horror film that is monstrous and heroic. (Mathijs 2008, 39)

I would like to comment in passing on a few of these references before unpacking the film's allusion to *The Resurrection of Eve*. First, like *Rabid*, *Carrie* fused the character-functions of the menacing monster and the damsel in distress to stunning effect, and created one of the most influential modern incarnations of the monstrous-feminine. Second, the pseudo-lesbian and quasi-softcore-pornographic "hot tub scene" prefaced by Judy's reading of Freud's biography bears (or bares) some discussion. During his commentary on the film, Cronenberg comments a number of times on the degree to which *Rabid* represents a technologically driven modernization of the vampire myth.[14] He emphasizes this especially during his discussion of the hot-tub scene, which he describes as "strangely traditional," affirming that it "definitely relates to all the lesbian vampire scenes you might have seen – there are many of them in the history of cinema."[15] As this suggests, the scene is chiefly a visual homage to the spate of lesbian vampire films of the late 1960s and 1970s,[16] most of them very loosely inspired by Le Fanu's story *Carmilla* (1872).

Disregarding the scene's vampiric-generic qualities, Beard emphasizes its association with a common pornographic formula. He notes that Judy is a sexualized figure here – though once again not narratively and not for her "'partner' Rose, but only for the male heterosexual viewer. Rose's approach and attack here are resolute, self-possessed, and commanding ... She is, more than in any of the other attacks, truly the 'male' in this coupling; although as a sexual spectacle for the male viewer the scene more resembles perhaps the 'lesbian' conventional pornographic skit" (2001, 55). Here, and throughout his chapter on *Rabid*, Beard reads Rose as a metonym for the film itself, imagining her/it as singling out particular (salacious, voyeuristic, heterosexual, male) members of the audience and punishing them for the kinds of pleasure they are presumed to have taken from her sexual exploitation in previous films, and by extension for the pleasure they are presumed to try to take from her role in *Rabid*. This reading reinforces another of the ways that *Rabid* plays with its own generic parts as well as its actor's parts in attaining its provocative hybridity. The film's punishment of certain types of "illicit" pleasures, in this case the predatory sexuality of many of Rose's male victims, parallels the reactionary moralism of many slasher films of the late 70s in which a variety of (typically young) characters are "punished" for hedonistic, and most often sexual, behaviours.[17]

The major difference is that, at least if we accept Beard's interpretation, *Rabid* seeks to punish certain types of *audience* response by extension. In effect, Beard suggests, Rose is a diegetic embodiment of the film itself, and the various predatory males she consumes embody a certain segment of the audience, who want to consume Rose as a typical (i.e., pornographic) Marilyn Chambers part – something that the film also clearly *invites* them to do.

Beard's argument becomes more fully articulated in his discussion of the scenes that circulate around the Eve adult theatre. He claims that the scene in which a "sleazebag" (Mathijs's term) audience member attempts to pick up Rose while publicly viewing a (Cinépix) softcore porn film "makes it clear that *Rabid* is not a film that shares the assumptions of the average porno movie and is quite prepared to turn its wrath grimly on viewers who might wish to see it simply in that light – whether as sexual spectacle, violence/horror spectacle, or any combination of the two" (Beard 2001, 58). These scenes are prefaced, as Mathijs has pointed out, by the allusion to Chambers's earlier role in *The Resurrection of Eve*, as though reminding the audience of the truth of Braudy's observation that "the other life of a film character is the continuity in other films ... of the actor" (1999, 421). But what can be gleaned from this allusion? How does it "frame" the audience's experience of *Rabid*?

In suggesting one possible answer to this question, I turn to Williams's observation about the basic, and basically sadomasochistic, duality that structures much of the "mainstream" pornography of the 1970s and 1980s. Williams observes that under "a patriarchal double standard that has rigorously separated the sexually passive 'good' girl from the sexually active 'bad' girl, masochistic role-playing offers a way out of this dichotomy by combining the good girl with the bad: the passive 'good girl' can prove to her witnesses (the super-ego who is her torturer) that she does not will the pleasure that she receives. Yet the sexually active 'bad' girl enjoys this pleasure" (1989, 8). *The Resurrection of Eve* welded these contradictory aspects by its portrayal of Eve's gradual trajectory from the former to the latter, ambiguously connecting her transformation, in a manner reminiscent of Masoch's *Venus in Furs*, to the desire of her husband. *Behind the Green Door,* on the other hand, achieves this combination by the plot device of Gloria's hypnosis; while her "good," sexually innocent, conscious persona presumably abhors the series of sexual acts she engages in, her unleashed libidinous side glories in them.

Rabid's reference to *Eve* foregrounds the degree to which it engages with the same dualism in its (male-imaginary) presentation of Rose's desire (in this case, cathected *from* semen, which constitutes the "money shots" of the porn world, *into* blood, which constitutes those of the horror world). Indeed, *Rabid*'s solution to this sadomasochistic dichotomy is closer to *Green Door*'s, as it similarly emphasizes Rose's unnaturally and suddenly fused duality, but in a characteristically Cronenbergian grotesque literalization, this fusion is fleshy, as Keloid's experimental surgery has in effect welded Rose-the-passive-victim with Rose-the-seductive-vampiric-phallus-monster.[18] In Andrew Parker's apt phrase, "Dr. Keloid's experiment and Cronenberg's film thus commonly go astray" in that they obey "the logic of a different graft" (Parker 1993, 18).

An even more poignant and distressing instantiation of Braudy's observation may be the closing scene in *Insatiable*, the first major porn film Chambers headlined after her work in *Rabid*. The film ends, after having shown Sandra's epic masturbatory fantasy of serial partners, with a close-up of her sweat-gleaming naked body, flexing and twitching as she desperately moans and mutters, "more, more, I need more." I suspect I am not alone in finding the scene (like much else in *Insatiable*) more horrifying than erotic. It reverberates unsettlingly with *Rabid*'s scene of Rose on the floor of her friend's tidy bathroom, shuddering and sweat-streaked in convulsions of blood withdrawal. This is one of the many scenes in which, as Parker notes, even though Chambers appears in her underwear, she is "not thereby highly eroticized" (1993, 13). On the contrary, this is one of *Rabid*'s most pathos-laden scenes, effectively inviting the audience to identify with Rose's abject sufferings, and it is a watershed moment in Cronenberg's film-making career, one that makes the film far more memorable and potent than its precursor, *Shivers*.

Williams has read *Insatiable*, and particularly its closing scene, as something of a parallel watershed moment in the world of hardcore porn. She writes: "I am not sure just when the change begins to occur, but sometime in the early eighties, and especially in the dissolved category of hard-core utopia (most markedly in the 1980 *Insatiable* and its 1984 sequel *Insatiable II*), the phallus falters: it no longer acts as the standard of measurement for either male or female pleasure" (Williams 1989, 180). The frenzied desperation of Sandra's insatiability suggests both the limits of the phallus-as-signifier-for-pleasure, and the limits of pleasure-through-visual-representation.[19] If one considers *Insatiable*'s closing scene with both Braudy's and Williams's observations in mind, it begins to seem as if the American pornographic film world became infected by a kind of contagious inadequacy, transmitted from Cronenberg's sexuality-scrutinizing cinema via the carrier of Chambers, and as if the phallic lack emphasized by *Insatiable* and related films was prefigured by *Rabid*'s remetaphorization of the phallus as a signifier of violation, exploitation, and addiction.

Of course, the contagion passes both ways, and Chambers's sense of disappointment and betrayal with her adult film career has, for me at least, indelibly inflected *Rabid*'s bleak conclusion with a kind of pathos which I doubt the film could sustain without it. Reminiscent of the overt nihilism of *Night of the Living Dead*'s closing scenes, *Rabid* ends with Rose's body, lying on a garbage heap in the streets, being gnawed upon by a Dobermann, until a group of biohazard-suited men indifferently toss it into a garbage truck to be taken away for disposal. Interviewed in 2003, after *Rabid*'s DVD release, Chambers remarked, with characteristically witty bitterness, "I'm kind of pissed off that I didn't get over the hump, pardon the expression, and get to do my major film." In the same interview, Chambers cites the spectre of AIDS (which many, Cronenberg included, have seen *Rabid* as anticipating)[20] and the exploitative tendency of the industry, in which performers are often poorly paid while filmmakers and their backers make millions, as her major reasons for leaving the adult film industry. She goes on to state, "My advice to somebody who wants to go into adult films is: Absolutely not! It's heart-breaking. And it's really not ... (she searches for words, sounding emotional) ... it leaves you kind of empty. So have a day job and don't quit it."[21]

The commingled horror and absurdism that often characterized the big-budget porn films of the 1970s are not lost on Ottawa-based film-maker Lee Gordon Demarbre, who remarks that "*Deepthroat, Behind the Green Door*, all those ... movies *weren't* sexy, not for a second. They're all about *freak show*,"[22] and Demarbre's ambivalent fascination for these films, and the porn industry in general, partially informed his creation, thirty years after *Rabid*'s release, of a film that very differently engages with some of the horror-porn intertexts (dis)entangled by Cronenberg's film. In particular, Demarbre's giddily inventive horror-comedy, *Smash Cut*, invokes the controversy that surrounded Chambers's casting in *Rabid*. Like *Rabid*, *Smash Cut* is the first non-pornographic film feature for a well-known American porn-star, in this case Sasha Grey.[23]

Demarbre affirms that one of his reasons for casting Grey was as an allusion to Cronenberg's film, while freely admitting that another was to capitalize on the notoriety associated with her name and reputation.[24] However, in contrast with *Rabid*'s producers' enthusiasm for Chambers's casting, Grey's casting was a source of anxiety for the film's producers, who were concerned that her presence in the film would interfere with funding due to a now-retired piece of Canadian legislation, the Tax Amendments Act, 2006. Many Canadian film-makers (including Cronenberg) raised an outcry against the passage of this act, maintaining that it would effectively put in place a fiscally based policy of government censorship.[25] *Smash Cut*'s completion roughly coincided with the Harper government's scrapping of the act, making its restaging of issues raised by *Rabid* especially timely.

In contrast with *Rabid*'s contagion motif, *Smash Cut* is, at base, a satirical parody of the slasher film genre and, perhaps even more importantly, but certainly even more blatantly, an affectionate imitation of and homage to American exploitation-film legend Herschell Gordon Lewis.[26] The film is insistent on this lineage, and opens with an epigraph that also serves to contextualize its satirical thrust: "I see filmmaking as a business and pity anyone who regards it as an art form" (Herschell Gordon Lewis). This epigraph is followed by a warning delivered to the audience by Lewis himself, who cautions them to watch "only if [they] must." *Smash Cut* prefaces itself with a big wink, knowing that the pleasure its ideal audience expects will come not from its *terror*, but from its deliberate *terribleness*. Demarbre is a *soi-disant* disciple of Lewis, viewing him as a cinematic mentor, and his reverence for the "Godfather of Gore" is shared by many fans and creators of exploitation-inflected indie films. Jeffrey Sconce writes:

> Though aficionados of low-budget science-fiction and horror may have first watched these films as objects of ridicule, many also went on to identify with the role of the exploiter in exploitation cinema. Director/ producers like Corman, David F. Friedman, William Castle, H.G. Lewis, and others have become folk heroes in this community by acknowledging, indeed embracing, the fundamental hucksterism of all cinema, each in his own way a cynical pragmatist unencumbered by the delusions of art and gravitas that afflict more deluded filmmakers. (Sconce 2007, 288)

Unlike Demarbre's *miglior fabbro* Lewis, however, *Smash Cut's* antic antihero, Able Whitman (David Hess), is decidedly one of these "deluded filmmakers," whose pathological auteurist pretensions and delusions of mythic grandeur (worthy of his American literary eponym) are matched only by his epic failure and vast absence of talent. The name "Able" both ironically underpins his lack of talent and sticks its tongue in the cheek of Judaeo-Christian Scripture by suggesting an affinity between Able's (human) sacrifices for his art and the flesh-and-blood sacrifices offered by the biblical Abel. While Whitman repeatedly compares himself to Shakespeare, tirelessly haranguing anyone who will listen with his theory about Hamlet ("Do you know what the greatest work in the history of English literature *is*? It's a fucking *horror film!*"), his last name ironically invokes the nation-defining songs of the American poet, but perhaps more importantly is a further reference to Lewis, who described his sanguine, seminal schlock-shocker *Blood Feast* (1963) as "like a Walt Whitman poem. It's no good, but it's the first of its kind, therefore it deserves recognition" (Miller 2010, 81).

Following Lewis's caveat to viewers, *Smash Cut's* narrative proper begins with a few ably awful moments from what turns out to be Whitman's most recent production, as the audience recognizes when scenes from this film within a film alternate with reaction shots from a fictional audience watching the film in an Ottawa revue theatre. Throwing popcorn at the screen, the dissatisfied filmgoers shout condemnations including "This movie is lame!" "That was the death of cinema!" and, most memorably, "that guy [Whitman] makes Ed Wood look like Orson Welles." These scenes are followed by a reaction shot to this reaction shot, as we see the ill-starred auteur, Able Whitman, dressed as Bobo the Killer Clown from the film within a film; in tears and enraged, he declares that the audience deserves "to die before they get to see the end of the film!"

Appropriately enough, from this point on *Smash Cut*'s plot begins to roughly parallel that of *Blood Feast*, fused with occasional elements from other slasher films. *Blood Feast*'s premise is one of Orientalism run rampant, as Egyptian caterer Fuad Ramses (Mal Arnold) slaughters a series of young women in order to set the glittering tables of his elite clientele in the style to which they have become accustomed. In his quasi-biographical study of Lewis's films, Christopher Wayne Curry argued that Fuad Ramses was "the original machete-wielding madman" (Curry 1998, 67) and thus the prototype of the killers that came to define the slasher genre from the late 70s on. While this specific claim is debatable, it cannot be denied that Lewis's film was a major precursor to the genre, particularly in terms of its increasing preoccupation with explicit gore and inventive (and often deliberately ridiculous) death scenes.

Instead of an Egyptian caterer, *Smash Cut*'s (only, Demarbe insists, semi-autobiographical) killer is, of course, a Canadian filmmaker[27] who comes unhinged after witnessing first the "death" of his last film at the hands of audiences and critics, and second, the death of his stripper girlfriend, Gigi Spot (Jennilee Murray), in a car crash, and subsequently decides that real carnage is the only way he can attain the authentic visions of horror he has spent his life trying to realize. Other major elements of *Smash Cut*'s plot are also drawn from different Lewis films. Sasha Grey's character April Carson in particular owes something to Kathy Baker (Gretchen Wells), the persistent heroine of *The Gruesome Twosome* (1967), a film whose title appears in a newspaper description of the murder of producer Ozzy Coburg and his stripper girlfriend within *Smash Cut*. Her role also has marked parallels with that of Lila (Vera Miles), Marion Crane (Janet Leigh)'s sister from *Psycho* (1960) another vital precursor to the slasher genre that *Smash Cut* sends up with such aplomb.

Like Lila in Hitchcock's film, April is in search of her missing sister, the same unfortunate Gigi whom the audience realizes has been killed in a car crash and subsequently converted into a rapidly rotting post-mortem muse by Whitman. Also like Lila, April enlists the aid of a professional investigator, in this case the eccentric Isaac Beaumonde (portrayed by professional clown and physical comedian Jesse Buck) in trying to uncover her sister's whereabouts. The film, through facial close-ups and subjective shots that emphasize April's investigating gaze, frames her as the quintessential "woman who looks" in Williams's memorable phrasing (Williams 1996). In this way, it also ironically parries the expectations of audiences who expect Sasha Grey, porn star, to be primarily a recipient, rather than a source, of the gaze. While *Smash Cut* cannot resist a few coyly fetishistic close-ups of (clothed) parts of Grey's anatomy (in particular, her feet are framed in a couple of comically conspicuous shots), it more often emphasizes Grey as a watcher. This tendency is doubly emphasized during the scenes when she plays a part (in playing with the body parts of his victims, including, unbeknown to her, the head of her sister Gigi) for Whitman's camera. These scenes are marked out by the presence of crosshairs over the camera's subject, emphasizing their status as films within the film of *Smash Cut*. In most of these scenes, April seemingly breaks the fourth wall at Whitman's instruction, by delivering all of her lines directly to the camera/audience, often while offering the camera (which in this case incarnates Bobo, the killer clown-puppet) body parts which Whitman persuades her are fake (and which of course look *fromageously* unreal), but which the audience recognizes as the "real" parts of Whitman's various victims.

Demarbre recounts that he and Lewis discussed many different potential titles for the film, including *Cinemaniac*. Most of these were drawn from ideas that Lewis had at one point contemplated making; many of these titles appear on promotional posters within the film, attributed to Whitman and his producers. The title *Smash Cut*, however, is particularly apt for a number of reasons pertinent to my framing of the film here. A smash cut refers to an abrupt cut from one scene to another, and usually very different, scene without contextualizing transition. It is a technique usually used to surprise or startle the audience, or to create juxtaposition, often through irony, between scenes. Less literally, the "cut" of the title is redolent of the slasher genre, and emphasizes the film's generic parody. It also suggests Grey's "break" into non-pornographic film, a break that both she and Demarbre consciously designed to make with this film. Retrospectively, the title also reflects the smashed expectations of both some of the film's producers and some of its viewers, as the former marketed it as, and many of the latter apparently expected it to be, a horror film in the most literal, affective sense of the word. The film further departs from the expectations of some of its producers and audiences in that it is widely advertised as starring Sasha Grey, but it involves no scenes of explicit sex, and Grey remains fully clothed throughout the entire film. In fact, she is deliberately played "against type," as an innocent ingénue, in keeping with the film's installation of the slasher film's stereotyped final girl, generally characterized by her virginity, or at least sexual reticence.

This smash cutting of expectations is effectively the film's modus operandi. Like *Rabid*, it relies on the audience's awareness of its character-contagion for some of its effects, but unlike *Rabid*, it does so by playing its character-actors against expectation to comedic effect; in Demarbre's words, "Sasha Grey keeps her clothes on, David Hess isn't always raping and Michael Berryman has hair – everyone is playing against type."[28] In short, the film critically challenges the expectations of its audience by deliberately "cutting up" the implicit viewing contract its marketers and distributors helped to create. However, it is clear that Demarbre's film is not designed to "punish" audiences (except perhaps those members of the audience who are also producers!) for wanting to view it as a horror or a pornographic spectacle; rather, it is coloured by a consistent and infectious giddiness, and obviously prides itself on its own promiscuous intertextuality and saturation with generic codes.

Another apparent allusion to *Rabid* occurs during the establishing shot for what will become *Smash Cut*'s climax. In what must have been one of the film's most expensive scenes to shoot, the front of the Bytowne Theatre is initially framed with an eye-level, potentially subjective shot, which then rises across the face and over the roof of the building, the theatre's vertical red-lit sign tracing across the screen in a surprisingly lovely arc (one which occurs, ironically enough, shortly after Able's murder of his own cinematographer, Armand). The strategy of this shot, with the suggestion of a subjective viewpoint that moves into an elevated perspective that belies this impression, is similar to the sequence which opens *Rabid*, where the camera dollies around Rose. And, even more so, it also echoes *Rabid*'s shot outside the Eve adult theatre, which establishes the scene when Rose claims the first of her victims, also *literally* an audience member. This parallel is appropriate, for it is within the Bytowne that Whitman attempts to create his ultimate cinematic expression by using poisoned gas released from his own film[29] as it plays on the projector to kill his audience, while he, wearing a gas mask (and visually echoing the killer of the 1981 seminal Canadian slasher flick *My Bloody Valentine*), records the entire event.

Clearly, *Smash Cut*'s framing of a cinema within its own diegesis does not "frame" the adult film industry in the same way that Cronenberg's incorporation of the Eve porn theatre does. And yet Grey's contrapuntal characterization in the film necessarily brings it into critical dialogue with the world of porno. Unlike Cronenberg, Demarbre does not deny having had some familiarity with Grey's porn movies prior to casting her for his film; it was seeing her work in porn that led to his desire to work with her. Nevertheless, his decision to cast Grey in *Smash Cut*, against the advice of many of his producers, can also be read as something of a jab (stab?) at the porn industry, and one which is tied to the film's homage to Lewis's movies. Demarbre states that "what I hate about porn is that it killed erotic cinema, it killed a lot of my favourite film-makers. Ken Russell stopped making movies because of porno. Russ Meyer, to a degree, stopped making sexy movies because porno was where it was at."[30] His comment stresses an ambivalence towards the pornographic film industry, in part because the advent of commercial hardcore porn seemed to spell the collapse of a particularly rich vein of exploitation cinema, including Lewis's early "nudie-cuties," like *The Adventures of Lucky Pierre* (1961). Lewis, of course, was able to survive this collapse, which he foresaw in the early 1960s, by shifting his focus from nudie-cuties and soft-core sexploitation films to "hardcore" splatter films including the genre-defining *Blood Feast*. If we bear this in mind, Grey's transplantation from the "multiple penetration" world of porn into the "multiple penetration" world of slasher films with *Smash Cut* can be seen as a curious gloss of Lewis's transition from the sexploitation into what could be called the *gore-sploitation* film, and is yet another facet of the film's referential play.

It is hilariously driven home by the film's conclusion in which, during a sustained duel between Able Whitman (wielding phallic axe) and Isaac Beaumonde (brandishing phallic cane), Whitman, about to finish Beaumonde off, triumphantly declares "I have final cut, Mr Beaumonde!" – only to have April bury a knife in his back, followed by Beaumonde's driving of his own axe into his chest. As Whitman lies dying, he reveals the contents of the cooler he has carried throughout the film to be Gigi's head, at which point April, the avenging sister, uses a heavy-duty nailgun to drive another sort of point home into his head. For the generically competent viewer, this conclusion is an orgy of referential inversion and over-the-top visual puns, as Sasha Grey (famous for multiple-penetration scenes) multiply penetrates David Hess (famous for being typecast as a psychotic rapist and killer following his role in Craven's *The Last House on the Left*, 1972) in a splatstick three-way that ends with Beaumonde, in a bit of vaudevillery, using his cane to draw the curtains on the audience, informing them "I think *you've* seen enough."

Beaumonde's final line can be interpreted as a chiding of the audience for their desire to see more: more explicit sex, more explicit violence, more visual excess which the film, in a spirit very different from *Rabid*, "punishes" them by withholding. While *Smash Cut*, in this respect at least, echoes the audience-punitive sadomasochistic strategy that earlier linked *Rabid* to the slasher genre, it does so in an entirely different tone. Its satiric laughter is ultimately much lighter; where *Rabid* seeks to strike certain viewers in the groin with Rose's stabbing cock-proboscis for their preferences in cinematic pleasures, *Smash Cut* instead gleefully elects to "punish" them by having Sasha Grey in a vinyl nurse's outfit trepan them with outrageous allusions, and pleasure them with painful puns.

This lighter tone is in keeping with Grey's attitude towards the porn industry, an attitude in sharp contrast to Chambers's perspective later in her career. Grey has stated, "All women have the right to be feminist whether you're pro-porn or anti-porn," and that she sees her work, both in and outside the porn industry, as "sending a positive message to our society that every girl in porn is not abused and cracked out."[31] Unlike Chambers, who wanted to leave behind her career in pornographic film for "straight" film, only to find herself trapped in the former, Grey doesn't think the two need to be mutually exclusive, and her conception of her own career, and identity, is one which is readily compatible with the character-contagion on which both *Smash Cut* and *The Girlfriend Experience* rely: " I really want to blend the two together ... and focus on my career as a whole, not as two separate entities. They're all in one for me."[32] Whatever one might think of Grey's pro-porn stance, her insistence that the audience look at (i.e., *recognize*, as opposed to *watch*) her porn career, informs her investigative part as the "woman who looks" in *Smash Cut*, and is vital not only to the film's humour, but also its invitation to its audience to investigate their own assumptions, preferences, and judgments.

NOTES

1 Vatsndal (2004, 16). He adds: the "factors against which the average Canadian horror movie must struggle as it is conceived and made – principally, a shaky sense of national identity; a cinematic, not to say artistic, tradition in diametric opposition to horror; the paradox suggested by those first two components, and a host of economic issues on top of that – insure that most of them founder in their quest for greatness" (17).

2 This association is of course not unique to Canada insofar as many other
   national cinemas are predicated on the same "low cultural" affinity. Linda
   Williams has influentially linked this to the perception of each genre as
   predicated on a kind of excess; "pornography and horror films are ...
   systems of excess. Pornography is the lowest in cultural esteem, gross-out
   horror is next to lowest" (Williams 1991, 3).

3 According to the *OED*, the first definition is "the mental and moral
   qualities distinctive to an individual," in this case, Marilyn Chambers,
   while the second is "a person in a novel, play, or film," "a part played by
   an actor," in this case, the film's unfortunate heroine, Rose.

4 Dennis Giles, for example, explains that "what the film industry sells
   to the viewer is not a material thing but an experience, or promise, of
   pleasure," a tacit contract between audience and film. Giles adds that "the
   good movie experience is the result of a viewing contract scrupulously
   observed by the producers, the exhibitors, and the consumers of the show"
   (Giles 1984, 39).

5 The same effect is visible in the careers of "scream queens" from Barbara
   Steele to Danielle Harris and horror icons from Bela Lugosi to Robert
   Englund.

6 Kim Newman writes that *Rabid* "suffers from its son-of-*Shivers* place
   in Cronenberg's career," and is "a slightly more elaborate, slightly less
   startling footnote to its predecessor" (Newman 2011, 159). Nevertheless,
   one of the things that, to my mind, makes *Rabid* a much more effective
   and interesting film is its central focus on Rose as both locus of audience
   identification and epicentre of contagion ... not to mention Cronenberg's
   abandonment of "turd on a wire" (Vatnsdal's apt term) creatures for
   invisible virus particles (albeit ones discharged from a prosthetic penile
   stinger in Rose's armpit).

7 Clover notes that it was "between 1974 and 1986" that "the formula
   evolved and flourished in ways of some interest to observers of popular
   culture, above all those concerned with the representation of women in
   film" (Clover 1993, 26).

8 Adam Lowenstein (1998) has noted this, and persuasively linked
   Cronenberg's engagement with horror's spectatorial structures to the
   "Canadianness" of the director and his films. Cronenberg would go on to
   further stretch and modify the conventions of the slasher film in *The Brood*.
   There, the "stalk and slash" format of the slasher is reduplicated, and the
   role of the phallic-weapon-brandishing male killer is again superimposed
   on a woman, an archetypal embodiment of the monstrous-feminine that

Barbara Creed has considered at some length. However, in that film Cronenberg has abandoned the identificatory structure that makes *Rabid* so unique in his corpus.

9 However, Wood famously failed to appreciate this quality in Cronenberg's early films, which he dismissed as misogynistic and reactionary, as attested by his response to *Shivers*: "The most striking of this year's batch of exploitation movies, by virtue of its detestability, was David Cronenberg's *The Parasite Murders*. Its derivation is from *Invasion of the Body Snatchers* via *Night of the Living Dead*, but the source of its intensity is quite distinct: all the horror is based on extreme sexual disgust." Quoted in Ernest Mathijs (2008, 49).

10 *Rabid*, DVD commentary.

11 Ibid.

12 Ibid.

13 The scene also looks a great deal like an ad for the motorcycle, featuring a conventionally attractive woman gazing off into the distance, invoking Chambers's earlier role as the face of Ivory Soap. This is doubly ironized given Cronenberg's remarks about the total unreliability of the Norton, one of the reasons he elected to use that brand of machine for the film's accident sequence.

14 He states that Rose has "become a strange kind of vampire … without the mythology and the supernatural elements of the normal vampire story, which is a kind of filmmaking and storytelling that I've never been really very drawn to for myself. I mean I used to enjoy the Hammer Dracula films and so on, but they never appealed to me as a filmmaker" (*Rabid*, DVD commentary). It is noteworthy that, despite the preponderance of scholarly attention paid to the vampire in popular culture, critics have had relatively little to say about *Rabid* qua vampire film, aside from connecting both to the AIDS crisis.

15 *Rabid* DVD commentary.

16 Presumably including *Daughters of Darkness* (1971), *Lust for a Vampire* (1971), and *Vampyres* (1974).

17 A reading which parallels James Twitchell's (1985) early, and highly problematic, interpretation of horror film audience-types in *Dreadful Pleasures*.

18 In addition, it is hard to miss the degree to which this biological fantasy, *Rabid*'s key device, parallels the biological fantasy which is at the heart of *Deep Throat*. In the latter, a (mutant) woman is the centre of narrative attention due to the existence of a clitoris down her throat at the base of

her tongue. In the former, a (mutant) woman has a piercing penis in a vaginal sheath hidden in her armpit. See Linda William's discussion of this film in *Screening Sex* (2008, 131–43).

19 Gertrud Koch's discussion of the ejaculating penis as "a sign of inadequacy, an inadequacy of representation" is also insightful on this point (Koch 1993, 41–2).

20 Andrew Parker's remains the most salient and balanced consideration of the film's retrospective relationship with media coverage of the AIDS crisis (Parker 1993).

21 Marilyn Chambers, Jam Canoe interview, http://jam.canoe.ca/Movies/Artists/C/Chambers_Marilyn/2004/06/05/pf-757225.html.

22 Interview with author.

23 Contrary to the promotional materials for Soderbergh's *The Girlfriend Experience* (2009), released after *Smash Cut* had been shot and edited, but before its release. Soderbergh is similarly open about his desire to work with Grey, and stated: "We would be drafting off her notoriety rather than vice versa. I needed her. That's no different than getting Brad Pitt to be in your movie, albeit in a different context." Quoted in the *L.A. Times*, http://articles.latimes.com/2009/may/21/entertainment/et-sasha-grey21. It is interesting that, like Cronenberg on Chambers, Soderbergh identifies the actress's *notoriety* as central to the character-contagion on which his film depends.

24 Demarbre states: "I thought Sasha Grey would work, because Marilyn Chambers was in *Rabid*, and I thought not only was it a nice reference to the David Cronenberg movie, but it was also something that Herschell would do." Interview with author.

25 See, for example, Charlie Smith's Straight.com article at http://www.straight.com/article-149268/canadas-new-culture-war?rotator=1.

26 In pitching the script to Grey, Demarbre grinningly told her that Lewis was "his Godard," a statement which she has said clinched the deal for her. http://independentfilmquarterly.net/online-exclusives/sasha-grey-no-boundaries-left-to-cross.html.

27 The filmmaker-as-killer device is another of the film's numerous homages, in this case to Michael Powell's *Peeping Tom* (1960) and perhaps the Brazilian *Coffin Joe* films of José Mojica Marins.

28 *Ottawa Express* interview: http://www.ottawaxpress.ca/film/film.aspx?iIDArticle=18749.

29 It is worth noting that Demarbre had written the script for the film before Tarantino's *Inglourious Basterds* (2009) used a similar metacinematic method of mass murder.

30 Personal interview.
31 *L.A. Times* interview, http://articles.latimes.com/2009/may/21/entertainment/et-sasha-grey21.
32 *Independent Film Quarterly* interview, http://independentfilmquarterly.com/index.php?option=com_content&task=view&id=723&Itemid=116.

"Canadian Mental-Case": A Conclusion

GINA FREITAG AND ANDRÉ LOISELLE

While *The Canadian Horror Film: Terror of the Soul* may not offer one absolute, concise definition of Canadian horror cinema, as a whole, it is (to borrow Moreland's turn of phrase) an "invitation to an audience to investigate their own assumptions." If Frye conceives of the Canadian imagination as an interval between the terrifying outside and the unbearable inside, then we can certainly reflect on the "ins" and "outs" of Canadian horror as a confrontation of these physical and mental landscapes. This anthology examines many of the familiar aspects of horror cinema (slashers, eco-horror, body-horror, the experimental, and so on), but its reflections consistently return to Frye's determination that "there is something, say an attitude of mind, distinctively Canadian" (Frye 1971, 131) which contextualizes terror into Canadian spaces. Frye might have written these words decades ago, and mention of his famous name in certain circles might cause much eye rolling. But the fact remains that no one before or since has so convincingly argued that there are certain typically Canadian fears. It might be utterly futile to search for commonalities among Canadians; perhaps Canada is peopled by 30-odd million people who have *absolutely nothing in common with one another*; perhaps it is high time to burn *The Bush Garden* and never, *ever*, refer again to Northrop Frye. But we don't think so. We believe that this "terror of the soul" evokes something that is, somehow, fundamentally Canadian. We also believe that it is worth going back to Atwood and visualizing what she describes as "Canada as a state of mind": it is a space which "you inhabit not just with your body but with your head. It's that kind of space in which we find ourselves lost" (Atwood 1972, 26). And a way in which we can make sense of this "Canadian mentality" is to recognize familiar nasty, persistent anxieties which are projected, in this case, through horror cinema. But first, we must ask ourselves one question: have we also lost our minds?

Caelum Vatsndal's monster-by-monster approach reminds us not only that Canada does have a history of violence, but that the creatures of our making are often ones which erupt from within ourselves. In other words, monsters can assume any shape or form, and may be closer to home than we realize. Andrea Subissati talks of cracking into the core of our fears, of the cringe-inducing apprehension of cultural extinction, that the hold on our creative autonomy is slipping. Similarly, Keir-La Janisse expresses the fear of artistic hegemony and the impact of commercial success, how artistic "voices" may be sold to the figurative devil when independent artists suffer and struggle under industry pressures. In these discussions there is an underlying sense that we are battling an anxiety of cultural inferiority. At times, we can hear the echo of *Pontypool*'s Grant Mazzy, who amid the delirium of social breakdown, expresses the feeling of being trapped in the "basement of the world," a small, confined place in which we, too, feel secluded from the outside, tucked just beneath the surface of things, out of sight, out of mind. It is this "out-of-mind" that we cannot quite escape, for we are compelled to remain trapped in the garrison of our minds, telling ourselves neurotic stories which we now perpetuate through the national myth-making of cinema. Aalya Ahmad describes the "imaginative frontier" that we have forged for ourselves, so that physical and mental landscapes really do come alive. She underscores Frye's image of the settler, adding those exploits of natural resources which have included that of indigenous myth and folklore. This iconography, once mined, is imbued with an imaginative power that takes on a life of its own.

And with this constant undermining and questioning of identity, we tend to lose sight of that which is closest to us, the "horrifying normality" or "ordinary hell" that is the subject of André Loiselle's chapter. At times, the most profound anxiety is one in which "the mundane and the monstrous coexist"; there are connections, affinities to be made between the two which we do not always immediately recognize. But in confronting these "disturbing truths" and "unpleasant realities," we sense the instability of identity, which is strangely and quite often mirrored in the insecure male character types mentioned in Paul Corupe's account. Of course, gender politics is an anxiety whose presence is heavily felt in horror cinema. But it gives way to explorations of character types who "refuse to evolve" and resort to horrific violence in order to maintain some semblance of control. These flaws and doubts are very telling in the Canadian space; they are actualized by the explosive violence of outward actions and external landscapes.

Male characters hold a great focus in several of these chapters, returning again in Mark Hasan's discussion of the forest slasher subgenre, though the focus does shift to the environment of the killer, from the mundane to the forest domain, where isolation is just as, if not more, salient. The space of unknown territory, often raw and treacherous, voices another anxiety of that which lurks around us; it is "not only the fear of nature, but what it conceals." We tell ourselves "just don't go into the woods," because our surroundings can bring out a madness that further destabilizes us. How strange it is that despite the space of nature, and our affinity for "cottage life" where we are drawn to the woods for its offering of peace and solitude, that space is also known to be "claustrophobic."

With this connection to our environment, and the way in which it mirrors the wildness of our internal workings, it is easy to see how we can become intimidated by the vastness of the landscape around us; it is a constant reminder of our own smallness in the grand scheme of things. It is only logical that this constant reminder will have an impact on how we view our relationship with nature; even with this innate sense of anxiety about the future state of our environment, we mistreat it, exploit it, and in some ways, as Gina Freitag writes, we actually sense that the wildness of nature cannot be contained, even by our own shaping hand. These environmental anxieties do seem to be guided by a sense that nature is the solution, that we allow nature to reprimand us in the effort to correct itself after our mistakes. When we discuss "survival," especially in relation to nature, it is not necessarily clear whose survival we are actually talking about – ours, or nature's? This environmental anxiety is also informed partly by the ever-present concern for the management (or mismanagement) of resources, and the way in which we undermine certain thresholds in nature through such exploitation; in other words, we have a severe preoccupation with borders – a border anxiety – of which we are already made conscious in relation to the giant powerhouse to our south. At the same time, the border, which distinguishes spaces, domains, and territories, suggests a distinction of "insiders" and "outsiders." The question of who exactly is being referred to by each of those terms is another matter as well, one for which there is an indeterminate answer, a consequence of postcolonial anxiety, as Peter Thompson points out. And so we ask yet another question: "Who belongs"? This is simply part of the "deep questioning" of the Canadian mentality, which is, at times, as indefinite as the sensation of horror that Scott Birdwise contemplates. He, too, relates a concern for border anxiety, where "space" threatens to engulf "place," though his concentration shifts to the way in which we know horror, as a method of "narrativizing social anxiety," which we have thus fleshed out.

We also acknowledge fear through what Bill Beard defines as a "profound uneasiness" and "queasiness" of the mind-body relation. Through Cronenberg, our main proponent of body-horror in Canadian horror cinema, we see a "blending of fascination and disgust" at the way in which the body reacts often in relation to the instability of the mind. This "alarming destabilization" is also reflected in the anxiety surrounding medical institutions, outlined by James Burrell. Our fear and mistrust extend to those immediately concerned with the health and care of our bodily landscapes – physicians – whose image is often interpreted on-screen in relation to transformations, disease, mutations; in short, the madness of medical power has destructive consequences. This is certainly a theme which is intertwined with our other anxieties – power assumed or exerted over the environment, over natural resources, and of course, over ourselves. This power is sensationalized even further through Sean Moreland's suggestion of the character-contagion, an element found in body-horror that further interrogates sexual anxieties, which are often so closely linked with gender anxiety. In this case, the female gender takes on the power of "locus of identification," which is constantly undermined, shaken, and questioned, especially when there is a slippage between character and celebrity. It is yet another aspect of the Canadian mentality which is rendered unstable.

Each one of these anxieties can be found in horror cinema in general, it is true. But the unique combinations of these concerns, misgivings, and fears certainly have power over the Canadian imagination. One of the most important elements which is interlaced throughout Canadian horror cinema is the idea of an "unsettled" nation, one which is bothered, made "uneasy" by the wildness of its landscapes, the continual uprooting and refining of identity, and one which is constantly disrupted by such specific anxieties which are never fully quelled; they hold a special place in the Canadian state of mind. And it is because they are never fully quelled that they are continually exploited by Canadian horror cinema.

Just as Frye, Atwood, and a slew of others have offered critical theory to guide the "lost" through the mindset of "the Canadian mentality," we hope that this collection of original essays has provided a reflection on the "Canadian mental-case," a supposed collective imagination plagued by unrelenting anxieties which constantly threaten violent outbursts, particularly in Canadian horror cinema. We may not fully be able to navigate the menace of the wild which lurks within and without, but we can certainly try to imagine its terrifying contours, give form to its monstrous shadows, and speak of its shattering silences.

Bibliography

Alaimo, Stacy. 2001. "Discomforting Creatures: Monstrous Natures in Recent Films." In *Beyond Nature Writing: Expanding the Boundaries of Ecocriticism*, ed. Karla Armbruster and Kathleen Wallace, 279–96. Charlottesville: University of Virginia Press.

Allen, Robert C. 1999. "The Role of the Star in Film History (From *Film History: Theory and Practice*)." In *Film Theory and Criticism: Introductory Readings*, ed. Leo Braudy and Marshall Cohen, 547–61. New York: Oxford

Angus, Ian. 1997. *A Border Within: National Identity, Cultural Plurality, and Wilderness*. Montreal and Kingston: McGill-Queen's University Press.

"L'année 2010 au cinéma." 2010. *La Voix de l'Est*. 31 December.

Atwood, Margaret. 1972. *Survival: A Thematic Guide to Canadian Literature*. Toronto: Anansi.

– 1995. *Strange Things: The Malevolent North in Canadian Literature*. Oxford: Clarendon Press.

– 2010. "Act Now to Save Our Birds." *Guardian*, 9 January. Accessed August 2011. http://www.guardian.co.uk/books/2010/jan/09/margaret-atwood-birds-review.

Beal, Timothy. 2002. *Religion and Its Monsters*. London: Routledge.

Beard, William. 1994. "The Canadianness of David Cronenberg." *Mosaic* 27, no. 2: 113–33.

– 2001. *The Artist as Monster: The Cinema of David Cronenberg*. Toronto: University of Toronto Press.

– 2002. "Thirty-Two Paragraphs about David Cronenberg." In *North of Everything: English-Canadian Cinema since 1980*, ed. William Beard and Jerry White, 144–59. Edmonton: University of Alberta Press.

Beaty, Bart. 2008. *David Cronenberg's A History of Violence*. Toronto: University of Toronto Press.

Bindi, Irene. 2008. "The Films of Jack Chambers." Curatorial essay accompanying the *Films of Jack Chambers* program screened at the Winnipeg Film Group's Cinematheque on 12 and 13 November. https://www.winnipegfilmgroup.com/wp-content/uploads/The-Films-of-Jack-Chambers-by-Irene-Bindi.pdf.

Blackwood, Algernon. 1910. *The Human Chord*. London: Macmillan.

Bowen, John W. 2009. "A Very Careful Hatred." *Rue Morgue* 9, no. 12: 20–4.

Brakhage, Stan. 2003. "Space as Menace in Canadian Aesthetics: Film and Painting." In *Telling Time: Essays of a Visionary Filmmaker*, 87–108. Kingston, NY: Documentext.

Braudy, Leo. 1999. "Acting: Stage vs Screen." In *Film Theory and Criticism: Introductory Readings*, ed. Leo Braudy and Marshall Cohen, 419–25. New York: Oxford.

Broadcasting Regulatory Policy CRTC. 2010-905. http://www.crtc.gc.ca/eng/archive/2010/2010-905.htm. Accessed 18 February 2015.

Brownmiller, Susan. 1975. *Against Our Will: Men, Women, and Rape*. New York: Bantam Books.

Burroughs, William. 2009. *Naked Lunch: The Restored Text*. New York: Grove Press.

Caillois, Roger. 1965. *Au coeur du fantastique*. Paris: Gallimard.

Callahan, Vicki, ed. 2010. *Reclaiming the Archive: Feminism and Film History*, 17–31. Detroit: Wayne State University Press.

Campbell, Mary B. 2004. "Biological Alchemy and the Films of David Cronenberg." In *Planks of Reason: Essays on the Horror Film*, revised edition, ed. Barry Keith Grant and Christopher Sharrett, 307–20. Lanham: Scarecrow Press.

CanWest MediaWorks Publications. *No Genie Nominations for Vancouver's Juno*. Accessed 10 December 2011. http://www.canada.com/vancouversun/news/business/story.html?id=fd0f69cc-a564-413f-9535-d25f0546d1c2

Carroll, Noel. 1987. "The Nature of Horror." *Journal of Aesthetics and Art Criticism* 46, no. 1 (Autumn): 51–9. http://dx.doi.org/10.2307/431308.

Castex, Pierrre-Georges. 1951. *Le conte fantastique en France de Nodier à Maupassant*. Paris: José Corti.

Chafe, Paul. 2009. "'All the qualities o' th' isle.' *The Shipping News* as Island Myth. In *The Geographical Imagination of Annie Proulx: Rethinking Regionalism*, ed. Alex Hunt, 87–98. Lanham: Lexington Books.

Chevrier, Louise. 2003. "La littérature populaire: Pauvre auteur, seul son éditeur le sait." *La Presse*. 6 April.

Clover, Carol J. 1992. *Men, Women, and Chain Saws: Gender in the Modern Horror Film*. Princeton: Princeton University Press.

Collins, Anne. 1998. *In the Sleep Room. The Story of CIA Brainwashing Experiments in Canada*. Toronto: Key Porter Books.

Conrich, Ian. 2010. "Introduction: Horror Zone: The Cultural Experience of Contemporary Horror Cinema." In *Horror Zone*, ed. Ian Conrich, 1–10. London, New York: I.B. Tauris.

Crane, Jonathan. 2000. "A Body Apart: Cronenberg and Genre." In *The Modern Fantastic: The Films of David Cronenberg*, ed. Michael Grant, 50–68. Westport: Praeger.

Creed, Barbara. 1990. "Phallic Panic: Male Hysteria and *Dead Ringers*." *Screen* 31, no. 2: 125–46. http://dx.doi.org/10.1093/screen/31.2.125.

Creed, Barbara. 1993. *The Monstrous-Feminine: Film, Feminism, Psychoanalysis*. London, New York: Routledge.

– 2000. "The Naked Crunch: Cronenberg's Homoerotic Bodies." In *The Modern Fantastic: The Films of David Cronenberg*, ed. Michael Grant, 84–101. Westport, CT: Praeger.

– 2002. "Horror and the Monstrous-Feminine: An Imaginary Abjection." In *Horror: The Film Reader*, ed. Mark Jancovich, 7–76. London: Routledge.

Cresswell, Tim. 2004. *Place: A Short Introduction*. Oxford: Blackwell Publishing.

CRIC (Centre for Research and Information on Canada). 2005. "Portraits of Canada 2005." Montreal: CRIC. http://www.library.carleton.ca/sites/default/files/find/data/surveys/pdf_files/cric-paper_19-2005.pdf.

Curry, Christopher Wayne. 1998. *A Taste of Blood: The Films of Herschell Gordon Lewis*. London: Creation.

Davis, Susan. 1997. *Spectacular Nature: Corporate Culture and the Seaworld Experience*. Berkeley: University of California Press.

Dean, Malcolm. 1981. *Censored! Only in Canada: The History of Film Censorship – The Scandal Off the Screen*. Toronto: Virgo Press.

Delaney, Marshall [Robert Fulford]. 1975. "You Should Know How Bad This Film Is. After All, You Paid for It." *Saturday Night*, September, 83–5.

Deleuze, Gilles. 2003. *Francis Bacon: The Logic of Sensation*. Trans. Daniel W. Smith. Minneapolis: University of Minnesota Press.

Denison, Merrill. 1949. "That Inferiority Complex." In *The Empire Club of Canada Addresses*, 254–67.Toronto: Empire Club of Canada.

Denton, Clive. 1976–7. "Film Reviews: William Fruet's *Death Weekend*." *Cinema Canada*, December/January, 57–8.

Druick, Zoe. 2006. "Framing the Local: Canadian Film Policy and the Problem of Place." In *Canadian Cultural Poesis: Essays on Canadian Culture*, ed. Garry Sherbert et al., 85–98. Waterloo: Wilfrid Laurier University Press.

Ebert, Roger. 1980. Review of *I Spit on Your Grave*. 16 July. Online version. Accessed 24 August 2011. http://www.rogerebert.com/reviews/i-spit-on-your-grave-1980.

Edwards, Justin D. 2005. *Gothic Canada: Reading the Spectre of a National Literature*. Edmonton: University of Alberta Press.

Eggerston, Laura. 28 February 2006. "Quebec Strain of C. Difficile in 7 Provinces." *Canadian Medical Association Journal* 174, no. 5: 607–8. http://dx.doi.org/10.1503/cmaj.060105 http://www.cmaj.ca/content/174/5/607.2.

Elder, R. Bruce. 1984. "Forms of Cinema, Models of Self: Jack Chambers' *The Hart of London*." In *Take Two: A Tribute to Film in Canada*, ed. Seth Feldman, 264–74. Toronto: Irwin Publishing.

– 1989. *Image and Identity: Reflections on Canadian Film and Culture*. Waterloo, ON: Wilfrid Laurier University Press.

– 2003. "The Foreignness of the Intimate, or the Violence and Charity of Perception." In *Subtitles: On the Foreignness of Film*, ed. Atom Egoyan and Ian Balfour, 439–48. Cambridge, MA, and London: Alphabet City and MIT Press.

– 2005. "Goethe's Faust, Gertrude Stein's *Doctor Faustus Lights the Lights*, and Stan Brakhage's Faust Series." *Canadian Journal of Film Studies* 14, no. 1 (Spring): 51–68.

Falk, Dan. 1992. "The Earth According to Suzuki: Testing the Methods of a Scientist Turned Journalist Turned Environmental Activist." *Ryerson Review of Journalism* (June). Accessed August 2011. http://rrj.ca/the-earth-according-to-suzuki/.

Fee, Margery. 2009. "Retrieving the Canadian Critical Tradition as Poetry: Eli Mandel and Northrop Frye." In *Northrop Frye's Canadian Literary Criticism and Its Influence*, ed. Branko Gorjup, 184–202. Toronto: University of Toronto Press.

Feldman, Seth. 2001. "Canadian Movies, Eh?" In *The Fifteenth Annual Robarts Lecture*. Toronto: York University.

Fothergill, Robert. September 1973. "Being Canadian Means Always Having to Say You're Sorry." *Take One* 4, no. 3: 24–30.

Foy, Joseph J. 2010. "It Came From Planet Earth: Eco-Horror and the Politics of Postenvironmentalism in *The Happening*." In *Homer Simpson Marches on Washington: Dissent through American Popular Culture*, ed. Timothy M. Dale and Joseph J. Foy, 167–88. Kentucky: University of Kentucky Press.

Francis, Daniel. 1992. *The Imaginary Indian: The Image of the Indian in Canadian Culture*. Vancouver: Arsenal Pulp Press.

Francoeur, Martin. 1998. "Sur le seuil de la consécration: Patrick Sénécal s'affirme comme un des maîtres du roman d'horreur." *Le Nouveliste*, 10 October.

Frayling, Christopher. 2005. *Mad, Bad and Dangerous? The Scientist and the Cinema*. London: Reaktion Books.

Freitag, Gina. 2011. "Unleashing the 'Furious Feminine': The Violence of Gender Discourse in Canadian Horror Cinema." MA thesis in Film Studies, Carleton University.

Freitag, Gina, and André Loiselle. June 2013. "Tales of Terror in Québec Popular Cinema: The Rise of the French Language Horror Film since 2000." *American Review of Canadian Studies* 43, no. 2: 190–203. http://dx.doi.org/10.1080/02722011.2013.795025.

Freud, Sigmund. 1953–74. In *The Standard Edition of the Complete Psychological Works*. Vol. 17. Ed. and trans. James Strachey. London: Hogarth.

– 2003. *The Uncanny*. Trans. David McClintock. New York: Penguin.

Frye, Northrop. 1965. "Conclusion." In *Literary History of Canada*, ed. Carl F. Klinck et al., 821–49. Toronto: University of Toronto Press.

– 1971. *The Bush Garden: Essays on the Canadian Imagination*. Toronto: House of Anansi Press.

Giles, Dennis. 1984. "Conditions of Pleasure in Horror Cinema." In *Planks of Reason*, ed. Barry Keith Grant, 38–52. Metuchen, NJ: Scarecrow Press.

Goldie, Terry. 1989. *Fear and Temptation: The Image of the Indigene in Canadian, Australian, and New Zealand Literatures*. Montreal and Kingston: McGill-Queen's University Press.

– 2004. "Semiotic Control: Native Peoples in Canadian Literature in English." In *Unhomely States: Theorizing English-Canadian Postcolonialism*, ed. Cynthia Sugars, 191–203. Peterborough: Broadview Press.

Goldman, Marlene, and Joanne Saul. Spring 2006. "Talking with Ghosts: Haunting in Canadian Cultural Production." *University of Toronto Quarterly* 75, no. 2: 645–55. http://dx.doi.org/10.3138/utq.75.2.645.

Grant, George. 1969. "In Defence of North America." In *Technology and Empire*, 13–40. Toronto: Anansi.

Grant, Michael, ed. 2000. *The Modern Fantastic: the films of David Cronenberg*. Westport, CT: Praeger.

Griffiths, Linda, and Maria Campbell. 1997. *The Book of Jessica: A Theatrical Transformation*. Playwrights Canada Press.

Halberstam, Judith. 1995. *Skin Shows: Gothic Horror and the Technology of Monsters*. Durham: Duke University Press.

Handling, Piers. 1977. "Bill Fruet: 2 or 3 Things … " *Cinema Canada* (September): 43–6.

– 1983. "A Canadian Cronenberg." In *The Shape of Rage*, ed. Piers Handling, 98–114. Toronto: General Publishing.

Haraway, Donna. 1991. *Simians, Cyborgs, and Women: The Reinvention of Nature*. New York: Routledge.

Harris-Zsovan, Jane. 2010. *Eugenics and the Firewall: Canada's Nasty Little Secret*. Winnipeg: J. Gordon Shillingford.

Huet, Marie-Hélène. *Monstrous Imagination*. 1993. Cambridge, MA.: Harvard University Press.

Ingram, David. 2000. *Green Screen: Environmentalism in Hollywood Cinema*. Devon, UK: University of Exeter Press.

Jancovich, Mark. 1992. *Horror*. London: Batsford.

Karpenchuck, Dan. 2009. "Oil Outweighs Environment in Canada's 'Paradise Lost.'" *Radio Netherlands Worldwide*, 15 December. Accessed 27 July 2011. http://www.rnw.org/archive/oil-outweighs-environment-canadas-paradise-lost.

Kashmere, Brett. 2004. "In the Realm of Mystery and Wonder: R. Bruce Elder's *Book of Praise*." *Take One* 45 (March-June): 36–8.

Kelly, M.T. 1987. *A Dream Like Mine*. Holstein, ON: Exile.

Kerekes, David, and David Slater. 2000. *See No Evil: Banned Films and Video Controversy*. London: Headpress.

Kerridge Richard. 2000. "Eco Thrillers: Environmental Cliffhangers." In *The Green Studies Reader: From Romanticism to Ecocreiticism*, ed. Laurence Coupe, 242–9. London: Routledge.

Kertzer, Jonathan. 1998. *Worrying the Nation: Imagining a National Literature in English Canada*. Toronto: University of Toronto Press.

Koch, Gertrud. 1993. "The Body's Shadow Realm." In *Dirty Looks: Women, Pornography, Power*, ed. Pamela Church Gibson and Roma Gibson, 22–45. London: British Film Institute.

Kristeva, Julia. 1982. *The Powers of Horror: An Essay on Abjection*. New York: Columbia University Press.

Kroker, Arthur. 1985. *Technology and the Canadian Mind: Innis/McLuhan/Grant*. Montreal: New World Perspectives.

Laurin, Danielle. 2009. "Il fait saigner la banlieue." *L'Actualité* 34, no. 16 (15 Octobre): 68.

Lawson, Alan. 2004. "Postcolonial Theory and the 'Settler' Subject." In *Unhomely States: Theorizing English-Canadian Postcolonialism*, ed. Cynthia Sugars, 151–64. Peterborough: Broadview Press.

Leach, Jim. 2006. *Film in Canada*. Oxford, New York: Oxford University Press.

Levinas, Emmanuel. 2003. *On Escape*. Trans. Bettina Bergo. Stanford, CA: Stanford University Press.

Loiselle, André. 2008. "Quebecus Horribilis: Theatricality, the 'Moment of Horror' and Quebec's 'Satanist' Cinema." *Nouvelles "Vues" sur le Cinéma Québécois* 8 (Winter). http://www.cinema-quebecois.net/pdfs/LoiselleNVCQ8.pdf

– 2010. "Popular Genres in Quebec Cinema: The Strange Case of Horror in Film and Television." In *How Canadians Communicate III*, ed. Bart Beaty, Derek Briton, Gloria Filax, and Rebecca Sullivan, 141–59. Edmonton: Athabasca University Press.

– 2014. "Canadian Horror, American Bodies: Corporeal Obsession and Cultural Projection in *American Nightmare, American Psycho*, and *American Mary*." *Brno Studies in English* 39, no. 2: 123–36.

Loiselle, André, and Tom McSorley. 2006. "Appendix." In *Self-Portraits*, ed. Loiselle and McSorley, 321–3. Ottawa: Canadian Film Institute.

Lowenstein, Adam. 1998. "Canadian Horror Made Flesh: Contextualizing David Cronenberg." *PostScript* 18, no. 2 (Winter): 37–51.

Mackey, Eva. 2000. "Death by Landscape: Race, Nature, and Gender in Canadian Nationalist Mythology." *Canadian Women's Studies* 20, no. 2 (Summer): 125–30.

Marzluff, John M., and Tony Angell. 2005. *In the Company of Crows and Ravens*. New Haven, CT: Yale University Press.

Massey, Doreen. 1994. *Space, Place and Gender*. Cambridge: Polity.

Mathijs, Ernest. 2008. *The Cinema of David Cronenberg: From Baron of Blood to Cultural Hero*. London: Wallflower.

Mazurkewich, Karen. 1999. *Cartoon Capers: The Adventures of Canadian Animators*. Toronto: McArthur.

McCallum, Gary J. 1977. "The Leopard Is Loose." *Take One* 5/6 (January): 38–40.

McGregor, Gaile. 1985. *The Wacousta Syndrome: Explorations in the Canadian Langscape*. Toronto: University of Toronto Press.

– 1992. "Grounding the Countertext: David Cronenberg and the Ethnospecificity of Horror." *Canadian Journal of Film Studies / Revue Canadienne d'Études Cinématographiques* 2, no. 1: 43–62.

– 2003. "A Case Study in the Construction of Place: Boundary Management as Theme and Strategy in Canadian Art and Life." *Invisible Culture* 5 (Winter): 1–32. http://www.rochester.edu/in_visible_culture/Issue_5/IVC_iss5_McGregor.pdf.

Miller, Cynthia J. 2010. "Exploring Cinema's Sordid Side." In *From the Arthouse to the Grindhouse*, ed. John Cline and Robert G. Weiner, 75–85. Lanham, MD: Scarecrow Press.

Modleski, Tania. 1988. *The Women Who Knew Too Much: Hitchcock and Feminist Theory*. New York, London: Methuen.

Morris, Peter. 1978. *Embattled Shadows: A History of Canadian Cinema, 1895–1939*. Montreal and Kingston: McGill-Queen's University Press.

Mowat, Farley. 2005. *A Whale for the Killing*. Toronto: Key Porter Books.

Muir, John Kenneth. 2002. *Horror Films of the 1970s*. Vol. 2. Jefferson: McFarland.

Murray, Robin L., and Joseph K. Heumann. 2009. *Ecology and Popular Film: Cinema on the Edge*. Albany: State University of New York Press.

Nancy, Jean-Luc. 1997. *The Gravity of Thought*. Trans. François Rafoul and Gregory Recco. Atlantic Highlands, NJ: Humanities Press.

– 2005. *The Ground of the Image*. Trans. Jeff Fort. New York: Fordham University Press.

Newman, Kim. 2011. *Nightmare Movies*. London: Bloomsbury.

"Ontario NDP Perplexed as to Why There Was No Provincial Oversight for Company that Watered Down Chemo Drugs." 2013. *National Post*, 10 April. http://news.nationalpost.com/2013/04/10/ontario-ndp-perplexed-as-to-why-there-was-no-provincial-oversight-for-company-that-watered-down-chemo-drugs/.

Overton, James. 2000. "Sparking a Cultural Revolution: Joey Smallwood, Farley Mowat, Harold Horwood and Newfoundland's Cultural Renaissance." *Newfoundland Studies* 16, no. 1 (Fall): 166–204.

Panagia, Davide. 2009. *The Political Life of Sensation*. Durham, London: Duke University Press.

Parker, Andrew. 1993. "Grafting David Cronenberg: Monstrosity, AIDS Media, National/Sexual Difference." *Stanford Humanities Review* 3, no. 1: 7–21.

Pendakur, Manjunath. 1990. *Canadian Dreams and American Control: The Political Economy of the Canadian Film Industry*. Detroit: Wayne State University Press.

Peritz, Ingrid. 2010. "Cursed by 'Miracle Drug,' Thalidomide Victims Wait for Canada's Apology." *Globe and Mail*, 5 February. http://www.theglobeandmail.com/news/national/thalidomide-victims-wait-for-canadas-apology/article4352125/?page=all.

Phillips, Arthur Angel. 1958. "A.A. Phillips on the Cultural Cringe." In *The Australian Tradition: Essays in Colonial Culture*, 89–96. Melbourne: Cheshire.

Picard, André. n.d. "Krever Inquiry." *The Canadian Encyclopedia*. http://www.thecanadianencyclopedia.com/articles/krever-inquiry

Pinedo, Isabel Cristina. 1997. *Recreational Terror: Women and the Pleasures of Horror Film Viewing*. New York: State University of New York Press.

Plumwood, Val. 1993. *Feminism and the Mastery of Nature*. New York: Routledge.

Podruchny, Carolyn. 2004. "Werewolves and Windigos: Narratives of Cannibal Monsters in French-Canadian Voyageur Oral Tradition." *Ethnohistory* 51, no. 4 (Fall): 677–700. Durham, NC: Duke University Press. http://dx.doi.org/10.1215/00141801-51-4-677.

Pratley, Gerald. 1987. *Torn Sprockets: The Uncertain Projection of the Canadian Film*. Toronto: Associated University Presses.

Pratley, Gerald. 2003. *A Century of Canadian Cinema*. Toronto: Lynx Images.

Rodley, Chris. 1997. *Cronenberg on Cronenberg*. London: Faber and Faber.

Rothenburger, Sunnie. 2010. "'Welcome to Civilization': Colonialism, the Gothic, and Canada's Self-Protective Irony in the *Ginger Snaps* Werewolf Trilogy." *Journal of Canadian Studies / Revue d'Études Canadiennes* 44, no. 3 (Fall): 96–117.

Saad, Gad. 2012. "Don't Romanticize the Canadian Healthcare System." *Psychology Today*, 14 June. http://www.psychologytoday.com/blog/homo-consumericus/201206/don-t-romanticize-the-Canadian-healthcare-system.

Sammon, Paul M. 1981. "David Cronenberg." *Cinefantastique* 10, no. 4 (Spring): 21–34.

Sconce, Jeffrey. 2007. "Movies: A Century of Failure." In *Sleaze Artists: Cinema at the Margins of Taste, Style, and Politics*, ed. Jeffrey Sconce, 273–309. Durham: Duke University Press. http://dx.doi.org/10.1215/9780822390190-013.

Segrave, Kerry. *American Films Abroad: Hollywood's Domination of the World's Movie Screens from the 1890s to the Present*. Jefferson, NC: McFarland, 1997.

Senécal, Patrick. 1998. *Sur le seuil*. Quebec: Éditions Alire.

– 2001. *5150, rues des ormes*. Quebec: Éditions Alire.

– 2002. *Les septe jours du talion*. Quebec: Éditions Alire.

Shaviro, Steven. 1993. *The Cinematic Body*. Minneapolis: University of Minnesota Press.

Silverman, Kaja. 1999. "On Suture." In *Film Theory and Criticism Introductory Readings*, ed. Leo Braudy and Marshall Cohen, 137–47. New York: Oxford.

Silversides, Ann. 2009. "Public Reports of Infection Rates Urged." Canadian Medical Association Journal 181, no. 9 (27 October) (First published 21 September 2009). http://www.cmaj.ca/content/181/9/573.full?sid=14d0d2b2-9d96-4ecd-9fbd-c8df9af88e3a.

Simpson, Catherine. 2010. "Australian Eco-Horror and Gaia's Revenge: Animals, Eco-nationalism and the New Nature." *Studies in Australasian Cinema* 4, no. 1: 43–54. http://dx.doi.org/10.1386/sac.4.1.43_1.

Sinclair, Iain. 1999. *Crash*. London: BFI.

Sobchack, Vivian. 1987. *Screening Space: The American Science Fiction Film*. New York: Ungar.

Starr, Marco. 1984. "J. Hills Is Alive: A Defence of *I Spit on Your Grave*." In *The Video Nasties: Freedom and Censorship in the Media*, ed. Martin Barker, 48–55. London: Pluto Press.

Stoffman, Daniel. 2002. *The Nelvana Story: 30 Animated Years*. Toronto: Nelvana.

Sugars, Cynthia. 2006. "The Impossible Afterlife of George Cartwright: Settler Melancholy and Postcolonial Desire." *University of Toronto Quarterly* 75, no. 2 (Spring): 693–717. http://dx.doi.org/10.3138/utq.75.2.693.

– "Genetic Phantoms: Geography, History, and Ancestral Inheritance in Kenneth Harvey's *The Town That Forgot How to Breathe* and Michael Crummey's *Galore*." *Newfoundland and Labrador Studies* 25, no. 1: 7–36.

Sugars, Cynthia, and Gerry Turcotte. 2009. *Unsettled Remains: Canadian Literature and the Postcolonial Gothic*. Waterloo: Wilfrid Laurier University Press.

Suzuki, David. 2010. *The Legacy*. Vancouver: D&M Publishers.

– 2011a. "Humans May Have the Bases Loaded, but Nature Bats Last." *Science Matters*. David Suzuki Foundation. 2 June. Accessed July 2011. http://www.davidsuzuki.org/blogs/science-matters/2011/06/humans-may-have-loaded-the-bases-but-nature-bats-last/.

– 2011b. "A Murder of Crows." *The Nature of Things* (CBC). Television broadcast date 12 June. Accessed July 2011. http://www.cbc.ca/video/#/Shows/The_Nature_of_Things/ID=1385855962.

Suzuki, David, and Faisal Moola. 2011a. "Aflockalypse Now: Mass Animal Die-Offs and the Ongoing Extinction Crisis." *Science Matters*. David Suzuki Foundation. 13 January. Accessed July 2011. http://www.davidsuzuki.org/blogs/science-matters/2011/01/aflockalypse-now-mass-animal-die-offs-and-the-ongoing-extinction-crisis/.

– 2011b. "If a Tree Falls in the International Year of Forests, Does Anybody Hear?" *Science Matters*. David Suzuki Foundation. 10 February. Accessed July 2011. http://www.davidsuzuki.org/blogs/science-matters/2011/02/if-a-tree-falls-in-the-international-year-of-forests-does-anybody-hear/.

Talaga, Tanya, and Robert Cribb. 2007. "Coming Clean on Medical Mistakes." *Toronto Star*, 19 March. http://www.thestar.com/News/article/193502.

Testa, Bart. 1989. *Spirit in the Landscape*. Toronto: Art Gallery of Ontario.

– 2002. "Chambers' Epic: *The Hart of London*, History's Protagonist." In *The Films of Jack Chambers*, ed. Kathryn Elder, 141–74. Toronto: Cinematheque Ontario.

Todorov, Tzetan. 1975. *The Fantastic: A Structural Approach to a Literary Genre*. Ithaca: Cornell University Press.

Tremblay, Odile. 2009. "Cinéma – L'année 2009 a ramené les spectateurs québécois devant leurs longs métrages." *Le Devoir*, 30 Decembre.

Trudeau, Pierre. 1969. Press Club in Washington, DC, 25 Mar.

Turbide, Diane. 1997. "Dr. Cameron's Casualties: A Series Revisits Canada's 1950s Brainwashing Scandal." *Maclean's*, 21 April, 61.

Twitchell, James. 1985. *Dreadful Pleasures: An Anatomy of Modern Horror*. Oxford: Oxford University Press.

Vacante, Jeffrey. 2006. "Liberal Nationalism and the Challenge of Masculinity Studies in Quebec." *Left History* 11, no. 2: 96–117.

Vatnsdal, Caelum. 2004. *They Came from Within: A History of Canadian Horror Cinema*. Winnipeg: Arbeiter Ring.

Vax, Louis. 1960. *L'art et la littérature fantastiques*. Paris: Presses Universitaires de France.

Wainwright, J.A. 1999. "Invention Denied: Resisting the Imaginary Indian in M.T. Kelly's *A Dream Like Mine*." *World Literature Today*, edited by On Contemporary Canadian Literature(s) (Spring): 256–60.

Williams, Linda. 1989. *Hardcore: Power, Pleasure and the Frenzy of the Visible*. Los Angeles: University of California Press.

– 1991. "Film Bodies: Gender, Genre, and Excess." *Film Quarterly* 44, no. 4 (Summer): 2–13. http://dx.doi.org/10.2307/1212758.

– 1996. "When the Woman Looks." In *The Dread of Difference: Gender and the Horror Film*, ed. Barry Keith Grant, 15–34. Austin: University of Texas Press.

– 2008. *Screening Sex*. London: Duke University Press. http://dx.doi.org/10.1215/9780822388630.

Willoquet-Maricondi, Paula. 2010. "Introduction: From Literary to Cinematic Ecocriticism." In *Framing the World: Explorations in Ecocriticism and Film*, ed. Paula Willoquet-Maricondi, 1–24. Virginia: University of Virginia Press.

Wood, Robin. "An Introduction to the American Horror Film." In *The American Nightmare*, ed. Andrew Britton, Richard Lippe, Tony Williams, and Robin Wood, 7–28. Toronto: Festival of Festivals, 1979.

Woodman, Ross. 2002. "Jack Chambers as Filmmaker." In *The Films of Jack Chambers*, ed. Kathryn Elder, 45–58. Toronto: Cinematheque Ontario.

Woolf, Virginia. 1996. "'The Cinema' (1926/50)." In *The British Avant-Garde Film: 1926 to 1995 – An Anthology of Writings*, ed. Michael O'Pray, 33–6. Luton, Bedfordshire: University of Luton Press.

Filmography

5051, rue des ormes (2009, Éric Tessier)
Les 7 jours du talion (2010, Daniel Grou)
The Adventures of Lucky Pierre (1961, Herschell Gordon Lewis)
American Mary (2012, Jen Soska, Sylvia Soska)
American Pop (1981, Ralph Bakshi)
Behemoth (2011, David Hogan)
Behind the Green Door (1972, Artie and James Mitchell)
Black Christmas (1974, Bob Clark)
Blood Symbol (1992, Maurice Devereaux)
Blue Monkey (1987, William Fruet)
The Brain (1988, Ed Hunt)
The Brood (1979, David Cronenberg)
Candyman (1992, Bernard Rose)
The Care Bears Movie (1985, Arna Selznick)
Carrie (1976, Brian DePalma)
The Christmas Martian (1971, Bernard Gosselin)
Clearcut (1991, Ryszard Bugajski)
Le collectionneur (2002, Jean Beaudin)
Contamination .7 (aka *Creepers*) (1997, Joe D'Amato and Fabrizio Laurenti)
Coonskin (1975, Ralph Bakshi)
A Cosmic Christmas (1977, Clive A. Smith)
Cosmopolis (2012, David Cronenberg)
Crack, Brutal Grief (2000, Bruce Elder)
Crash (1996, David Cronenberg)
Crimes of the Future (1970, David Cronenberg)
Cube (1997, Vincenzo Natali)
A Dangerous Method (2011, David Cronenberg)

The Dark (1993, Craig Pryce)
The Dark Hours (2005, Paul Fox)
Daughters of Darkness (1971, Harry Kümel)
The Day after Tomorrow (2004, Roland Emmerich)
Deadly Eyes (1982, Robert Clouse)
Dead Ringers (1988, David Cronenberg)
Death Weekend (1976, William Fruet)
The Devil and Daniel Mouse (1974, Clive A. Smith)
Le diable est parmi nous (1972, Jean Beaudin)
Dys- (2014, Maude Michaud)
Eastern Promises (2007, David Cronenberg)
End of the Line (2007, Maurice Devereaux)
eXistenz (1999, David Cronenberg)
The Eye (2002, Pang Brothers)
Eye of the Beast (2007, Gary Yates)
Fast Company (1979, David Cronenberg)
The Fly (1958, Kurt Neumann)
The Fly (1986, David Cronenberg)
The Food of the Gods (1976, Bert I. Gordon)
Friday the 13th Part 3 (1982, Steve Miner)
Fritz the Cat (1972, Ralph Bakshi)
The Gate (1987, Tibor Takács)
The Gate II: The Trespassers (1990, Tibor Takács)
The Ghostkeeper (1986, Jim Makichuk)
Gina (1975, Denys Arcand)
Ginger Snaps (2000, John Fawcett)
Ginger Snaps II: Unleashed (2003, Brett Sullivan)
Ginger Snaps Back: The Beginning (2004, Grant Harvey)
The Girlfriend Experience (2009, Steven Soderbergh)
Gnaw: Food of the Gods II (1989, Damien Lee)
Goin' Down the Road (1970, Don Shebib)
The Gruesome Twosome (1967, Herschell Gordon Lewis)
Halloween (1978, John Carpenter)
Hardcore Logo (1996, Bruce McDonald)
The Hart of London (1968–70, Jack Chambers)
Heavy Metal (1981, Gerald Potterton)
Heavy Traffic (1973, Ralph Bakshi)
Highway 61 (1991, Bruce McDonald)
A History of Violence (2005, David Cronenberg)
The Host (2006, Joon-ho Bong)

Humongous (1982, Paul Lynch)
Ice Quake (2010, Paul Ziller)
Incubus (1982, John Hough)
Inglourious Basterds (2009, Quentin Tarantino)
Insecticidal (2005, Jeffery Scott Lando)
I Spit on Your Grave (1978, Meir Zarchi)
Jack Brooks: Monster Slayer (2007, Jon Knautz)
Jaws (1976, Steven Spielberg)
Karla (2006, Joel Bender)
Kaw (2007, Sheldon Wilson)
The Keeper (1976, T.Y. Drake).
Killer Pickton (2005, Ulli Lommel)
The Lure of the Wendigo (1914, Francis J. Grandon)
Lust for a Vampire (1971, Jimmy Sangster)
The Making of "Naked Lunch" (1992, Chris Rodley)
Maps to the Stars (2014, David Cronenberg)
The Mask (1961, Julian Roffman)
M. Butterfly (1993, David Cronenberg)
Monster Brawl (2011, Jesse Thomas Cook)
Mourir à tue-tête (1979, Anne Claire Poirier)
Naked Lunch (1991, David Cronenberg)
Of Unknown Origins (1983, George P. Cosmatos)
Open Water (2003, Chris Kentis)
Orca (1977, Michael Anderson)
Paperback Hero (1973, Peter Pearson)
Peeping Tom (1960, Michael Powell)
La petite Aurore, l'enfant martyre (1952, Jean-Yves Bigras)
Phantom of the Paradise (1974, Brian DePalma)
The Pit (1981, Lew Lehman)
Planet of the Apes (1968, Franklin J. Schnaffner)
Le poil de la bête (2010, Philippe Gagnon)
Polytechnique (2009, Denis Villeneuve)
Pontypool (2009, Bruce McDonald)
Psycho (1960, Alfred Hitchcock)
The Pyx (1973, Harvey Hart)
Rabid (1977, David Cronenberg)
Ravenous (1999, Antonia Bird)
Resurrection of Eve (1973, Jon Fontana and Artie Mitchell)
Rip-Off (1971, Don Shebib)
Roadkill (1989, Bruce McDonald)

Rock & Rule (1983, Clive A. Smith)
Rock 'n' Roll Nightmare (1987, John Fasano)
The Rowdyman (1972, Peter Carter)
Sasquatch (2002, Jonas Quastel)
Scanners (1981, David Cronenberg)
Severed: Forest of the Dead (2005, Carl Bessai)
The Shipping News (2001, Lasse Hallström)
Shivers (1975, David Cronenberg)
Slipstream (1973, David Acomba)
Smash Cut (2009, Lee Demarbre)
Spider (2002, David Cronenberg)
Splice (2009, Vincenzo Natali)
Stereo (1969, David Cronenberg)
Sur le seuil (2003, Éric Tessier)
Swarmed (2005, Paul Ziller)
Sweet Prudence and the Erotic Adventures of Bigfoot (2011, William Burke)
The Thaw (2009, Mark A. Lewis)
The Thing (2011, Matthijs van Heigningen Jr.)
The Tracey Fragments (2006, Bruce McDonald)
Vampyres (1974, José Ramón Larraz)
Videodrome (1983, David Cronenberg)
The Vulture (1967, Lawrence Huntington)
Wedding in White (1972, William Fruet)
Wendigo (2001, Larry Fessenden)
The Werewolf (1913, Henry MacRae)
Yellow Submarine (1968, George Dunning)
Yeti: Curse of the Snow Demon (2008, Paul Ziller)

Contributors

Aalya Ahmad is an adjunct professor in the Pauline Jewett Institute of Women's and Gender Studies, Carleton University, Ottawa. She has taught and published research in the areas of horror fiction and film, zombies, popular culture, diaspora, introductory women's and gender studies, and feminist activism. She has also co-edited *Fear and Learning*, a collection on the pedagogy of horror, as well as the dark fiction anthology, *Postscripts to Darkness*.

William Beard is a professor of Film Studies in the Department of English and Film Studies at the University of Alberta, where he has taught since 1978. He is the author of *The Artist as Monster: The Cinema of David Cronenberg*, as well as monographs on the work of Clint Eastwood and Guy Maddin and numerous essays and book chapters on Canadian and American cinema.

Scott Birdwise is a PhD candidate in the Graduate Program in Film at York University. He has published several articles and three collections of essays on Canadian filmmakers, most recently *The Transformable Moment: The Films of Stephen Broomer* for the Canadian Film Institute. His dissertation investigates the role of documentality—the conjunction of documentary and governmental practices and discourses—in the documentary imagination of "the people" in four different national/global contexts and artistic practices.

James Burrell is a Toronto-based writer who has written extensively about Canadian exploitation cinema for such publications and online sites as *Rue Morgue Magazine* and Canuxploitation.com. His recently-released guide to Canadian horror films, *Horrorwood North: The Extraordinary History and Art of Canadian Genre Cinema,* is the fourth volume from The Rue Morgue Library, and is published by Marrs Media Inc.

Paul Corupe is the founder of the Canadian B-film site Canuxploitation. com, and a Toronto-based writer/editor who regularly writes about genre film and Canadian cinema in publications including *Rue Morgue* magazine, *Take One: Film and Television in Canada* and *Cinema Sewer.* In addition to serving as the managing editor of the *Spectacular Optical,* an independent small-press publisher of collectible film and pop culture books, he has appeared in several documentaries about Canadian film and scripted episodes of Bravo's *On Screen!* television series.

Gina Freitag is an independent scholar. She received an M.A. degree in Film Studies at Carleton University, where she completed a thesis project on female archetypes in horror cinema. She has co-authored an article on Québec horror cinema with André Loiselle (Carleton University), which is published in *The American review of Canadian Studies* (43.2, June 2013). Her main research interests include horror cinema, Canadian cinema, and gender studies. She is the founder of and co-organizer for the Cellar Door Film Festival in Ottawa, ON (www.cdff.ca).

Mark R. Hasan is a York University Film Production graduate, Toronto-based accredited journalist (*Rue Morgue, Canadian Screenwriter, Film Score Monthly, Music from the Movies, The Toronto Star*) and media review writer + publisher (KQEK.com) specializing in classic, cult, and documentary films. As a recognized authority on film music, Hasan has aided film festivals (Toronto Jewish Film Festival), and publishes a monthly podcast on iTunes, Libsyn, and YouTube. His film work is profiled in detail at www.bigheadamusements.com, and he is currently completing *BSV 1172,* an experimental documentary on local video store Bay Street Video.

Kier-La Janisse is a film programmer and writer based in Toronto. She is the Editor of Spectacular Optical Publications, the founder of The Miskatonic Institute of Horror Studies and the author of *House of Psychotic Women: An Autobiographical Topography of Female Neurosis in Horror and Exploitation Films* (2012). With Paul Corupe, she co-edited the book *Kid Power!* (2014) and the forthcoming *Satanic Panic: Pop-Cultural Paranoia in the 1980s.*

André Loiselle is a professor of Film Studies and Assistant Vice-President (Academic) at Carleton University in Ottawa. His main areas of research are Canadian and Québécois cinema, the horror film and theatricality on screen. He has published ten books, including *Stages of Reality: Theatricality in Cinema* (2012, with Jeremy Maron), *Denys Arcand's 'Le Déclin de l'empire américain' and 'Les Invasions barbares'* (2008), *Cinema as History: Michel Brault and Modern Quebec* (2007) and *Canada Exposed* (2009, with Pierre Anctil and Christopher Rolfe).

Sean Moreland has published numerous essays, primarily on literary and cinematic horror and the Gothic, as well as poetry and short fiction. He co-edited the essay collections *Fear and Learning: Essays on the Pedagogy of Horror* (McFarland, 2013) and *Monstrous Children and Childish Monsters: Essays on Cinema's Holy Terrors* (McFarland, 2015) and is currently editing *The Lovecraftian Poe: Essays on Influence, Reception and Transformation* (forthcoming, late 2015). He is editor of *Postscripts to Darkness* (pstdarkness.com) and sometimes teaches in the English Department at the University of Ottawa.

Andrea Subissati is a sociologist and writer on cultural studies and horror film. In 2010, her first book on the social impact of zombie cinema was published under the title *When There's No More Room In Hell: The Sociology of the Living Dead*. She is a contributing writer for *Rue Morgue* Magazine, producer and co-host of the Faculty of Horror podcast, and co-founder of The Black Museum horror lecture series in Toronto, Ontario.

Peter Thompson is an associate professor in the School of Canadian Studies at Carleton University in Ottawa, Ontario. He has published several articles on representations of the natural environment in contemporary literature and popular culture, with a particular focus on Atlantic Canada.

Caelum Vatnsdal is a director and writer based in Winnipeg, Manitoba. He is the author of a history of Canadian horror movies entitled *They Came From Within* (2004). His films include *Target Practice* (2012), *Micro-Nice* (2002) and *Black as Hell, Strong as Death, Sweet as Love* (1998). He has made rock videos, commercials, dramas and documentaries and has worked on many projects with Guy Maddin.